BRICKS & MORTALS

August Sander, Bricklayer *(1928)*

BRICKS & MORTALS

Ten Great Buildings and the People They Made

Tom Wilkinson

BLOOMSBURY PRESS

NEW YORK · LONDON · NEW DELHI · SYDNEY

Published by Bloomsbury Press, New York
Bloomsbury is a trademark of Bloomsbury Publishing Plc

All papers used by Bloomsbury Press are natural, recyclable products made
from wood grown in well-managed forests. The manufacturing processes
conform to the environmental regulations of the country of origin.

LIBRARY OF CONGRESS CATALOGING-IN-PUBLICATION DATA HAS BEEN APPLIED FOR.

ISBN: 978-1-62040-629-8

First published in Great Britain in 2014
First U.S. Edition 2014

1   3   5   7   9   10   8   6   4   2

Typeset by Hewer Text UK Ltd, Edinburgh
Printed and bound in the U.S.A. by Thomson-Shore Inc., Dexter, Michigan

Bloomsbury books may be purchased for business or promotional use. For
information on bulk purchases please contact Macmillan Corporate and
Premium Sales Department at specialmarkets@macmillan.com.

To my parents

Contents

Introduction

The First Hut
Architecture and Origins

What is found at the historical beginning of things is not the inviolable identity of their origin; it is the dissension of other things. It is disparity.

Michel Foucault, 'Nietzsche, Genealogy, History'[1]

I saw something nasty in the woodshed.

Stella Gibbons, *Cold Comfort Farm*

Composing hut, Toblach

On the flower-spattered flank of an Alpine valley stands a prefab pitch-roofed shed (did architecture begin like this, with a simple wooden dwelling in the wilderness?). The building is small, neither picturesquely dilapidated nor unusually luxurious, and enclosed by a pine palisade topped with barbed wire. Behind it shady trees creep up like assassins. Leaves rustle, peasant children shout – this is 1909, and peasants have not yet vanished from this part of the world – and from within the hut comes the sound of a piano. The notes flow uncertainly from the machine, now stumbling, now mellifluous, and carry clearly in the still mountain air. Suddenly something dark and feathered hurtles towards the hut, and there is a cymbal crash of shattered glass. The piano falls silent and Gustav Mahler, shed dweller, emits a startled yell as a jackdaw pursued by a hawk bursts through his window-pane and the two flap fighting around his head.

For thousands of years people have tried to imagine the genesis of architecture in such terms: a sylvan scene, a wooden hut and the creative spark that initiated the history of building (jackdaws and composers aren't regular features of these fantasies, I admit). Returning to the origin of building isn't just something historians do: like Mahler, many artists have worked in 'primitive' structures, and the popularity of beach huts, tree houses and garden sheds suggests that the idea has wide appeal. There is a comfort in the purity of origins for artists, holidaymakers and historians alike, a narrative neatness in going back to the start. But beginning at the beginning creates as many problems as it solves. For one thing, we might ask, was there just one beginning of building or many? Do we discard the attempts that led nowhere and end up with a history

3

of the victors? How can we know about prehistoric building? And when do we draw the line between simple early buildings and Architecture with a capital A?

I'm afraid the last question is a bit of a red herring – in other words, I'm not going to answer it. Architectural historian Nikolaus Pevsner began his *Outline of European Architecture* by loftily declaring that a bicycle shed was unworthy of his attention because it was not architecture, but I'll be spending a lot of time lurking behind the bike sheds of history. And as for the problem of origins, well, I've cheated. I haven't begun at *the* beginning (for all his flaws, Mahler was no Neanderthal); instead, I've selected a point – which could have been any point at which a human retreated to a primitive hut – that harks back to the beginning of things. In the process I've exchanged the parabola of time's arrow for a game of snakes and ladders, less elegant perhaps, but more appropriate for mapping my tangled subject. Throughout this book, though it is arranged chronologically in ten object-focused chapters, I'll follow a similarly meandering path, pinballing through time and space in order to flesh out my themes – sex, power, morality and so on – as they connect to architecture. So let's slide down Mahler's snake to the primordial swamp: his humble choice of workplace suggests an atavistic hankering for my present theme, architectural origins.

Mahler went to the mountains to escape the distractions of the modern city, completing most of his major works in a succession of three Alpine *Häuschen* – 'houselets' – in breaks from directing orchestras in Vienna and New York. The wooden structure I described above was to be his final hut, standing on land belonging to the farmhouse where he stayed for the last three summers of his life in the Tyrolean commune of Toblach. Far from the heat and noise of Vienna, Toblach was still a scene of pre-industrial rural life at the beginning of the twentieth century. Rural life drove Mahler mad. He wrote exasperated letters to his wife about the racket his hosts made. 'What a joy it would be to stay in the country if the peasants came into the world as deaf-mutes!'[2] ran one, and on another occasion, 'The world would be a wonderful place if one had a few acres of land with a fence round it, and were all alone in the middle.'[3] But his *Häuschen* was not safe from the world and its exasperating inhabitants. Peasants scrambled over the five-foot fence to ask for money, so he had barbed wire strung along the top. Even then he was plagued by less tangible intrusions: driven to distraction by farmyard noises, he asked his landlord, 'How can we teach the cock not to crow?' 'Simple,' came the reply. 'Wring its neck.'[4]

Besides the usual irritations of country life, Mahler's rural idyll turned out to be anything but: it was on an Alpine holiday in 1907 that his young daughter died of pneumonia, and in 1910 he had a nervous breakdown in Toblach after discovering that his wife had been having an affair with the architect Walter Gropius – later head of the Bauhaus, and builder of another primitive structure, the wooden Sommerfeldhaus in suburban Berlin. Broken-hearted and heart diseased, Mahler died the following spring; it seems that, even boxed up and fenced in, there was no way to keep the world out.

Mahler was not alone in his shed; many artists and writers have worked in similarly basic structures. Inspiration for some seems to depend on solitude and on going back to the beginning, to the most elemental building – on wiping the slate clean before the act of creation. Mark Twain, Virginia Woolf, Dylan Thomas, Roald Dahl and George Bernard Shaw all wrote in huts (Shaw's pivoted on its base to follow the sun); Heidegger and Wittgenstein philosophised in shacks; and Gauguin died in a cabin in the South Pacific surrounded by underage islanders – he called it his *maison du jouir*, 'house of orgasm'. Gauguin had travelled to Polynesia on a grant from the French government, who wanted him to depict the locals and their customs as a record and perhaps as an advertisement to encourage other colonials. Fleeing bourgeois domesticity, he painted an imaginary untouched culture while poisoning it with syphilis.

The granddaddy of all shed-based artists was the American writer Henry David Thoreau, who in 1845 built a hut on his friend Emerson's land in order to commune with nature but without the inconvenience of backwoods isolation. Thoreau's retreat, as recorded in his book *Walden*, was not a rejection of modernity. In his chapter on the sounds he hears in his hut, he lists pastoral standbys like birdsong, the bells of distant churches and 'the lowing of some disconsolate cow', but he also describes the sounds of passing trains: 'The whistle of the locomotive penetrates my woods summer and winter, sounding like the scream of a hawk.' Unlike Mahler, Thoreau is not perturbed by these man-made and natural sounds, but welcomes them as communications from the outside world. For Thoreau, humans and our machines are in a kind of harmony with nature, not some aberrant imposition. He walks to the nearest village along the railway and observes that he is 'related to society by this link'.[5]

A little log cabin at Todtnauberg in the Black Forest without running water or electricity was the refuge of a writer with a more troubling relish for reverse gear. This was the place where German philosopher Martin Heidegger wrote many of his works. It was also where he hosted a bonfire party for students and teachers from Freiburg University, of which he was rector, in 1933. They met there, in the darkness of the wood with the firelight flickering on their eager faces, to discuss the Nazification of the German universities, for Heidegger had proclaimed his allegiance to the new regime. I'm not suggesting that hut dwellers are evil. Despite his deeply problematic politics, some of Heidegger's ideas about building are still valid. His notion that inhabitation creates buildings just as much as builders do and his emphasis on vernacular structures are useful correctives to views of architecture that exclude experience and the non-professional. But there is something troubling about his return to architectural origins. In Heidegger's philosophy architectural complexities tend to be reduced to the concept of dwelling. In order to 'dwell authentically', Heidegger suggests that we give up technologies that sever our metaphysical connection with things and places. This is a big change from Thoreau's harmonic view of technology and nature, but then Thoreau belonged to a vanished world. Technological advance seemed very different to Germans a century after *Walden* – especially those with right-wing tendencies (Heidegger's obsession with rootedness has affinities with the Nazi theory of 'blood and soil', the spurious connection of races and places that inspired the erection of folksy cottages for Aryans – and genocide). But although the idea of dwelling is meant to be a corrective to over-rationalised views of architecture, ironically it tends to abstraction. Likewise, for Heidegger history itself became historicity, an abstract condition of being rather than a succession of specific social circumstances. Cause and effect were unhinged by this metaphysics of experience, as were ethics; he never really apologised for supporting the Nazis. His hut, cut off from society, modernity, and – by returning to the origin of building – from history itself, was a good place to put his feet up and forget about his responsibilities.

Beyond the eccentric orbit of composers and philosophers, whose problems may seem far removed from everyday concerns, hut dwelling is also a popular leisure activity. Dachas, those clapboard country houses that make Russia the most populous second-home-owning nation; wonkily perfect Japanese tea houses; five-star beach shacks in atoll resorts; gnome-filled garden colonies (those allotments with summer houses that cling to the side of German railways); and British beach huts alike attest to a widespread desire for the simple life – although of course few holidaymaking hut dwellers have to shit in a bucket; *nostalgie de la boue* (literally 'nostalgia for mud') doesn't usually stretch that far. We, and many of the artists I mentioned earlier, owe our present hankering after the simple life to Rousseau and his followers: by adopting the hovel of the noble savage, Romantic logic goes, we too can wash away the corrupting influence of civilisation.

As for the shed workers above, it seems a place without history where you can make a fresh start, although there is something suspect about playing primitives. Huts, in the real world, do have a history – usually one of disenfranchisement. They also have leaky roofs, inadequate sanitation and are filled with pests and freezing draughts. They are the kind of houses that get crushed by landslides, flattened by earthquakes and swept away by wildfires and tsunamis. If we go looking for a pre-Romantic English hut, we'll find instead a hovel (the word hut didn't come into currency until the seventeenth century), and a hovel was not a home for a noble savage but for a serf. King Lear is exiled from his castle to a hovel, a reversal of such enormity that sense and language go on the blink as all around is buffeted by pathetic fallacy. Horror of the hovel dissipated after political and industrial revolutions swept away the *anciens régimes* of Europe, when the muddy reality of feudal life began to fade from popular memory and sheds could be safely idealised. But some features of feudalism survive to this day. Five-star beach huts in Bali are the modern equivalent of Marie Antoinette's fake farm cottage at Versailles, where she aped a milkmaid artfully dressed in silken rags; they are places for the jaded rich to play at rural misery while all around the locals inhabit the real deal.

Historians looking in their rear-view mirrors face the same problems as artists, philosophers and tourists who try to turn back time on architecture. A Roman military engineer of the first century BC named Vitruvius wrote a treatise *On Architecture* – the earliest surviving work on the topic – that retells the genesis of building. His account, largely forgotten in the Middle Ages and then rediscovered by Renaissance scholars, became almost scriptural for later architects.

At the beginning of time, he says, humans were like animals, foraging for food and living in caves and woods. One day a forest fire drew humans together by its warmth. United by this source of heat and light, people began to talk, and since they were now living together, to build simple homes – some of branches and leaves, some in covered burrows, and others, inspired by swallows' nests, of wattle and daub. These structures improved over time, as humans strove to better their homes in a spirit of peaceful competition. Finally, Vitruvius adds, 'That houses originated as I have written above, we can see for ourselves from the buildings that are to this day constructed of like materials by foreign tribes' (the past has ever been another country).[6] Vitruvius was a military engineer whose job involved working on forts in colonial outposts, and this brought him into contact with the tribes whose structures he cites as examples of primitive architecture, a very particular context – aggressive, arrogant and paranoid – in which to build, look at and think about architecture, and a funny one in which to surmise that 'peaceful competition' is the spur to architectural innovation.

Vitruvius imagined that his own Gracco-Roman architecture had begun just as humbly as that of the foreign tribes he fought, arguing that even the grandest temples were modelled on wooden predecessors – according to his theory the decorative motifs carved in the marble were originally functional elements of the timber construction. However it was the genius of the Greeks – Vitruvius asserts – to have given these petrified huts the perfect proportions of the human figure. The orders of classical architecture – the traditional division of buildings into different types according to the proportions of their columns and type of ornament – were first described in his treatise. Each of the orders, he says, was derived from a human type: the Doric order, simple and robust, was derived from the proportions of a man; the Ionic, refined and ornamented, from the proportions of a woman; and the Corinthian, slender and highly decorative, was based on the figure of a virgin.

Vitruvius' explanations of the origin of Architecture with a capital A are charmingly fanciful, but there is also a dark side to his fairy tale: Italian bodies were, of all races, the most beautiful, and destined to take over the world – as must their buildings. This kind of preposterous architectural bigotry was also popular with Nazi theorists, who thought that German cottages looked like the smiling faces of Aryan peasants, whereas modernist buildings were like the 'blank' and 'pulpy' faces of 'others'.[7]

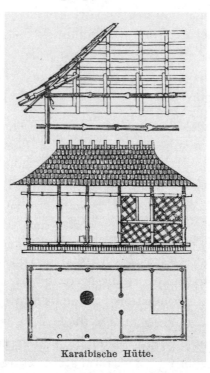

Karaibische Hütte.

Semper's abstract Caraib cottage

Let's skip forward 1,500 years from Vitruvius to another encounter with architectural origins. The year is 1851, and in the Crystal Palace an exiled German revolutionary and erstwhile court architect to the King of Saxony named Gottfried Semper is studying the spoils assembled by the world's largest empire. Among the jumbled loot of the Great Exhibition his attention is drawn to a humble West Indian dwelling – what he referred to as a 'Caraib cottage' – made from woven bamboo. It was during these years of London exile that Semper planned his huge, unreadable, yet enormously influential book, *Style in the Technical and Tectonic Arts*, in which he was to argue that architecture originated in simple huts like the one he had seen in the Crystal Palace. Semper's inspirational brush with the primitive may seem a straightforward reiteration of Vitruvius' experience of barbarian buildings, but unlike Vitruvius, who had insisted on the importance of human proportions, Semper focused on four basic techniques – weaving, ceramics, carpentry and masonry – and on the abstract spaces these create. The Caraib cottage was significant because, he said, 'It shows all the elements of antique architecture in their pure and most original form: the *hearth* as the centre point, raised earth as a *terrace* surrounded by posts, the column supported *roof*, and the woven enclosure as a *spatial termination* or *wall*.'[8] This view would have an enormous influence on the development of modern architecture, with its tendency to stress the abstract interplay of spaces and volumes. You might think that chucking out the racist allegories left over from Vitruvian thinking might be an improvement, but Semper's abstracting vision also brackets the circumstances that made possible his encounter with a West Indian hovel in the middle of the world's biggest, most industrial city in 1851. The hut got there because the British empire had transformed the Caribbean into a money factory worked by slaves. The hut was not some abstract space but the former home of a displaced indigenous person (the Caribs resisted slavery and were quickly eradicated from their island homes). Like Vitruvius' imaginary first hut, the first hut of nineteenth-century science was also the home of a colonial subject, brought to the awareness of the theorist by expansionary warfare and, though preserved in his writing, very likely burned, smashed and eradicated in reality.

Belgian station on the Congo River, 1889

The beginning of architectural history, imagined in ancient Rome or Victorian London, has often meant the end of someone else's architecture. This violent dialectic is explored in Joseph Conrad's 1899 tale *Heart of Darkness*, in which the narrator journeys up the Congo River in search of a renegade Belgian trader named Kurtz. It is also, we are made to understand, a journey back in time. Along the way various Europeans encountered by the narrator sing Kurtz's praises: he is eloquent, artistic, a genius. But when we finally get to Kurtz's station, we're in for a nasty surprise. Something has gone deeply wrong with the European about whom we've heard so much, and tellingly the first sign of the man's return to barbarism is architectural. The narrator, looking through his binoculars, glimpses a tumbledown building in the distance. After remarking on the gaping holes in its roof, he adds,

There was no enclosure or fence of any kind; but there had been one apparently, for near the house half-a-dozen slim posts remained in a row, roughly trimmed, and with their upper ends ornamented with round carved balls . . . Then I went carefully from post to post with my glass, and I saw my mistake. These round knobs were not ornamental but symbolic; they were expressive and puzzling, striking and disturbing – food for thought and also for vultures if there had been any looking down from the sky.[9]

The knobs on the top of the fence posts are grinning, desiccated human heads, 'expressive and puzzling' ornaments symbolising the violence at the point of origin, the violence that lies beneath Semper's spatial abstractions and Vitruvius' Arcadian myth. If we accept the dubious notion that a journey up the Congo is also a journey back in time, then the idea that architecture began with human cooperation is questioned by those heads on sticks. Certainly, the assertion that the genius of the Greeks lay in giving their temples human proportions is given a dark twist by this extreme anthropomorphism. Conrad's tale, told on the brink of the twentieth century, comes at the high-water mark of European expansion, and though almost the entire world was now under the thumb of Westerners, some – Conrad included – began to realise that something had gone wrong. But although Conrad attempts to lay bare the violence of colonialism, his language is shot through with the same contempt for African lives that created the horror of the Belgian Congo, in which ten million people died (his comparison of a technically adept African to a dog in breeches sticks in the mind).[10] The horrors of European barbarism were finally brought home when, between 1914 and 1945, we turned techniques practised on the rest of the world against ourselves. These techniques included a special kind of primitive dwelling first invented by the British in the Boer War: the concentration camp.

★

After the world wars Europe was shell-shocked, its relationship to its own past traumatised, its view of history unhinged. This extended to imaginings of architectural primitivism, as in Samuel Beckett's 1946 novella *First Love*, composed shortly after the author's time with the French Resistance.

> Now that the air was beginning to strike chill, and for other reasons better not wasted on cunts like you, [I] took refuge in a deserted cowshed marked on one of my forays. It stood in the corner of a field richer on the surface in nettles than in grass and in mud than in nettles, but whose subsoil was perhaps possessed of exceptional qualities. It was in this byre, littered with dry and hollow cowclaps subsiding with a sigh at the poke of my finger, that for the first time in my life, and I would not hesitate to say the last if I had not to husband my cyanide, I had to contend with a feeling which gradually assumed, to my dismay, the dread name of love.[11]

Beckett's narrator invites us into his primitive refuge, a deserted cowshed. This harks back to another kind of primitivism, which precedes Romantic ideals of the purity of origins: the simple shepherd's hut as hymned by ancient poets like Virgil. Traditionally a site of pastoral maunderings, Beckett points out the shit on the floor; nevertheless, it's still a place of love – creator of life – and also of literary creation, for it is here, the narrator says, 'I found myself inscribing the letters of Lulu in an old heifer pat.' Beckett's cruel exposure of love and art's feet of clay comes after a digression on the topic of history, and on its enduring fascination for the Irish:

> What constitutes the charm of our country, apart of course from its scant population, and this without help of the meanest contraceptive, is that all is derelict, with the sole exception of history's ancient faeces. These are ardently sought after, stuffed and carried in procession. Wherever nauseated time has dropped a

nice fat turd you will find our patriots, sniffing it up on all fours, their faces on fire.[12]

He innocently adds, 'I see no connexion between these remarks,' but at this moment in time, love, history and creation seemed united in excrementality. However, there were now significantly fewer ancient architectural turds left to sniff in the cities of Europe – the Luftwaffe and the RAF had seen to that. The slate had been wiped clean, and it was time for a new beginning.

Patio and Pavilion (1956)

A more hopeful – moderately more hopeful – post-war primitivism rose from these ashes. The exhibition This is Tomorrow, held in London in 1956, is often seen as the birth of pop art, that moment when high culture incorporated commercial imagery in an orgy of lightly ironic celebration. One exhibit at the show had a distinctly different tone, however: entering a high wooden enclosure (are we back in Mahler's alpine valley?) visitors found themselves on a sandy wasteland strewn with debris (emphatically not). In the middle stood a ramshackle shed full of holes with a corrugated-plastic roof. Walking around the structure to its open front, the visitor was confronted by its inhabitant, a huge collaged head, grotesque and ancient, flayed, burned and ossified, and, on closer inspection, made up of fragments of enlarged microscopic images, photographs of charred wood and rusted metal, and a picture of an old boot. This installation, called *Patio and Pavilion*, was the contribution of a group of four architects and artists: Alison and Peter Smithson, pioneers of brutalism and architects of the controversial public housing project, Robin Hood Gardens; artist Eduardo Paolozzi and photographer Nigel Henderson. Together they imagined a shed after the nuclear apocalypse, that destroying angel that hovered over the 1950s. The products of Western consumerism, celebrated and enshrined in the show's other installations, became here bent and twisted archaeo-logical relics of a past civilisation reconfigured into weird new constellations, and the new human sheltering in their midst is made from those same fragments. It is an insistent reminder that new beginnings depend on the destruction of the past. Reminiscing about the exhibition, the Smithsons noted their closeness in this period to Beckett, and there is something of Beckett's exhausted persistence in this scrabbled-together dwelling: 'I can't go on, I'll go on.' These words compress the vexing complexity of architectural history. In the face of the horrors of the last century, the myth of progress, including architectural progress, has often seemed a busted flush. The writing of history, too often a myth-making exercise, comes into question itself, and yet to abandon it is even more dangerous; perhaps, from the fragmentary remains, something habitable can be put together.

In this book I'll be looking at ten buildings from times and places as far-flung as ancient Babylon, early-modern Beijing and contemporary Rio. Instead of trying to join these dots I'll be paying attention to differences, to the specificity of times and places. Though each chapter follows a theme, like origins, as in this introduction, or sex or work, I'll try not to bracket out history, as Semper or Heidegger did, in favour of abstract concepts like volume or dwelling or any one of those meaningless words so beloved of architectural critics. As this discussion of origins has (I hope) shown, my themes are protean, squirming and changing to escape giving up their secrets. Like the buildings themselves, they mutate over time, as people bring new meanings to them, reuse them, pervert them, expand them and destroy them. They require a variety of specialised approaches, like the snark in Lewis Carroll's poem, which has to be hunted with railway shares, forks and hope (the snark turned out to be a fatal boojum, of course). What *does* unify my approach to all these buildings is an interest in how architecture shapes people's lives *and vice versa* (we can still shape it today, if we try). It is the most inescapable of art forms: you can avoid paintings and chamber music, you can, at a push, avoid films and photography, but even Bedouin have their tents. Everywhere, people are in architecture, and architecture is in us – an integral part of our societies, our lives, our minds.

The Tower of Babel, Babylon
(c.650 BC)
Architecture and Power

And Babylon shall become heaps, a dwelling-place for dragons, an astonishment, and a hissing, without an inhabitant.

Jeremiah 51:37

An oil gusher at Baba Gurgur oilfield in Iraq, formerly Babylon (c.1932).
In the foreground a river of oil flows through the desert

When British forces entered Baghdad in March 1917, so securing the crucial oilfields of the former Ottoman empire, German archaeologist Robert Koldewey was forced to abandon one of the most fabulous discoveries of the twentieth century: the ancient city of Babylon. Since 1898 Koldewey had been digging in Mesopotamia (present-day Iraq), the fertile 'land between rivers' where Babylon once stood, and where archaeologists tell us that writing, architecture, and the city were invented.[1] He had already shipped the magnificent Ishtar Gate back to Berlin and was now excavating the Hanging Gardens (or so he thought: his identification of those particular remains turned out to be wrong).

One of his most intriguing finds, admittedly not much to look at compared with the glistening blue tiles of the Ishtar Gate, was a rectangular pit filled with stagnant water. But this pit revealed the foundations of a building that had for millennia existed only in legends: the Tower of Babel. Called by its Babylonian builders *Etemenanki* – House of the Foundation of Heaven and the Underworld – the tower was an enormous ziggurat or step pyramid with a temple on its summit consecrated to the god Marduk, the fearsomely bearded creator of mankind and patron deity of Babylon. But although Babylon and its gods were wiped off the map centuries before the birth of Christ, the Tower of Babel has lived on for over two thousand years, haunting our imaginations in paintings, legends, wars and revolutions. A potent double image, it stands for the power of architecture over people, and vice-versa. Depending on the way you read the story of Babel, its tower either oppressed the people forced to build it, or it was liberating, bringing its makers together in a common endeavour of self-empowerment.

These twin towers – positive and negative images of the same building – face off like two mirrors creating an infinite echo of receding towers. Babel, Bastille, World Trade Center ... Monumental structures like the Tower of Babel have been built since the dawn of history. They are very obvious manifestations of architectural power, as are prisons, palaces, parliaments and schools, but even architecture built by ordinary people – whether houses or garden sheds – expresses and perpetuates power relations in everyday life. This theme comes up again and again in the story of bricks and mortals, but the present chapter is a tale of grandiose structures, and the fight against them – whether in Paris, New York or Baghdad, where the ruins of the Tower of Babel sit on one of the biggest oilfields in the world. There is no greater power in the world today than oil, and its story is intimately entwined with that of architecture. Telling it will take us through some unexpected twists and turns. Brecht wrote that 'petroleum resists depiction in five acts: today's catastrophes do not unfold in linear fashion, but in cycles of crises in which each fungible "hero" changes with the individual phases'; likewise, the story of the Tower of Babel has many protagonists – hijackers, archaeologist-spies, iconoclasts and kings.[2] So let's drill down through the layers of history – back through the invasion of Iraq, 9/11, the world wars, the rediscovery of the Tower of Babel, the search for oil in the Middle East – and beyond, to the beginning of scriptural time.

The most familiar account of the Tower of Babel appears in the Bible. According to the author of the Book of Genesis, the people of the world (who were united at the dawn of history) decided to build 'a tower, whose top may reach unto heaven' in order to 'make a name, lest we be scattered'.[3] But when God noticed what his creations were up to, his reaction was typically curmudgeonly. 'Behold,' he kvetched, 'the people is one, and they have all one language; and this they begin to do: and now nothing will be restrained from them.'⁴ In order to bring a halt to their antics he gave the people different languages and scattered them to the four corners of the world – 'therefore is the name of it called Babel; because the Lord did there confound the language of all the earth'.⁵

In this succinct tale the Bible illustrates both the utopian aspirations of builders and the ultimate limit of architecture's possibilities. It is usually read as a warning against hubris, for example by Flavius Josephus, a Romanised Jew of the first century. He misidentified the leader of Babylon as Nimrod, great-grandson of Noah, a tyrannical monarch who convinced the people that they didn't need God because it was within their own power to be happy. 'He also said he would be revenged on God, if he should have a mind to drown the world again; for that he would build a tower too high for the waters to be able to reach! And that he would avenge himself on God for destroying their forefathers!'⁶ This reading ingeniously provides a motive for the builders, but if you look more closely at the biblical tale, the text doesn't explicitly say that hubris is their crime. Despite the apparent simplicity of the tale, there is a deep ambiguity at play: depending on the way you see it, either the builders of the tower or the vengeful deity are working for the benefit of mankind. From the former perspective, the tower is an expression of the unity of humanity, and God stops it because he jealously refuses to accept any challenge to his power. Alternatively, you could say that God freed mankind from the implied tyranny of the Babylonian monarch, and the unity he enforced in order to build a massive and pointless vanity project. It's an ambiguity that recurs throughout the history of architecture: buildings have great potential as a means of empowering people, but they can also enslave them. Sometimes these two forces are united in one structure.

The Tower of Babel isn't just an enormous allegory; there is also a core of historical truth to the story. Indeed, the Jews were much more closely acquainted with the city of Babylon than they might have liked. Many of them spent fifty years there during the Babylonian Captivity, which followed an unsuccessful uprising against their imperial master King Nebuchadnezzar II. Ruler of a recently resurgent empire, Nebuchadnezzar had spent years restoring his capital to the glory of its early days – with a little help from his army of slaves. Building was a way of controlling an intensely hierarchical society, and like the Pyramids, the Great Wall of China (in the construction of which an estimated million workers died) or Stalin's White Sea Canal, Nebuchadnezzar's works were completed by captives, making life for the builders 'bitter with hard bondage, in mortar, and in brick'[7] – as the Jews later found in Egypt.

At the centre of Nebuchadnezzar's shiny new capital stood a reconstruction of the huge ziggurat dedicated to the god Marduk, a structure that had been destroyed by invading Assyrians in 689 BC. It took the Babylonians a century to rebuild their tower, and it was finally crowned with a blue-tiled temple during Nebuchadnezzar's reign. The proportions of the tower's rectangular plan may have been based on the constellation the Greeks named Pegasus. 'Reaching to the stars' was how the Tower of Babel is described on ancient tablets, and the temple on its summit would have made a fine observatory for the country's astrologer-priests. This sidereal alignment slotted the structure, like the Pyramids and Stonehenge, into the overarching structure of the cosmos. It's a way of making architecture – and culture as a whole, including the systems of belief, administration and coercion that organise it – appear to be an unchangeable, unquestionable part of nature itself. A *second* nature. By extension, the power of Nebuchadnezzar is made to feel as inexorable as the solidity of the ziggurat and the trajectory of the constellations. Architecture like this can have a petrifying effect on society, creating an impression that existing institutions should always be the way they are – there is a reason, after all, that so many of our banks, government buildings and universities mimic ancient temples.

Apart from being a great patron, Nebuchadnezzar was also a wrecker of architecture. In 588–7 BC he razed the Temple in Jerusalem – the holiest site of Judaism – in retaliation for the Jewish uprising. He then exiled the Jews to his own city in order to keep a closer eye on his recalcitrant subjects. This was the beginning of the diaspora, the great exodus from the Promised Land, so it is no wonder that the Jews had an enduringly negative memory of the architecture of their colonial overlords and dreamed up divine devastations of Nebuchadnezzar's capital. The prophet Jeremiah, who was probably a captive in Babylon, made an horripilating prophecy of the destruction of that proud city: 'And the land shall tremble and sorrow: for every purpose of the Lord shall be performed against Babylon, to make the land of Babylon a desolation without an inhabitant.'[8] Jeremiah's prediction is reiterated when the city makes one final, show-stopping appearance at the very end of the New Testament in the form of a woman riding a seven-headed beast. St John's hallucinatory Babylon is a stand-in for contemporary Rome, oppressor of the Christians. Rome may have been too risky to criticise directly, but the message is clear: 'Babylon is fallen, is fallen, that great city, because she made all nations drink of the wine of her fornication.'[9] Babylon has by this point become the sin city par excellence, and for millennia since it has been a touchstone of anti-urbanism, standing for metropolitan decadence wherever it might be found or imagined – Disraeli called London 'a modern Babylon' in 1847. In Rastafarianism and the reggae music it inspired the image-city of Babylon has sprawled even wider to encompass the whole of Western civilisation, with its bureaucratic corruption of natural man.

For centuries Christian travellers to Mesopotamia mulled over these biblical stories as they contemplated the obliteration of the Babylonians; unlike the still-impressive remains of ancient Egypt,

here absence was significance. Visitors found in the total blankness
of the desert a confirmation of biblical truth and a powerful political parable: a 'most terrible example to all impious and haughty
tyrants' in the words of sixteenth-century German traveller
Leonhard Rauwolf.[10] There was something in that, for in the end
it actually *was* hubris that destroyed the Tower of Babel, without
any need for divine intervention. Alexander the Great – self-
declared deity, hubris personified – earmarked the city of Babylon
for the capital of his empire during the course of his many rampages
back and forth through the ancient world. Its ancient splendour
and cyclopean scale doubtless appealed to his inflated ego, as its
still-massive walls (8.4 kilometres long and 17–22 metres thick)
appealed to his paranoia. But when Alexander entered the city in
331 BC, he found it in a state of decayed grandeur, and the Tower
of Babel crumbling. Like Nebuchadnezzar before him, he decided
to rebuild the structure, but – never one for half measures – he
wanted to do it from scratch. He commanded an army of ten thousand to clear the site, carting mud bricks away from the imposing
heap over a period of two months. But one month later he was
dead, aged only thirty-two, and the tower was never rebuilt.

The Bible doesn't tell us much about how the tower actually
looked, but we can get some idea of its appearance from other
sources. The Greek historian Herodotus claimed that it consisted
of eight levels with a temple on the top. A cuneiform tablet from
229 BC roughly confirms his description, although it is very unlikely
that Herodotus actually went to Babylon; his account, used to
justify Greece's war against Persia, is a dodgy dossier of cobbled-
together rumours, like his prurient story about the god descending
for intercourse with his priestess on the summit of the tower. Such
loose descriptions left a great deal of room for later invention, and
artists in the Renaissance developed an image of a circular multi-
storeyed tower spiralling up into the clouds. The most famous
depiction of the tower is a 1563 painting by Pieter Bruegel in which

Pieter Bruegel, Tower of Babel (c.1563)

a monstrous structure looms over a very un-Middle-Eastern land-scape – it looks more like the Netherlands. The tower in Bruegel's painting seems to be partly constructed from the living rock, the ultimate unification of architecture and nature, and in the fore-ground builders break off from carving huge blocks of stone in order to genuflect before their imperial master.

Because Babylon was a city of the imagination, it tended to look like whatever your oppressors looked like at the time. This has been the case ever since St John wrote his Book of Revelation, in which already-long-gone Babylon, oppressor of the Jews, stood in for imperial Rome, oppressor of the Christians. This got an update in 1520, when Luther wrote 'the papacy is truly the kingdom of Babylon, yes, the kingdom of the real Antichrist!', and Protestants have been comparing the Roman Church to Babylon ever since. For Bruegel too – a subject of the Spanish who at that time counted the Netherlands as part of their empire – Rome echoes Babylon. The superimposed arches of his circular tower are like the ruins of the Colosseum, which the artist had visited twelve years previously, and Rome was the seat of the Catholic faith of his Habsburg rulers. But the Netherlands was experiencing a rising tide of Protestantism, and Spanish enforcement of Catholic conformity rankled. Like the builders of the Tower of Babel, the Catholics spoke one tongue – Latin – in their religious services, whereas Protestantism was polyglot. For the Protestants of the Low Countries, the enforced uniformity and religious intolerance of the Spanish was an insufferable imposition. But the tower is unfinished, in fact unfinishable, because its foundations are already cracking as work continues at the pinnacle, and not one of its many layers seems to be complete. For Bruegel the Spanish are Babylonian in their arrogance and similarly doomed to failure.

Only three years after Bruegel painted his crumbling, unfinishable tower, a wave of iconoclastic devastation known as the *Beeldenstorm* – 'statue storm' – broke out in the Netherlands. Many of those taking part were Calvinists reacting to a recent Spanish crackdown on their heretical beliefs. According to an exiled English Catholic named Nicolas Sander, who was present at the desecration of the church of Our Lady in Antwerp:

> Followers of this new preaching threw down the graven and defaced the painted images, not only of Our Lady but of all others in the town. They tore the curtains, dashed in pieces the carved work of brass and stone, brake the altars, spoilt the clothes and corporesses, wrested the irons, conveyed away or brake the chalices and vestiments, pulled up the brass of the gravestones, not sparing the glass and seats which were made about the pillars of the church for men to sit in . . . The Blessed Sacrament of the altar . . . they trod under their feet and (horrible it is to say!) shed their stinking piss upon it.[11]

Lavatorial protests soon erupted all over the Netherlands. As historian Peter Arnade drily records, 'one Isabeau Blancheteste in Limburg urinated in the priest's chalice; iconoclasts in 's-Hertogenbosch did the same in priest's chests; an iconoclast in Hulst outside Antwerp threw a crucifix he had pulled down into his pigsty; and the Count of Culemborg fed the Eucharist wafer to his pet parrot'.[12] As well as vandalism, carnivalesque inversions of authority took place: one protestor gleefully dunked a sculpture head down in a font, shouting, 'I baptise thee!' and crowds pelted a famous statue of the Virgin with stones as she was being processed around Antwerp, crying, 'Little Mary, little Mary! This is your last time!'

By purging their churches and public places of Spanish and Catholic imagery, the iconoclasts hoped to cleanse their architecture – and nation – of tyranny. But it wasn't long before the empire struck back. A local branch of the Inquisition was set up, and around a thousand people were executed in inventive ways. A man named Bertrand le Blas, for example, who had pulled the wafer from a priest's hands during Mass and stamped it into the ground, was tortured to death in the main square at Hainault; as a prelude he was scorched with red-hot pincers, then he had his tongue torn out, and finally he was tied to a stake and slowly roasted to death over a low flame. But the Protestants weren't so easily dissuaded, and during the ensuing Eighty Years' War the Netherlands split into two provinces – the northern, Protestant Dutch Republic winning independence from Spain and eventually becoming the modern state we call the Netherlands, while the predominantly Catholic south initially remained Spanish and ultimately became Belgium. In contrast to the biblical tale, the *Beeldenstorm* was a case of the people, not God, fighting tyranny in its architectural manifestations. Two hundred years later the people of France would take this fight even further, and demolish the edifice of monarchy itself.

★

'Smoke as of Tophet; confusion as of Babel; noise as of the Crack of Doom!' So Thomas Carlyle described the fall of the Bastille in his own rather babbling history of the French Revolution. Here the name of Babel recurs, not as a symbol of tyranny, but as a synonym for, as the Bible tells us, 'confusion'. Carlyle, hagiographer of Frederick the Great, was no fan of democracy – the essence of Babel, a confusion of tongues – neither was he too keen on revolutionaries, who were to him at worst a crazed mob and at best mere figures of fun. 'A distracted "Peruke-maker with two fiery torches" is for burning "the saltpetres of the arsenale"; had not a woman run screaming; had not a Patriot, with some tincture of Natural Philosophy, instantly struck the wind out of him (butt of musket on pit of stomach)': so Carlyle gleefully reports from the scene of the Bastille.[13] But Carlyle's portrayal of the revolutionaries as a rabble says more about his own fears and prejudices than about the French Revolution. He's a Babylonian of the first order, a subscriber to the view that there should only be one architect – god or monarch – and that the confused people shouldn't pester him.

However, the Bastille wasn't toppled by Babylonian confusion, but by the people united against the architecture of oppression. And if any building could be called a modern Tower of Babel (Mark II: tyrannical mode) it would be this grim eight-towered fortress, 'a labyrinthic Mass, high-frowning there, of all ages from twenty years to four hundred and twenty'.[14] The French certainly understood it as a symbol of despotism, but also, after its fall, as a symbol of freedom. Like the Tower of Babel it was a double image, transformed by revolutionary action from a negative to a positive symbol. The image, however, didn't entirely correspond with reality.

Despite rumours of oubliettes full of innocents chained to mouldering skeletons, upon its fall the Bastille was found to contain only seven prisoners: four counterfeiters, one madman and two aristocratic sex pests. None of these was a particularly satisfactory symbol of tyrannical oppression. Instead, just as the attack had been inspired by the literary creations of prisoners past, among them Voltaire, Diderot and several writers of lurid misery-memoirs, it was also post-rationalised by the invention of illustrious and mysterious captives, including the man in the iron mask (loosely based on a real prisoner) and the entirely fictional Count des Lorges. This made-up count was a sort of mass hallucination, conjured by the fervent wish of the people to objectify their revolutionary beliefs. Eyewitnesses swore they had seen him stumbling from the smoking ruins, bent double by forty years in a dungeon, his white beard a foot long and his mole-like eyes squinting at the strange sun. By 1790 this imaginary prisoner had attained such celebrity that several accounts of his unjust incarceration had been written on his behalf, and his image was on show at Philippe Curtius' famous waxworks.

More palpably, the tower itself had a long afterlife as a twin symbol of tyranny and freedom. Though it was almost immediately razed to the ground by a canny property developer named Pierre-François Palloy, the Bastille's stones lived on as knick-knacks commemorating the extinction of tyranny. Rings and earrings were set with fragments from the ruins, its rusty chains were melted down and recast as medals, and Palloy, who had transformed himself from a nouveau riche into a devoted son of the revolution, used his considerable fortune to have large models of the Bastille carved from its fallen blocks. The stones, which he called 'Relics of Freedom', were dispatched under the protection of 'Apostles of Freedom' to each of France's eighty-three departments, where they were (mostly) received with great ceremony. 'France is a new world,' Palloy proclaimed in a speech in 1792, 'and in order to hold on to this achievement, it is necessary to sow the rubble of our old servitude everywhere.'[15] He was true to his word, and continued his mission – ruining himself in the process – by sending slabs from the ruins of the Bastille inscribed with the Declaration of Rights to all 544 districts of France. But this wasn't the end of the Bastille's journey. Like the wind-borne spores of some virulent disease, invisible fragments of the ruined tower spread ever further, far beyond the borders of the nation and of the eighteenth century, even to the supposedly unchanging Orient – to the wastes of Mesopotomia where the Tower of Babel had once stood.

'Where past and present are woven so closely together, the habitual appreciation of the divisions of time slips insensibly away.' So Gertrude Bell – explorer, archaeologist, kingmaker and spy – began her Mesopotamian travel memoir *Amurath to Amurath* (1911) with a cliché of eternal Orient-mongers.

> And yet there was a new note. For the first time in all the turbulent centuries to which those desolate regions bear witness, a potent word had gone forth, and who caught it listened in amazement, asking one another for an explanation of its meaning. Liberty – what is liberty? . . . Idly though it fell from the lips of the Bedouin, it foretold change. That sense of change, uneasy and bewildered, hung over the whole Ottoman Empire.[16]

The aftershocks of the Bastille's fall were finally being felt across the Bosporus, where the Ottoman empire tottered under the pressure of reformers and the burgeoning nationalism of its subject peoples. The Young Turks had taken up the baton with their revolution in 1908, and soon the idea of liberty spread out into the desert lands of the empire, always somewhat tenuously mastered by Constantinople. This was why Gertrude Bell – the first woman to leave Oxford with a first in history, one of the most proficient mountaineers in Europe and an expert on the Middle East – had been tasked by British military intelligence with keeping an eye on the fractious Bedouin during her travels through Mesopotamia. The possibility of an Arab spring was of the keenest interest to the

British, who wanted control over the region. For most British officials, Mesopotamia's significance lay solely in its proximity to India; however, a small yet powerful group centred on the Admiralty, including Winston Churchill, who became first lord in 1911, had a different prize in mind – oil. The only problem was, they weren't the only ones to have spotted it.

Since the end of the nineteenth century a new force had been threatening the supremacy of the British empire, as a sustained boom pushed the German Reich's industrialists, bankers and administrators in search of new markets and raw materials. There was very little on offer in terms of colonial possessions, the British long having snapped up most of the world's weaker nations, so instead the Reich struck an alliance with the debt-ridden Ottoman empire on Europe's doorstep. By a momentous deal made in 1889, the Germans won the concession to build a railway through Anatolia. This was expanded ten years later to a route stretching all the way from Berlin to Baghdad, a colossal and colossally expensive undertaking that would have finally united the inaccessible lands of the Ottomans and given the Germans ready access to the Persian Gulf. This prospect terrified the British, who were already nervous about the rapid expansion of the German navy. In response they seized control of Kuwait in 1901, cutting off German access to the coast and resulting in an uneasy stalemate. This didn't last long: in 1903 an eccentric Anglo-Australian millionaire named William Knox D'Arcy discovered oil in neighbouring Persia (modern Iran), and everything changed.

D'Arcy had spent years and millions seeking oil in the Middle East, egged on by First Sea Lord Jacky Fisher, who was convinced that the future of the Royal Navy (and hence the empire itself) depended on its conversion to oil. Lighter, faster and less labour intensive than coal, it would give the British fleet a crucial edge over the Germans. But exploration and extraction proved more expensive than even D'Arcy's vast resources could support. Then the group set up to manage the oilfields, the Anglo-Persian Oil Company, which later became BP, also began to run out of money. By 1912 it was in dire straits and looking for a reliable backer. After long internal wrangles, in 1914 Her Majesty's Government secretly bought a controlling stake in the company at the behest of Winston Churchill, who was continuing Fisher's project of converting the navy to oil power – just in time, because eleven days after parliament approved Churchill's bill, an archduke was shot in Sarajevo.

The discovery of oil in the region didn't do much for British attitudes to the Berlin–Baghdad Railway, which now came too close for comfort to the oilfields of Persia. Furthermore, it was suspected that oil, possibly in colossal quantities, also lay beneath Mesopotamia. In 1912 the Germans cannily extracted mineral exploration rights for a forty-kilometre corridor along the proposed route of the railway, while a motley group of rival bankers, governments and investors fought it out for the approval of the wily and indecisive Sublime Porte, as the Ottoman government was metonymically known, to explore the rest of Mesopotamia.

There were other people making holes in Mesopotamia at the time, and not just for oil. Just as the Germans and British competed for the region's mineral wealth, and hence its future, they also struggled for control of its past. The two endeavours were inextricably intertwined in figures like T. E. Lawrence 'of Arabia' and Gertrude Bell, who mixed archaeology with espionage. (Lawrence was sent to keep an eye on the progress of the Berlin–Baghdad Railway under the pretext of archaeological exploration.) Adventurous Europeans had been poking about in the region for centuries, but as the Ottoman empire disintegrated they felt emboldened to explore more tenaciously and to take more home with them. Inspired by classical writers like Herodotus, a desire to prove the historical truth of Bible stories and the political expediency of understanding the terrain and its inhabitants, early explorers – usually gentleman diplomats – unearthed strange-looking fragments. As Magnus Bernhardsson put it, these early archaeologists 'demystified history, as its sources were no longer limited to the Bible or Classical works, and were made more tangible. In this process, history became property' – specifically, the property of Europeans and Americans.[17] However, because of deeply ingrained prejudices against 'oriental' civilisations, scholars back home thought these artefacts very poor compared to the productions of ancient Greece, and a public relations battle ensued to win financial and governmental backing for Near Eastern archaeology.

One champion of the nascent discipline was an Englishman named Henry Austen Layard, who had been digging in Mesopotamia since 1845. After failing to win the backing of the British Museum (one of the BM's trustees called his finds 'a parcel of rubbish' best displayed 'at the bottom of the sea'), he went public, shrewdly marketing his account of his discoveries, *Nineveh and its Remains*, to British and American Bible-bashers. One of Layard's friends had advised him: 'Write a whopper with lots of plates . . . fish up old legends and anecdotes, and if you can by any means humbug people into the belief that you have established any points in the Bible, you are a made man.'[18] Sure enough, *The Times* called it 'the most extraordinary work of the present age'; it was a transatlantic bestseller, and the British Museum finally opened a gallery dedicated to the Near East, where you can still see the reliefs that Layard discovered, guarded by two enormous winged beasts.

Now the Germans joined the fray, but as Gertrude Bell discovered they had a very different approach to the past. They didn't need to make populist appeals to biblical authority since their government – which had a warmer relationship with the Ottomans than the British did – supported their expeditions from the outset. Their methods were also quite un-English. Bell ran into archaeologists of various nationalities on her travels

Marduk (right) *chasing Anzu, from Henry Austen Layard's* Monuments of Nineveh *(1853)*

around the desert and told T. E. Lawrence, whom she liked, that his archaeological technique was 'prehistoric', but she was enormously impressed by the scientific rigour of the Germans. Many of them – including Robert Koldewey, discoverer of Babylon – had trained as architects in their native land, unlike the British, who were usually Oxbridge classicists. Informed by their architectural studies, the Germans tried to preserve the remains of buildings that they uncovered, instead of destroying anything that wasn't easily removed; hence Koldewey's massive pit uncovering the foundations of the Tower of Babel, its onion layers revealing, he theorised, its centuries-long history of ruination and reconstruction. Koldewey was by all accounts a strange and difficult man. Even his friends found him impossible – one of his closest associates called him 'a crank, through and through' – so it is striking to read that Bell thought him highly congenial. But Bell too was unconventional.

An aristocratic outsider, she never married but had two passion-ate (albeit mainly epistolary) affairs with married men. She was far too intelligent and forthright a woman for the taste of most Europeans. MP and baronet Mark Sykes, who was to have a massive influence on Middle Eastern geopolitics, met and quar-relled with Bell in the desert. Sykes thought her a 'silly chattering windbag of a conceited, gushing, flat-chested, man-woman, globe-trotting, rump-wagging, blathering ass'.[19] He also called her a liar and, I am afraid to say, a bitch, but then he found her threatening as a rival Arabist, one unencumbered by his racism (in another of his charming aperçus, he called the Bedouin animals).

An entry in Bell's diary from March 1914 records a more enlight-ened desert encounter – a conversation with Koldewey tinged with mingled affection and foreboding:

Photographed Koldewey and then walked out again with him to the Via Sacra and so along the Tigris to Babil. Here Alexander died . . . 'He was 32,' said Koldewey, 'at 32 I had barely left school and he had conquered the world.' Then came death, unfortunately and it all fell to pieces . . . 'He was mad in Babylon – the perpetual drunkenness, then the story of his killing his friend. Drunk night and day.' I said, 'You must be mad to conquer the world.'[20]

They never met again. War broke out that summer, and although Koldewey hung on in Mesopotamia – which as part of the Ottoman empire was allied with Germany – when the British entered Baghdad in 1917, he unhappily returned to his own coun-try. But Bell did not forget her strange friend, writing in 1918,

On my way home yesterday I stopped at Babylon . . . 'Tempi passati' weigh very heavily there – not that I was thinking of Nebuchadnezzar, nor yet of Alexander, but of the warm welcome I used to find, the good company, the pleasant days I spent with dear Koldewey – It's no good trying to think of him as an alien enemy and my heart ached when I stood in the empty dusty little room where . . . the Germans and I held eager conversations over plans of Babylon . . . What a dreadful world of broken friendships we have created between us.[21]

The outbreak of hostilities may have brought archaeology to a halt, but its spoils were not forgotten: faced with crate-loads of artefacts abandoned by the Germans in their flight, Bell put aside her sentimentality and advised that they be sent to the British Museum. The presence of oil was not forgotten either: how else to explain the presence of nearly 1.5 million British troops in this far-flung theatre of war? One million remained after peace was declared to defend the borders and oilfields of British Mesopotamia, or Iraq as it was now called.

Two of the architects of this new nation were Gertrude Bell and her erstwhile enemy Mark Sykes. Towards the end of the war Sykes, along with his French opposite Maurice Picot, had secretly divided the Middle East between their respective countries. According to the terms of the Sykes–Picot Agreement, after the war France would rule Syria, and Britain would get Iraq and Palestine. This carve-up was totally contrary to the promises of self-determination made to the Arabs in order to encourage them to rise against their Ottoman rulers, and has been responsible for much of the turmoil in the Middle East ever since. Bell and Lawrence, instrumental in liaising between the Arabs and the British government during the war, were well aware of the mendacity of their project but did it anyway. In doing so they proved, tragically, just how British they were: however much they loved the desert and its people, and however much they hated the constraints of life back home, their loyalties lay always with the empire – and so they helped to force the very constraints they loathed upon the rest of the world.

Bell was not untroubled by her role. Though she occasionally indulged in imperial masturbation – 'Truly we are a remarkable

people. We save from destruction remnants of oppressed nations' –
she was also beset by self-doubt, asking, 'How can we, who have
managed our affairs so badly, claim to teach others how to manage
theirs better?'[22] Even so she remained in Iraq after the peace, helping
to anoint Faisal king, after which she sighed, 'I'll never engage in
creating kings again, it's too great a strain.'[23] She also drew up the
nation's antiquities policy and established the famous Baghdad
Museum. Her role diminished, however, as the Iraqi government
became more autonomous, and in 1926 she overdosed on sleeping
pills. It was probably suicide: she couldn't foresee a future in Iraq, but
going home wasn't much of an option either.

Today the remains of the Tower of Babel lie much as Koldewey
left them in 1917: a shallow pit in a demilitarised zone. Unlike
other monuments in the region it was not restored by Saddam
Hussein, who proclaimed at the beginning of his rule that he
would recreate Babylon – hubris never goes out of fashion. He
went on to reconstruct the Ishtar Gate, Nebuchadnezzar's palace

John Martin, The Destruction of Babylon *(1831)*

Shock and Awe: Baghdad in 2003

and the Ziggurat of Ur, reviving an ancient practice by stamping the bricks of these buildings with the words: 'In the reign of the victorious Saddam Hussein, the president of the Republic, may god keep him, the guardian of the great Iraq and the renovator of its renaissance and the builder of its great civilisation, the rebuilding of the great city of Babylon was done in 1987.' Other inscriptions referred to Saddam as 'Son of Nebuchadnezzar'. This wasn't just megalomaniacal posturing, although it certainly was that too. The British had bequeathed Saddam a powder-keg nation of rival ethnic and religious groups, and in order to create a national myth to unite all these factions, he reached back to a time before Sunnis, Shias, Kurds and Bedouin had ever set foot in Iraq.

The post-war despoliation of the numerous national museums that Saddam erected around the country suggests that these efforts were not very popular or successful, but his attempts to restore Babylon were eagerly received in one unexpected quarter.

American evangelicals like Charles Dyer, whose book *The Rise of Babylon* identified Saddam's building projects as a herald of the apocalypse, developed an unhealthy fascination with the Iraqi leader. In a similar vein, the hugely successful *Left Behind* novel sequence detailed the adventures of a group of born-again Christians during an apocalyptic conflict in the Middle East, answering one of the most pressing questions of our time: 'While the world focuses on the chaos in New Babylon and the possible cause for this inexplicable darkness, what about Jerusalem?' This nonsense shifted over sixty-five million copies, helping to boost popular support for the Iraq War among the hugely influential fundamentalist lobby in the US.

Like the oil industry, religious wing nuts couldn't wait for the end times to get going, and self-anointed messiahs Tony Blair and George Bush were only too happy to oblige. Bush told Jacques Chirac on the eve of the invasion, 'This confrontation is willed by God, who wants to use this conflict to erase his people's enemies before a New Age begins.'[24] The shock and awe visited on Baghdad in 2003 was a stage-managed apocalypse, a real-time recreation of previous imaginings of the end of the world in the Middle East, such as John Martin's series of lurid Babylonian paintings and prints from the mid-nineteenth century. It also just happened to bring the world's second-largest oil deposit back under Anglo-American control.

Disappointingly for some, the invasion of Iraq didn't herald the end of the world, but it did cause untold damage to the remains of Babylon. The Baghdad Museum, founded by Bell in 1922 to house those Babylonian artefacts that had not yet been extracted from the country, was looted shortly after the invasion, and coalition forces transformed the site of Babylon itself into a military base, digging trenches and damaging the remaining walls. American marines also painted graffiti on the Ziggurat of Ur, where an enormous airfield was built, complete with a Pizza Hut and two branches of Burger King. Peace has not been much

kinder to Babylon: as the really important business of oil explo-
ration recommenced, a pipeline was laid through the site by the
Iraqi oil ministry in March 2012 despite the protestations of
UNESCO and Iraqi archaeologists.

American soldiers climb Saddam Hussein's restored ziggurat at Ur

Surrounded by the detritus of war, foreign occupation and the
oil industry, the foundations of the Tower of the Babel now lie
gently rotting in their bath of pond water. The tower's absence
mocks the many empires – Babylonian, Alexandrian, Persian,
Ottoman, British, Ba'athist and American – that have tried and
failed to impose unity on this corner of the world. From this
perspective, the destruction of the Tower of Babel can be read as a
tale of liberation instead of divine punishment, a release from
oppressive rule like the tower in Bruegel's painting, which stood
for the resented and doomed Spanish empire. This is also how the

destroyers of another tower – or two towers, to be precise – characterised their own attack on architecture.

The World Trade Center was selected by a small band of fanatical puritans as representative of American economic and cultural power. But such a minute force could not hope to overthrow the world's one remaining superpower, no matter how dramatic their deeds or how numerous their victims. This was instead a battle of images, a tactical hit calculated to elicit a violent response – in which it succeeded, since it was the ostensible rationale for the invasions of Iraq and Afghanistan. This then was a suicide mission not just for the hijackers but for the terrorist organisation as a whole, since there was absolutely no possibility of it surviving the repercussions of their attack. It was intended to polarise the Muslim and Western worlds, leading to the 'clash of civilisations' so fervently desired by both Christian and Islamic fundamentalists, and in that regard it has been a resounding success, as the ruins of Babylon can attest.

Muhammad Atta, the leader of the Hamburg-based cell and pilot of the first jet to crash into the Twin Towers, was well versed in the symbolic power of buildings. He had studied architecture in Cairo and Hamburg and had written his master's thesis on the Westernisation of the ancient Syrian city of Aleppo, a late result of the Sykes–Picot Agreement. Atta disliked the high-rises that stud Middle Eastern cities and the destruction that French modernist planners had wrought on the medieval tangle of Aleppo's streets. He detected the presence of a foreign, ideologically opposed power in these buildings and urban typologies which he wished to erase, so he advocated removing the towers in Aleppo's new town, which give views into the private courtyards where women are traditionally segregated. But this architect-manqué had no utopian tower of freedom to offer in place of oppressive structures: he simply wished to replace one architectural power-system with another, since in the place of

these skyscrapers and grids he argued that 'the traditional structures of the society in all areas should be re-erected' in order to
counteract 'emancipatory thoughts of any kind.'[25]

2

The Golden House, Rome
(AD 64–8)
Architecture and Morality

Something terrible is about to enter our world and this building is obviously the door.

Ghostbusters, directed by Ivan Reitman, 1984

The octagon suite in the Domus Aurea

The legend of its discovery is ripe with Plutonian allusion: some time around 1480, or so the story goes, a boy fell through a crack in a Roman hillside into a dark subterranean kingdom. Beneath the earth he found a network of caverns that had lain undisturbed since the time of the Roman empire, and as his eyes grew accustomed to the light, he discerned weird contorted figures painted on their walls. Contemporaries thought this underground structure was an ancient grotto; in fact it was the remains of the Emperor Nero's notorious first-century palace.

Called the Domus Aurea – 'Golden House' – because of its extravagant use of precious materials, it had been buried beneath a public bath by a succeeding dynasty that reviled Nero's memory, and then forgotten. The wall paintings, in which strange tendrils sprouted where columns should be and human forms were mingled with those of beasts and fabulous creatures, created a sensation in Renaissance Italy. They were the first ancient paintings to be seen for a thousand years and they contradicted everything that people expected from classical art, which was meant to be rational and mimetic, not nonsensical or unrealistic. Responses to these forms – named grotesques after the so-called grottoes where they were found – remained divided for centuries: they were imitated by Raphael and other painters up to the nineteenth century, and they helped inaugurate a new freedom in architecture, although many disapproved.

Vitruvius, the Roman theorist of architecture, was already griping about grotesques nearly a century before the Domus Aurea was painted.

Our contemporary artists decorate the walls with monstrous forms rather than reproducing clear images of the familiar world. Instead of columns they paint fluted stems with oddly shaped leaves and scrolls; and instead of pediments, arabesques; the same with candelabra and painted window frames, on the pediments of which grow dainty flowers unrolling out of roots and topped, without rhyme or reason, by figurines. The little stems, finally, support half-figures crowned by human or animal heads. Such things however, never existed, do not now exist, and shall never come into being . . . For how can a reed actually sustain a roof?[1]

Grotesques continued to raise hackles into the nineteenth century, when the great architectural moralist (and loquacious ranter) John Ruskin called them a 'monstrous abortion'. Such violent reactions to the decorations of the Domus Aurea and their ilk are not just disputes over taste, but responses to a much more provocative question: the morality of architecture. It isn't unreasonable to focus on architecture's moral dimension, which looms larger than in other art forms: unlike paintings and other rich men's trinkets, everybody uses architecture: everybody lives in it, its creation employs a lot of people, and it costs a lot of money – often public money.

Over the centuries people have detected a wide gamut of moral flaws in architects and patrons: some have been accused of building for a bad purpose – extravagance in the instance of Nero's house, greed in the case of property developers, cruelty in the case of supermax prisons (or, one might add, Vitruvius' own buildings – as I mentioned in the introduction he was a military engineer). Others are accused of building for a bad regime – Albert Speer's designs for Hitler spring to mind, but depending on your politics you might also include Lutyens' New Delhi, the constructivists' work for Stalin, Rem Koolhaas's Chinese state TV building or SOM's Burj Khalifa in Dubai. More frequently architects are accused of building badly, so that the results break the 'laws of architecture', whatever they might be. This might not seem a question of morality, but Vitruvius' famous triumvirate of architectural virtues – *utilitas, venustas* and *firmitas*, or utility, beauty and strength (or durabiltity) – have often been equated with moral laws. They've even been used to judge mere representations of architecture, as with the grotesques – 'For how can a reed actually sustain a roof?'

When Vitruvius complains that grotesques are unnatural, he's reiterating the first rule of ancient art: that it should represent nature. Though architecture may seem the least mimetic of the plastic arts, that hasn't stopped people from insisting that it should follow laws derived from, or imposed on, nature, and seeing infractions of those laws as leading not just to bad architecture, but moral badness. This may be questionable, but we can probably all agree with Vitruvius' third precept: a building that falls down on its inhabitants is bad. And the rule of utility, understood as fitness for purpose, has been used to justify two centuries of polemic against superfluous ornament, leading eventually to the white boxes of modernism. Finally, there is even an enduring notion that buildings themselves can be evil. This conceit underpins countless horror films – a personal favourite is the apartment block in *Ghostbusters*, designed by a deranged metallurgist-cum-occultist to focus the bad vibes of the universe – but this notion also gets taken seriously. It lies behind the idea that architecture can corrupt the morals of its users, for example in talk of 'sink estates' and their deleterious effects on the behaviour of their inhabitants.

As should be apparent, the problem of architecture's moral character is a vast and vexing one, so I'll focus on unpicking the twisted moral fibre of one structure rich in badness – it was extravagant, it broke the rules of art, and it was built for a bad ruler – Nero's Golden House.

Nero was one of the most reviled Caesars. The Middle Ages,

remembering his persecution of the early Christians, called him Antichrist. Many Romans too had found him monstrous (many but by no means all – there was a posthumous cult devoted to his memory); his disastrous reign brought down the first imperial dynasty and left Rome in a state of civil war, so it's hardly surprising that his personality got a drubbing, especially from republican-minded writers. According to his ancient biographers, Nero indulged in all kinds of outrageous debaucheries: he kicked his pregnant wife to death, slept with and then murdered his own mother, raped a Vestal Virgin and castrated a young boy before making him his wife. Suetonius concludes his catalogue of Neronian horrors with the following story.

> He so prostituted his own chastity that after defiling almost every part of his body, he at last devised a kind of game, in which, covered with the skin of some wild animal, he was let loose from a cage and attacked the private parts of men and women, who were bound to stakes, and when he had sated his mad lust, was dispatched by his freedman Doryphorus; for he was even married to this man . . . going so far as to imitate the cries and lamentations of a maiden being deflowered.[2]

As historian Edward Champlin remarks, this charade seems like a subversion of the *damnatio ad bestias* – 'condemnation to beasts' – with the emperor-as-beast punishing the condemned by fellating them. It's characteristic of a man who seemed hell bent on undermining what it meant to be emperor – by performing on stage as an actor, for instance, or by sexually submitting to a freedman (it is this diminution of imperial dignity that really appalled Suetonius).

Another of the counts against Nero was the allegation that he started the Great Fire of Rome, which lasted a full nine days in the summer of AD 64. Suetonius says that the emperor played his lyre while Rome burned, not the fiddle of legend; in any case, even the ancient sources are a bit sceptical about this. Much of the city, including parts of Nero's palace, was reduced to smoking rubble, but according to Tacitus the destruction was welcomed in one quarter: 'Nero meanwhile availed himself of his country's desolation, and erected a mansion in which the jewels and gold, long familiar objects, quite vulgarised by our extravagance, were not so marvellous as the fields and lakes.'[3] This wonder was the Golden House. Worried by suspicions that he'd started the fire to clear ground for his new palace, Nero placed the blame for the conflagration on the Christians, a persecution once instigated that led to the martyrdom of Saints Peter and Paul.

'Mockery of every sort was added to their deaths.' So notes Tacitus, who had little sympathy for the cult but nevertheless thought Nero's cruelty excessive. 'Covered with the skins of beasts, they were torn by dogs and perished, or were nailed to crosses, or were doomed to the flames and burned, to serve as a nightly illumination, when daylight had expired.'[4] These human torches lit the emperor's own pleasure gardens, piling unnaturalness on unnaturalness: he transformed the city into the country, and the human body into an object. Nero's unnaturalness was a common theme of his critics; conversely it made him deeply attractive to nineteenth-century decadents like Flaubert, who called Nero 'the greatest poet the world has ever had' for his inventive perversions of nature.[5] He was, like the hybrid grotesques, always pushing the boundaries of what it meant to be human, by playing the beast, making boys into girls and turning people into torches – candelabra in human form were, fittingly, a popular grotesque motif.

Could any building made by such a ruler be 'good'? Even Suetonius – to whom Nero's crimes were still politically dangerous – was able to separate the emperor from his works, some of which he praised. While Nero was taking advantage of the ravages of the fire to clear a huge expanse of central Rome for his palace, he also imposed new planning rules on the city in order to create a safer, more regulated environment and paid for much of the reconstruction from his own pocket. The emperor also constructed state-of-the-art public buildings, which provoked a contemporary to remark, 'What is worse than Nero? What is better than Nero's baths?'

Is it such a simple matter, though, to untangle a building from its patron? Nazi architecture is a good test case, since it was built by a thoroughly bad regime – indeed, there is something Neronian about the way the Nazis turned their victims into illuminating objects, making lampshades, it is alleged, of Jewish skin.[6] But is Nazi architecture morally bad? Jewish refugee Nikolaus Pevsner, in his *Outline of European Architecture*, skirted the subject with 'the less said the better'. For him it was too cack-handed in its attempt to throw off modernism and return to the classical or medieval past. The Italian fascists, on the other hand, he thought rather more successful, since 'for a noble, unvulgar display, no one can compete with the Italians'.[7] Donatella has long since trounced Donatello, but this was after Pevsner's time and we can forgive his ignorance of Versace, but his subscription to the same kind of racial essentialism that underpinned Nazi doctrine is harder to swallow.

Equally indigestible is Pevsner's reduction of Nazi architecture to folksy cottages and lumpish classicism. It's a strategy he employs to avoid conceding that some Nazi buildings *were* good, judged by his own criteria. Stripped-down classical buildings like the Air Ministry in Berlin are deeply banal, it's true. There is no sense in this jumble of blocks, none of the clarity that underpins even the wildest of baroque confections; it's merely dreary, a bathetically try-hard attempt to impress. There's nothing intrinsically fascist about it though – London and Washington are full of the same grey stodge. But the roads and bridges of the autobahn network are another creature entirely – sweeping, elegant, contoured to fit and enhance the landscape (their design was overseen by a talented architect, Paul Bonatz). And the Zeppelinfeld at Nuremberg, especially when floodlit for nocturnal rallies, certainly *works*: it impresses, it overwhelms, it cows. But despite their aesthetic or functional successes, these structures were built to be bad: the autobahns were intended to facilitate the quick movement of troops, and the Zeppelinfeld was used, via mass spectacles and the films of Leni Riefenstahl, to instill a grotesque ideology in the minds of a nation. The way that these buildings were built is even worse: the autobahns and their bridges were constructed by slaves, who died to embellish the German landscape with their graceful curves. So, can we say that the Nazis made good architecture? Only if we are willing to exclude all other considerations besides the aesthetic and fitness for purpose, and I think that would be a mistake.

Suetonius may have praised Nero's public works, but he was more ambivalent about the Domus Aurea:

> Its vestibule was tall enough to contain a colossal statue of the emperor a hundred and twenty feet high. So large was the house that it had a triple colonnade a mile long. There was a lake in it too, like a sea, surrounded with buildings to represent cities, besides tracts of country, varied by tilled fields, vineyards, pastures and woods, with great numbers of wild and domestic animals. In the rest of the house all parts were overlaid with gold and adorned with gems and mother-of-pearl. There were dining rooms with fretted ceilings of ivory, whose panels could turn and shower down flowers and were fitted with pipes for sprinkling the guests with perfumes. The main banquet hall was circular and constantly revolved day and night, like the heavens. He had baths supplied with seawater and sulphur water. When the edifice was finished in this style and he dedicated it, he deigned to say nothing more in the way of approval than that he was at last beginning to be housed like a human being.[8]

There is an implied critique of the emperor's extravagance in this catalogue of crimes against interior decorating. A degree of magnificence was acceptable or even necessary in an emperor, since it befitted his public status, but there were limits. Aristotle had defined the virtue of magnificence as being solely attainable by rich men spending neither meanly *nor too much*. Vitruvius called this Goldilocks virtue *decor* – decorum – which meant that every building should be as grand as its inhabitant or function. Cicero too praised magnificence, by which he thought patrons could demonstrate the splendour of their imaginations. But here, as elsewhere, Nero went too far. Overstepping magnificence into extravagance, he ended up demonstrating not the splendour of his imagination but its fevered weirdness.

Rich builders are perpetually belaboured with the brickbat of extravagance. Perhaps our cultural receptivity to the charge was ingrained along with the Christian virtue of humility and its inverse, sinful pride, but the dream of the simple life is an old one. Stoical Seneca – who was Nero's tutor, and whom Nero later ordered to slit his wrists for conspiring to assassinate him – wailed, 'Believe me, that was a happy age, before the days of architects!'

> In these our own times, which man, pray, do you deem the wiser – the one who invents a process for spraying saffron perfumes to a tremendous height from hidden pipes . . . who so cleverly constructs a dining room with a ceiling of movable panels that it presents one pattern after another, the roof changing as often as the courses, or the one who proves to others, as well as to himself, that nature has laid upon us no stern and difficult law when she tells us that we can live without the marble-cutter and the engineer . . . ? The things that are indispensable require no elaborate pains for their acquisition; it is only the luxuries that call for labour.[9]

All the while Seneca himself lived in hypocritical splendour. No wonder Nero didn't like him. In the Middle Ages, on the other hand, he was hailed as a pagan saint. Humility was then a favourite theme, but today it's long gone, killed off by the rebirth of the concept of *magnificenza* in the fifteenth century, propagated by scholars who just happened to be bankrolled by patrons of expensive palazzos. More convincing these days is the critique that extravagance is wasteful. It wastes resources, a problem especially pertinent to our era of overtaxed energy supplies and mineral deposits. It also wastes the time of builders, who could be better employed elsewhere (I'll return to this shortly). Economic wastefulness is another problem, especially when the patron is not a private individual. The cost of Versailles, for example, has been mooted as one of the causes of eighteenth-century France's economic problems; similarly, Ceaușescu's gargantuan palace in Bucharest impoverished ordinary Romanians. Extravagance also gets flak for being tasteless. Tastelessness may seem rather less serious a charge than wastefulness, but it often stands in for something quite serious indeed: it's levelled at people transgressing Vitruvian decorum and showing ideas above their station, in order to keep them in their place. Exhortations to Christian humility, as codified in sumptuary laws, were similarly meant to ensure social stasis, and if people today laugh louder at the extravagance of footballers' mansions than at the equally hideous interiors of Buckingham Palace, it's for the same reasons. Finally, extravagance has been criticised for risking social discord. Socrates warned in Plato's *Republic* that insatiable acquisitiveness leads inevitably to territorial war, to avoid which everyone in the ideal state was to live in humble dwellings built by their own hands. Envy too has been seen as a dangerously disruptive consequence of putting too much on display, potentially leading to theft or something worse. At the end of his famous 1923 manifesto *Towards an Architecture* Le

Corbusier warned his readers, 'architecture or revolution!'. This bit of scaremongering was, characteristically, a sales pitch – he meant that unless governments levelled the playing field by improving the housing of their citizens, they'd have an insurrection on their hands.

In the eighteenth century British philosopher Bernard Mandeville challenged such views with his *Fable of the Bees*, which championed the consumerist, trickle-down doctrine of *Private Vices, Publick Benefits*, as the subtitle of his poem puts it. He imagines human society as an enormous hive held together by the satisfaction of greed, pride and luxury: 'Thus every part was full of vice / Yet the whole mass a paradise.' And what would happen if society were to turn over a new leaf?

> Now mind the glorious hive, and see
> How honesty and trade agree:
> The show is gone, it thins apace;
> And looks with quite another face,
> For 'twas not only that they went,
> By whom vast sums were yearly spent;
> But multitudes that lived on them,
> Were daily forced to do the same.
> In vain to other trades they'd fly;
> All were o'erstock'd accordingly.
> The price of land and houses falls;
> Mirac'lous palaces whose walls,
> Like those of *Thebes*, were rais'd by play,
> Are to be let;
>
> . . .
>
> The building trade is quite destroy'd,
> Artificers are not employ'd;
> No limner for his art is fam'd,
> Stone-cutters, carvers, are not nam'd.[10]

Neoliberals continue in this vein today, albeit less lyrically. I've got some sympathy for their rejection of architectural sackcloth – egalitarianism doesn't mean mud huts for all – but until the ever-receding day arrives when every house is golden, or at least dusted with a little glitter, one might reply to Mandeville: what comfort is an architect's fame to those who live in slums? And might there not be better ways of employing builders than in the creation of, for instance, underground car museums for Chelsea oligarchs, especially when so many are entirely without homes? This disparity is even more pronounced in the developing world: the stunningly crass Mumbai house of Indian billionaire Mukesh Ambani, for example, was built on dodgily acquired land that had been earmarked for an educational facility for poor children. It's been valued at one billion dollars – this in a nation where 68.7 per cent of the population lives on less than two dollars a day.[11]

But perhaps there is also, dialectically speaking, a good side to this kind of extravagance – if it causes discord. While the Ambani house could only exist in an unequal society, it makes this inequality glaringly apparent: the 173-metre tower sticks out like a sore thumb. While this undoubtedly causes people who don't live in mansions a degree of anguish, it is more likely to make them question the mansion builders than wealth hidden in gated compounds or Swiss bank accounts. The political right talks dismissively about the 'politics of envy' (the phrase was popularised in the 1990s by American journalist Doug Bandow, who had to resign from the libertarian Cato think tank for taking bribes in 2005), but what's wrong with a slum kid envying the Ambanis? Envy is the first step to action – that's why it makes the rich uncomfortable.

Nero's house, with its rotating rooms and integral perfume delivery systems, must have rivalled the lily-gilding mansions of Ceaușescu and the Ambanis in its day. Though we might suspect that political antipathy spurred Suetonius and Tacitus to rhetorical excess, recent archaeological research confirms several points of their accounts: the palace grounds covered between one and three hundred acres, filling a great chunk of the city centre, and in the middle of the park was a huge rectangular lake surrounded by colonnades and overlooked by pavilions and villas. The most substantial remaining structure has around 150 rooms, including a domed octagonal chamber which may be the spinning dining room described by Suetonius. Its walls were originally covered in rare marble veneers, and the vaults lined with glittering gold and glass mosaics – another of the architect's innovations – but now we just see the brick facings of the concrete substructure, and even the grotesques have faded after centuries of exposure to daylight and tourists' breath.

Prosaic as it might now seem, this building was the finest product of the 'concrete revolution', a period of architectural and engineering innovation that coincided with Nero's reign. Although we think of concrete as the modern material par excellence, an ancient equivalent called *pozzolana* was already in use at the time Vitruvius was writing, nearly a century before the Domus Aurea was built. Vitruvius mentions the material as a natural wonder, but he seems to prefer the traditional system of post and lintel construction – trabeation to give it its technical name – which was used on ancient temples like the Parthenon. Vitruvius' traditionalism was perhaps due to the fact that he worked for the first emperor, Augustus, who wanted to create the illusion that his regime was a continuation of the republic and its familiar forms of building. But spurred on by Nero's ambitious projects, engineers in the first century gained a new confidence in concrete's possibilities. As a result entirely new forms were made, and a new sense of architectural space was achieved (or so it seems to modern eyes: the notion of 'architectural space' is a recent one). The rectilinear layouts of earlier trabeated buildings, descended from ancient Greek models, were replaced by more fluid vaulted and domed spaces of varying shapes and sizes, which played on the visceral experience of the person moving through them and led to that pinnacle of Roman concrete construction, the Pantheon.

Unusually, the names of the building's architects have come down to us. 'The directors and contrivers of the work were Severus and Celer, who had the genius and the audacity to attempt by art even what nature had refused.'[12] Tacitus doesn't explain exactly what constituted the unnaturalness of their design. It may have been the way they brought the countryside into the city, but from a Vitruvian perspective the innovations of the octagon suite would probably have seemed unnatural too. The room plays games with architectural seeming and being: the piers and lintels surrounding the entrances make a visible break with the conventions of trabeation by appearing far too thin to support the immense weight of the concrete dome, and in fact they don't; it's held up by a hidden structure of buttresses. In turn, this makes the dome seem lighter than it really is, creating a floating effect that adds to the psychological intensity of the space.

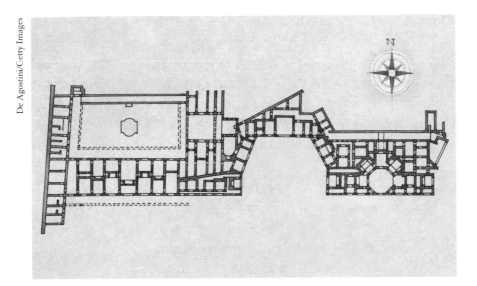

Plan of the Golden House, showing octagon suite to the right

Vitruvius insisted that the conventions of architecture had to be followed because to do otherwise would break the rule of artistic mimesis and would therefore be *unnatural.* Greek temples were first built to imitate earlier wooden structures, he asserts, and 'what is impossible in reality could not be based on sound principles if it was replicated in imitations of that reality'.[13] You can't, therefore, put mutules and guttae – those carved elements on a Doric temple that supposedly represent the ends of rafters and the wooden pegs that held them in place – in places where they wouldn't appear on a wooden structure. You can't raise a secretly buttressed dome over spindly piers because that would mask reality. And you can't even *paint* an architecture that sprouts from flowers, as in the grotesques: 'For how can a reed actually sustain a roof?' This insistence on architectural truth returned with a vengeance in the nineteenth century, stripped of its mimetic rationale and instead made into a moral imperative – a point I'll return to at the end of this chapter – but it didn't seem to bother the Renaissance artists who rediscovered the Domus Aurea, for all their classical learning.

The rediscovery of the grotesques in 1480 had an enormous impact on Renaissance art. Like many later tourists (the names of Casanova and the Marquis de Sade, among others, are carved on the walls of the chambers), countless artists had themselves lowered into the cramped caverns on a rope. The craze for visiting the 'grottoes' was recorded in a poem of the time:

> In every season they are full of painters,
> here summer seems cooler than winter . . .
> We crawl along the floor on our stomachs,
> armed with bread, ham, fruits, and wine,
> looking more bizarre than the grotesques . . .
> each person resembling a chimney-sweep,
> and our guide . . . shows us toads, frogs, barn-owls,

civet cats and bats,
while we are breaking our backbones on our knees.[14]

Raphael was one of the many artists who descended into the
Golden House. He and his assistant Giovanne da Udine used the
wall paintings they saw there to develop a complex scheme of
decoration for a long gallery in the Vatican, where scenes from the
Bible are surrounded by the writhing forms of grotesque imagery.
Raphael was well aware of Vitruvius and his criticisms of the
'unnatural' grotesques, but he seems to mock the charge by going
to the extremes of improbability – by allowing Udine to paint a
pot-bellied old man perched on the spindliest of tendrils, for example, while a cupid has to use a pole for balance. In this context
– directly beneath scenes from Genesis – the grotesques challenge
God's monopoly on creation. They show the artist as a demiurge,
a second albeit subservient god no longer slavishly imitating God's
works but equally capable of coming up with original forms. It's
striking that images associated with Nero ended up decorating a
papal palace, but their marginal status in the Vatican loggia makes
sense, and besides their true provenance wasn't yet known. They
were imported from the pagan past into the Christian present by
humanists, ostensibly reconciling the two – but here, in the subcon-
scious of history, the irrational lurks and strange desires are
expressed. These are dangerously unorthodox messages for the
Vatican to be promoting, but in sixteenth-century Rome, under
the rule of the first Medici pope, Leo X, even the palace of St Peter
could proclaim the supremacy of human genius.

In the nineteenth century, however, censorious souls saw something distinctly Neronian about Leo: he was extravagant, obsessed
by artistic patronage, contemptuous of convention, and he danced,
it was rumoured, at the Grecian end of the ballroom. To quote
from Dumas's *Celebrated Crimes*, 'Christianity then evinced a
paganism which, passing from works of art to the manners of

social life, became the peculiar characteristic of the period. Crime suddenly disappears to make way for vices, yet vices of good taste, such as those of Alcibiades and those of which Catullus sung.[15] The phrase 'passing from art into manners' is key, for here we have another example of the critical confusion of art and morality. Unsurprisingly, John Ruskin didn't approve of Leo's patronage much either. Abandoning Dumas's urbane irony, he called Raphael's design 'a poisonous root; an artistical pottage, composed of nymphs, cupids, and satyrs, with shreddings of heads and paws of meek wild beasts, and nondescript vegetables'. Ruskin's ostensible problem with the grotesques was the fact that supreme mimetic skill had been wasted on unnatural fripperies, but he also shared Dumas's belief that art affects morality: it was, he went on, 'almost impossible to believe the depth to which the human mind can be debased in following this species of grotesque'.[16] One can't help wondering about these depths to which Ruskin so tantalisingly alludes. Could it be that he is using artistic unnaturalness as a stand-in for charges of a more unnameable unnaturalness against Leo X?

Ruskin's reaction comes after three hundred years of grotesquery; Raphael's loggia inspired interior decorators from Renaissance Rome to nineteenth-century St Petersburg, and the hibernating hybrids of the Domus Aurea also had a huge impact on architecture itself. In the words of historian Manfredo Tafuri, there was a 'tendency that takes shape in Raphael's circle, that finds support in the taste for *license* connected to the discovery of the ancient *grotesques*, that develops into an intentionally *theatrical* architecture'.[17] This was the so-called mannerist movement, which blossomed in the sixteenth century, when the 'pure' classical language of the fifteenth century was 'deformed' by experimentation, the serenity and regularity of Brunelleschi's dome for Florence cathedral being replaced by the frivolous or sinister innovations of figures like Giulio Romano. The latter worked from 1524 to 1534 on a suburban villa known as the Palazzo del Te for Duke Federigo Gonzaga. Here on the outskirts of Mantua the duke could meet his mistress safe from prying eyes and loose tongues, and the building itself is appropriately licentious. In the incredible Sala dei Giganti – Room of the Giants – Romano painted scenes that terrified visitors: beneath a floating *trompe l'oeil* dome, flailing giants are crushed by crashing stones. The painting overwhelms with the seamless uniformity of its fictive space, and then confounds the conventional clarity and human-centred rationality of Renaissance perspective by bringing it all toppling down, seemingly on to the viewer. Like the octagon suite of the Domus Aurea before it, the Sala dei Giganti also undermines the classical tradition of architecture, with its slipping keystones and toppling columns, and these games are continued throughout the palazzo, with blocks, for example, that seem about to fall from architraves. Such architectural transgressions were soon all the rage in suburban villas and in garden structures like grottoes: places for pleasure, where the rules governing classical architecture – just as the rules of society – might be bent a little.

The rules might be bent by these spaces, but did the architecture itself encourage rule-breaking? Ruskin thought the whole of classical architecture corrupt and corrupting: 'It is base, unnatural, unfruitful, unenjoyable, and impious. Pagan in its origin, proud and unholy in its revival, paralysed in its old age . . . an architecture invented as it seems to make plagiarists of its architects, slaves of its workmen, and sybarites of its inhabitants.'[18]

Ruskin's diatribe was motivated more by his partisanship in contemporary British debates than by historical fact. A confirmed Goth, he rejected the classicism of the previous generation as derivative, boring, immoral and fake – all those gleaming Nash terraces are not marble but mere stuccoed brick, after all, and not very sturdy brick at that. The social changes wrought by industrialisation disturbed him: people, he thought, shouldn't ape the architecture of their betters with cheap mass-produced ornament. He was also reacting to the methods of modern construction, represented by the shoddy volume building of Regency developers. Ruskin thought this denied workers all pleasure in their labour, an argument he projected backwards in time, asserting that while medieval masons had been given free rein to express their imaginations, carvers of classical cornices were forced to follow petrified and petrifying precedent. There's little merit in his historical analysis (if medieval builders had really been allowed to go crazy with their chisels, the great cathedrals would probably not still be standing), but the emphasis he put on the experience of the labourer certainly added a new dimension to discussions of architectural morality. What about his assertion that buildings can turn their inhabitants into sybarites, though – can architecture really change our behaviour?

Only in Britain: a tweely detailed security wall prevents car bombs on Whitehall

Ruskin expressed his views in characteristically intemperate language, but anyone who cooks in an open-plan kitchen would agree that buildings modify behaviour – you wouldn't spit in the soup as guests watched from across the breakfast bar. All buildings imply certain actions by the way they are laid out: by placing front doors adjacently on terraced houses, for example, architects can try to foster interaction between neighbours and thus a sense of community, or conversely, by building a wall the Israeli state can attempt to exclude suicide bombers and Palestinians *tout court* (the British government did this rather more subtly in 2010, installing twee security balustrades along Whitehall styled to be in keeping with the rest of the neoclassical ensemble). It is now widely accepted that architecture can change behaviour in schools, calming students and encouraging learning by for example improving shared spaces and providing quiet areas for private study.[19] Meanwhile, a hugely lucrative retail design industry has sprung up on the promise of optimising sales: leading consultancy firm Envirosell, set up by a student of famous urban planner William H. Whyte, claims to promote what it calls 'shopping incidents, shopper conversion, store penetration and cashwrap operations' by changing the layout of shops.

Twin front doors in Trellick Tower

So architecture can change behaviour, but it's not the only factor in play, and it often gets the blame for more fundamental problems. The picture above shows two front doors in Trellick Tower, an enormous residential block in west London designed by Hungarian émigré Ernö Goldfinger (after whom the Bond villain is named – Ian Fleming allegedly disliked his buildings). It's the product of another concrete revolution, the brutalism that began in the 1950s in France and Britain, spread across the world in the 1960s, and was killed off by an impassioned backlash in the 1970s. Externally, Trellick Tower is an aggressive statement of modernist aesthetics: a huge, starkly geometric edifice of exposed concrete with a separate tower for the lifts and other services. To mitigate the potentially inhuman scale of the building and to make the lifts speedier, Goldfinger only put access corridors on every third floor, linking these to the lift tower by bridges. Along the corridors, paired front doors give entry to the building's maisonettes, with internal stairs allowing residents to move between the floors of their own flats. As well as encouraging interaction between the residents, who are funnelled together by the plan, this unusual layout also allowed the flats to cover the entire footprint of those floors without access corridors, thus creating some of the most spacious public housing in London, with windows on both sides taking advantage of the incredible views. But for all Goldfinger's thoughtful innovations, his building soon turned into a vertical hell.

Modernists had first advocated tower blocks in the 1920s as a replacement for the ground-hugging slums of the Victorian city, opening up green spaces for children to play and letting daylight in. When people moved in, many were ecstatic: for the first time they had indoor lavatories, modern kitchens and reliable and clean heating. But by 1972 when Trellick Tower was completed this utopian dream had soured. The reasons are complex. In many instances the designs of visionary architects had been imitated on the cheap by

A Mondrian for living in: Trellick Tower's facade is an abstract modernist composition

mercenary developers for corrupt city officials, leading to poorly finished, even dangerous structures – the 1968 collapse of Ronan Point in east London after a gas explosion was the beginning of the end, and a clearly immoral transgression of Vitruvian *firmitas*. However, even well constructed towers became associated with social decay. A degree of fragmentation is inevitable when communities are uprooted and rehoused, but tower blocks were meant to counter this by keeping urban networks together in dense proximity, rather than scattering them across suburbia. But being so high up inconvenienced some residents – as should have been obvious. Deprived of easy access to the communal life of the street and those vaunted green spaces opened up by the demolition of the slums, the elderly, young mothers and children were at risk of claustrophobic isolation. On the other hand, many later remembered their communities in the sky fondly. The account of Andrew Balderstone, a sheet-metal worker who lived in a twenty-storey block in Leith from 1964 to 1984, is worth quoting at length. His story encompasses the vagaries of architectural experience.

It wasn't anything to do with the block itself, really, it was a change in the kind of people who lived there, and how people behaved . . . For the first five or ten years, things were really great, everybody kept the block spotless, you were really proud of having such a nice new house. There were one or two practical problems, kids having to play outside, that kind of thing, but nothing's perfect in life, and in general we all loved it! The problems only started after about five or ten years, when they started putting a different kind of tenant in. It began with one couple especially, really rough-looking people straight from the worst slums. Well, to start off with it was just him beating her, but soon she got the hang of it, and started beating him back even worse! They were four storeys above us, but it was deafening – they'd come in steamin', well after midnight, loud music straight away, shouting the odds, great thuds and bangs, inside and out – you'd lie there in bed listening – crash, that's all their plates on the floor – clatter, that'll be his record collection landing in the street! After that, things started to go gradually downhill – soon there was four or five families like that, spread up and down the block. This was the idea of the Corporation housing management. 'Management' – what a sick joke! They had this crazy idea that by spreading the bad ones out among the normal tenants, you'd bring them up to your level – but what happened, especially in a big block like that, it was the opposite – they brought us down! It was like a kind of cancer. At first you still tried to keep your standards up, but you soon learnt it was a waste of time . . . Things started to vanish from the rooftop drying green, so people stopped using it – then the same happened with the launderette, and the drying cupboards. The lifts had always been fine before, but now they started breaking down all the time, and it took longer and longer to get someone out to mend them. Then one year there was a rubbish strike, and some of these new

68

families, they wouldn't take their bags downstairs, oh no, first they jammed the chute, and then they just started tipping rubbish bags out of a window in the chute room, straight on to my balcony. Can you imagine it! Rotting rubbish, waist high! At first I thought, let's not have a row, so I tried cleaning it up myself, but then the next few nights more bags just came crashing down. So in the end I got really mad. I lugged all these bags back up, dozens of them, and emptied them all out on the floor outside their doors – old tin cans, tomatoes, fish-heads, the lot! I shouted, 'Here's yer rubbish back, ya shower of scummy bastards!' Then I ran back downstairs as fast as I could, and back into my house. I could hear screaming and swearing up there – but that was the end of those people chucking down their rubbish bags. The awful thing was, though, you realised now you'd become the same as them! Well, the caretaker couldn't cope with all this, so he left, then more and more of the neighbours got fed up and got out – and all the Housing Department could do was fill the vacant flats with single-parent families. So it got worse and worse, faster and faster. After they started putting the druggies in, about the late seventies, the vandalism and the break-ins really got going, all-night parties with idiots using the rubbish chutes at 3 a.m., masses of bottles crashing down. That was the time when the craze for throwing things out suddenly started . . . One of the families at the top had been chucking doors down, and one of them had been caught by the wind and landed on my car. Then, after that, we had a bus stop, with a lump of concrete on the end, hurled down like a spear through the roof of a parked van, and embedded in the road beneath it. There were live cats as well. Finally somebody up on the 18th floor chucked a whole motorbike down one night, during an argument apparently. How they even got it out through the window I can't imagine. That's the real dregs for you! Respectable working-class folk, like we had at first in our block, wouldn't do that kind of thing. Then we had our first suicide – an addict took a header through a window on the nineteenth floor, and splatted in the car park – and then there was a murder in the block, about 1980, a guy got his face stamped in. Then some of these new people started agitating to get the block pulled down, saying it was a hell in the sky and all that stuff – well, of course that's what it was by then, after they and the Council had done their worst! By that time all I wanted was to get out. At last I managed to get rehoused – I shouldn't imagine there's any of the other original people left there now. It all seems such a terrible waste – they were perfectly good houses, if the Council had only bothered to look after them, rather than using them as a dumping ground![20]

Trellick Tower itself was bedevilled by violent crime. Its graffiti-covered corridors were haunted by destitutes, prostitutes and addicts, its floors strewn with bottles and syringes, its lifts – when they worked – reeked of piss. The tenants were soon desperate to get out, the waiting list for transfers grew to two years, and when they finally left, the council replaced them with 'troubled families' – to use the current official taxonomy. The problems got worse, and the tabloids took to calling Goldfinger's building the Tower of Terror.

But today Trellick Tower has a waiting list a mile long – to get in. The building still looks the same: it's still an uncompromising concrete monolith, and that upsets a particular English mindset that thinks everyone should live in cottages without wondering how this could be achieved short of concreting over that other English ideal, the rolling greensward. So what changed? In the mid-1980s a residents' association was formed, and this body pressured the housing authority to install an intercom and a twenty-four-hour concierge – incredibly, both had been lacking up to this point. The council also changed its policy on who was housed there, letting people choose to move in rather than forcing them to do so, and was surprised to find that people actually wanted to live in Trellick Tower. But perhaps this isn't such a great mystery. To this day, the majority of the units are publicly owned, and like many such properties they are very generously proportioned, especially when compared to the coffin-sized 'luxury' flats built by today's rapacious developers. The quality of the finish, the attention to detail in the interiors, is also remarkable. No longer a sink estate, the building, which was listed in 1998, became – and remains – a desirable address and a London emblem, appearing in films, songs and music videos.

But although some buildings like Trellick Tower have been rehabilitated, brutalism is still widely reviled as antisocial. As a result, many brutalist landmarks around the world have been and continue to be demolished – a fate, as Jonathan Meades reminds us in his requiem for the lost car parks of architect Rodney Gordon, that befell many great Victorian buildings in the 1960s, when they were similarly unfashionable.[21] The name doesn't help: it sounds cruel and inhumane, but it was popularised by erstwhile brutalist cheerleader Reyner Banham to evoke Le Corbusier's post-war use of *béton brut* – exposed concrete – that is, unpolished concrete still textured with the wooden grain of its timber moulds. (There was doubtless an element of mischievous provocation involved in Banham's phraseology too.) Exposed concrete doesn't take very well to northern climates, true, but then brick and marble also require regular cleaning in our polluted cities, and it hasn't helped that brutalist structures have often been neglected by neoliberal governments, who loathe everything they stand for.

Consider on the other hand the aesthetic ambition of the best of these structures, their cubist angularity, their sculptural brawn and bravura chiaroscuro. The age of brutalism was one of the very few times that Britain has really been at the forefront of the avantgarde, and much of it was, incredibly for such adventurous art, state funded. This state sponsorship also exercises a lot of brutalism's critics, because its fruits represent Britain during its most socialist phase (these critics also tend to lump all high-rises together as brutalist, which they most certainly are not, while simultaneously forgetting that tower block accommodation really took off under the Conservative MacMillan government, which offered generous tall-building subsidies to its friends in the construction industry). But if there is something jarring about the appearance of truly brutalist buildings, that's the point. They advertise the confidence and difference of the post-war technocratic welfare state, a state that no longer clung to its imperial past with the bony fingers of marble columns or hid its workers in dismal slums, but raised them in towers where they could be seen by all and could see all. That this didn't work out – many towers simply became aerial slums – has more to do with the political and economic crises of the 1970s and 80s than with the architecture of the 1960s; with the creation of sink estates by councils desperate to dump their problem families in places where they could be forgotten, with the deliberate unemployment of whole communities and with the equally deliberate neglect of their environments.

So the towers fell. Some of them had been shoddily constructed and needed to go, but the better ones could have been retained with the kind of minor changes made to Trellick Tower. Despite their many flaws, towers were not the cause of the social disintegration of the 1970s. The wilfulness of this misconception may seem obvious, but it was used to justify many reactions to modern architecture. As writers such as Owen Hatherley and Anna Minton have eloquently discussed, the battle over brutalism was more a cover for political factions fighting over ideology than a purely aesthetic dispute – as if such a thing exists – an excuse to replace inner city social housing and its tenants with privately owned developments and higher-band council-tax payers.[22]

Architects and planners have also done their bit to skew the argument through an understandable sense of professional *amour propre*. One of the most influential reactions to modernist planning was a 1972 polemic entitled *Defensible Space: Crime Prevention Through Urban Design*. Its author, American planner Oscar Newman, attributed the higher crime rates reported in New York tower blocks solely to questions of design, ignoring niggling little factors like

Brutalism is named for béton brut, *literally 'raw concrete'. Still marked by its timber moulds, it has an organic quality that belies its name*

socio-economic disparity, unemployment and drug abuse. He thought that the obscurity of the shared spaces in these buildings – stairwells, lobbies, bin stores – deterred any sense of ownership. The result was, he said, that people did not take part in their policing, leading to untrammelled criminality. Instead buildings should be designed around easily observed communal areas that encouraged territoriality in the residents.

Newman's theory seems logical enough – otherwise, surely, the installation of intercoms and concierges would not make towers safer. However, it is worth pointing out that it is not some design-conjured sense of territoriality that secures Trellick Tower but physical locks and twenty-four-hour security, expensive solutions that don't appeal so much to developers and city planners, who embraced defensible space theory instead. It was popularised in the UK by Essex County Council's influential *Design Guide* of

1973, which encouraged planners to replace towers with the now ubiquitous inner-city cul-de-sacs of suburban semis. This approach was appealing to developers because it gave them a reason to maximise density (and therefore profits) on irregular plots without resorting to expensive verticality; governments liked it because it promised a quick fix, and meant they didn't have to face up to the more intractable structural problems of their societies. But although cul-de-sacs were seen as the natural habitat for lace-curtain twitchers, they have turned out to be just as crime ridden as tower blocks. The lack of passing traffic means that dead-end streets are far less overlooked than highways, and therefore more attractive to light-fingered visitors. These transformations – Towers of Terror into desirable addresses, and cul-de-sacs into arseholes of the earth – reveal the problematic nature of the doctrine of architectural corruption. Brutalism does not necessarily brutalise, and cul-de-sacs do not – thank God – turn us into suburban vigilantes.

There's another moral to the story of brutalism, besides the question of what it does to its inhabitants: its advocates argued that the rough poetry of its concrete structures told the truth. We've come across the idea of architectural honesty before, when Vitruvius insisted that buildings should be mimetic – that stone temples, for example, should faithfully represent the wooden ones on which they were based. He also called the grotesques bad because they did not tell the truth about tectonics – a reed, he said, cannot sustain a roof.

Today we have returned to an infantile kind of mimetic architecture with iconic buildings 'inspired' by cheese graters, sea shells and the like, but in the mid-eighteenth century the idea that buildings should be structurally truthful, faithful to the essence of nature rather than to its outward appearance, took hold. This was partly a response to the perceived excesses of the baroque period, when no building was complete without being violently contorted, without taking outrageous liberties with classical precedent, or without pretending to be better than it was by augmenting or even disguising its structure with a rash of gilded stucco. (Borromini's church of San Carlo in Rome is a personal favourite; its queasily pulsating geometry was long considered to be the product of a diseased mind.) Instead, theorists like German art historian Johann Joachim Winckelmann advocated taking a more scientific look at antique buildings, and using these as the foundations for a renewal of architecture. This led to the birth of neoclassicism and the tedious historical accuracy of buildings like La Madeleine in Paris, but in nineteenth-century Britain similar ideas were applied to medieval architecture by Gothic revivalists like Augustus Welby Pugin – designer of the Houses of Parliament – and John Ruskin. They rejected classical building for a variety of reasons, one of the most prominent being its dishonesty. Pugin, with all the fervour of the Catholic convert, added a religious dimension to the argument.

> The severity of Christian [by which he means Gothic] architecture is opposed to all deception. We should never make a building erected to God appear better than it really is by artificial means. These are showy worldly expedients, adapted only for those who live by splendid deception, such as theatricals, mountebanks, quacks and the like. Nothing can be more execrable than making a church appear rich and beautiful in the eyes of men, but full of tricks and falsehood, which cannot escape the all-searching eye of God.[23]

A far less pious Goth, Eugene Viollet-le-Duc, was espousing the structural truth of medieval buildings at around the same time in France, but for quite different reasons. He held that 'to be true in respect of the constructive processes is to employ the materials according to their qualities and properties. What are regarded as questions purely belonging to art, symmetry, and external form, are only secondary conditions as compared with those dominant principles.'²⁴ This was a rejection of the superficial revival of historical styles that characterised the architecture of the latter half of the nineteenth century in favour of a 'style-less' structuralism that would harmonise with the zeitgeist. Significantly, he advocated the frank use of modern materials, which he thought could help architecture return to the honest state of its medieval past, when architects had been true to their age and its technologies, and when they weren't ashamed to show how they'd put buildings together, unlike people working in a revived historical idiom, who were always harking back to the ancient Greeks, making Gothic ornament out of mass-produced terracotta or repeating naughty tricks like the hidden buttresses of the Golden House's dome.

Now, said Viollet-le-Duc, cast iron should replace flying buttresses. This led him to advocate some pretty odd-looking structures that seem to be less about honesty than a sort of awestruck wonderment at the structural possibilities of iron, but perhaps there is something genuinely medieval *and* true to the mid-nineteenth century about this prostration before sublime structures. As well as dreaming up new hybrids, Viollet-le-Duc also strapped historical buildings into his architectural polygraph. Working as a restorer on many churches including Notre-Dame in Paris, and on the walled town of Carcassonne, he aimed to recreate medieval structures not as they were made but as they *should* have been made. This ruthless interventionism was controversial even in his day, and led him to make some very licentious additions: the famous gargoyles of Notre-Dame, for example, are entirely the nineteenth-century invention of Viollet-le-Duc. Is this honest? He would have said it was *super*-honest: more true to the spirit of the age in which the building was devised than mere stony remains could ever be.

Eventually this interest in the zeitgeist was given a more explicitly political cast by people associated with the arts and crafts movement in England. Wallpaper-designing socialist

William Morris eschewed modern materials because they were made by workers who had been alienated from each other and their products by piecework; instead, there should be a return to craft and to medieval workshop production. Of course, a few bearded lathe turners were never going to provide for the new industrial masses – hand-painted wallpaper is far beyond the means of most people – and Morris ended up complaining that he was left 'ministering to the swinish luxury of the rich'. Others took up where Viollet-le-Duc had left off, however, by embracing the materials of modernity – by insisting, in fact, that to do otherwise would dishonestly obscure the true conditions of capitalist society. In other words, it's no good cladding a brick or steel-framed building in marble panels because it disguises the way the building is constructed and thus leads to a misapprehension of political reality; marble harks back to an era of imperial majesty in order to sustain the servile mindset of feudal societies, and workers laboriously carving pediments could be better employed constructing housing for the masses.

This kind of historical honesty was increasingly demanded of architecture throughout the twentieth century – it was one of the reasons for Viennese architect Adolf Loos's polemic 'Ornament and Crime' of 1908, in which faithfulness to the zeitgeist is turbocharged with rhetorical zealotry.

> The Papuan covers his skin with tattoos, his boat, his oars, in short everything he can lay his hands on. He is no criminal. The modern person who tattoos himself is either a criminal or a degenerate. There are prisons where eighty per cent of the inmates have tattoos. People with tattoos not in prison are either latent criminals or degenerate aristocrats. The urge to decorate one's face and anything else within reach is the origin of the fine arts. It is the childish babble of painting . . . What is natural in the Papuan or the child is a sign of degeneracy in a modern adult. I made the following

discovery, which I passed on to the world: the evolution of culture is synonymous with the removal of ornamentation from objects of everyday use.[25]

This reasoning lay behind the unadorned white villas of architects like Loos and Le Corbusier. Fifty years later, however, the brutalists turned the argument of the first-generation modernists against them: for much of the twentieth century, the brutalists said, architects had been rather less scrupulously honest than they pretended. The early works of Le Corbusier looked like they were made of concrete, but they weren't; they were actually stuccoed brick. The Fagus Factory by Walter Gropius looked like it was made of iron and glass. It wasn't; it was held up by traditional brick walls. Now, however, following the example of Le Corbusier's post-war work (such as the Unité d'Habitation housing block in Marseille), there was to be a new honesty in architecture: concrete would henceforth look like concrete. It would not even be polished, and certainly not rendered. Brick would be brick and steel would be steel, and all the different functions of a building would be legible from the outside, like the detached lift housing of Trellick Tower.

This kind of argument appeals to puritanical types – I should know, I have a streak of (purely aesthetic) puritanism myself. There's something bracing about the indecent exposure of a totally naked building. When this is truly achieved, as in Hunstanton School by Alison and Peter Smithson, prime proselytisers for brutalism, or in Cedric Price's Inter-Action Centre, which was essentially just a group of Portakabins bolted together, there is a frisson of shock – yes, that's still possible after all these years of avant-garde nose-thumbing. Even better than these examples, though, and coming long before Le Corbusier's Unité d'Habitation, is the trades union school built by Hannes Meyer, then head of the Bauhaus, outside Berlin between 1928 and 1930.

It was stuck behind the Iron Curtain and presumed MIA until 1989, and that is perhaps why it didn't figure in the brutalist pantheon. The school's structural elements are completely visible on the exterior – there's no cladding or rendering. The various elements – gymnasium, staircase, dormitory blocks and cafeteria – are all clearly defined entities which can be read from the outside, and there is no attempt to embellish or inflate certain areas, such as entrances or meeting halls, out of some inappropriate sense of ceremonial hierarchy. The mass-produced 'democratic' materials – no Miesian marble or bronze here; it's glass, steel, concrete and brick all the way – are allowed to express what Michael Hays rather dauntingly called their 'factural indexicality': that is to say, they still bear the marks of their making, and thereby honestly reveal the social conditions of their production.[26]

This argument has a conceptual elegance that lends an aesthetic charm to even this most bloody-mindedly un-pretty of buildings, but that was not the ostensible point. To lie about structure or materials would have created a false understanding of the way society worked, and would therefore have been counter-revolutionary. To build with outdated methods would have been just as bad, and so Meyer tried to revolutionise the profession, as well as the aesthetic, by organising the classes in the Bauhaus as 'work brigades' and setting them real projects like the trades union school. However, when the building was taken over by the Nazis in 1933 and converted into an SS training camp, it didn't make its new users into nicer people. Likewise, the monumentality of brutalism didn't stop the welfare state from being dismantled – those cloud-capp'd towers were the very first bits of social democracy to melt into thin air, and their inhabitants clamoured to sign up to the privatisation that undermined them. Truth-telling, then, might be morally right in an abstract sense, but a building is not an abstraction, and architectural honesty's effect on public morality is hard to measure, if it exists at all. You could even take the opposing view that architectural dishonesty – loft-style basements, flagstone-patterned lino, double garages with plaster columns, stone-effect cladding – makes people's lives better because it gives them at least the semblance of luxury. If you think semblance is enough.

The immorality of Nero's house no longer exercises our indignation; today it's just an artefact prized for its aesthetic and historical value. Over time even the greatest of crimes lose their capacity to revulse. More recent buildings, however, still inflame our judgment – the Nazis' actions still resonate in Europe, America and the Middle East, and their ruins still emit the radiation of immorality. The battle of brutalism left even fresher wounds; we are still fighting it today in the planning departments and ballot boxes of Europe and North America, where social democracy and its monuments crumble simultaneously to dust. The current

baudenkmal bundesschule bernau

The SA marches past Hannes Meyer's Trades Union School outside Berlin in June
1933. The building later became a training school for the SS

resurgence of interest in these unloved structures in architecture schools, from writers like Owen Hatherley and in blogs like Fuck Yeah Brutalism is easily dismissed as left-wing melancholy, a crippling nostalgia for lost battles, or at worst a perverse affectation of middle-class aesthetes who never had to live in these monstrous carbuncles. (I once lived in a low-rise block, and the stairwells *were* filled with the sweet-and-sour smells of heroin and vomit, but apart from that it was sturdy, overlooked green tree-filled spaces, was more spacious than the newbuilds I have occupied since, and these days it has an intercom system to prevent unwanted visitors.) In any case, backward glances don't necessarily impede a forward trajectory. As Marx put it,

> The tradition of all dead generations weighs like a nightmare on the brains of the living. And just as they seem to be occupied with revolutionizing themselves and things . . . they anxiously conjure up the spirits of the past to their service, borrowing from them names, battle slogans, and costumes in order to present this new scene in world history in time-honoured disguise and borrowed language . . . The awakening of the dead in those revolutions served the purpose of glorifying the new struggles, not of parodying the old; of magnifying the given task in the imagination, not recoiling from its solution in reality; of finding once more the spirit of revolution, not making its ghost walk again.[27]

Buildings themselves assume historic dress, like the brutalists looking back to the heroic age of modernism or Pugin cladding the classically proportioned Houses of Parliament in Gothic filigree. They are tangible repositories of memory, which is the topic of the next chapter. But these backward glances must be critical if they are to refresh the moral immediacy of the past. Opening old wounds makes the past work for the present – in other words, helps us to recognise what in the past is wrong for us, take what we need from it, improve on it, and move on. That is equally the task of the critical historian – of the post-Neronian Romans who condemned the Domus Aurea for its transgressions of imperial propriety, the medieval scholars who damned Nero for his perse-cution of the Christians and the nineteenth-century moralists who censured his sexual and artistic depravity. As global inequality grows ever more apparent to a more connected world, and the Ambanis and the oligarchs of Chelsea blight our cities with their grotesque houses, the crimes of Nero resonate once more, albeit in a different key.

Djinguereber Mosque, Timbuktu
(1327)
Architecture and Memory

There never were any mosques in Zvornik.
Branko Grujic, Serbian mayor of Zvornik, after the expulsion of
the Muslims who made up 60 per cent of the town's population,
and the destruction of its dozen mosques[1]

The mud-brick minaret of Djinguereber Mosque, Timbuktu, Mali

In 1324 King Musa of Mali made a pilgrimage to Mecca of such breathtaking magnificence that people were still talking about it four hundred years later. 'He set off in great pomp with a large party,' according to the author of a seventeenth-century Malian chronicle, 'including 60,000 soldiers and 500 slaves, who ran in front of him as he rode. Each of his slaves bore in his hand a wand fashioned from two kilos of gold.'[2] There were dignitaries, there were palanquins, there were hundreds of camels and wives, and they carried with them a total of 2,200 pounds of gold; Musa's kingdom was one of the richest in the Middle Ages, when his mines supplied two thirds of the West's gold. His spending as he made his way cross North Africa completely unbalanced the Mediterranean economy. 'Gold was at a high price in Egypt until they came that year,' one Cairene recalled, but when Musa flooded the market the local currency fell dramatically in value, and, 'this has been the state of affairs for about twelve years until this day.'[3] Musa's wealth didn't just make a lasting impression on his hosts; his reputation spread far across Europe. A Spanish map from 1375 shows him holding a gleaming nugget as big as a goose egg, and his city of Timbuktu became a byword for wealth, mystery and extreme inaccessibility.

On the southern fringes of the Sahara, where the desert sands shade into the green savannah, lies the region of Africa known as the Sahel ('shore' in Arabic), a great strip of semi-arid land running from the Atlantic to the Red Sea. It was in the western part of the Sahel, by the northernmost bend of the Niger River, that Musa's fabulous kingdom lay. One of its greatest cities, Timbuktu was a crucial trading post, where slaves for the

Arabian trade and gold from the south were exchanged for rock salt from the desert, and caravans of up to three thousand camels would disgorge their exotic burdens after the arduous Saharan crossing. Trade – not conquest, as had been the case in North Africa – was what first brought Islam here in the eleventh century, although most of Musa's subjects remained unconverted. Itinerant Muslim scholars had also been attracted by the possibility of patronage from Mali's legendarily wealthy inhabitants. But the way from Mecca was not a one-way street: several of Musa's forebears had made the hajj before him, albeit never with as much pomp.

In the centres of Islamic civilisation Musa visited he evidently found much that appealed to him: in the course of his travels he picked up Islamic law books from Cairo, descendants of the Prophet from Mecca and an Andalusian poet-architect named al-Sahili. When the expedition returned to West Africa a year later, al-Sahili oversaw the construction of a magnificent domed audience chamber for the king, with a carved plaster ceiling decorated with elegant calligraphy. 'As architecture was unknown in this country, the sultan was entranced,' wrote the great philosopher of history and al-Sahili's fellow Andalusian Ibn Khaldun in the late fourteenth century.[4]

Khaldun never actually visited Timbuktu, but two hundred years later Leo Africanus, a Muslim scholar from Fez who ended up at the court of Pope Leo X, did, and he recorded an Arabic oral tradition that al-Sahili was also responsible for a great mosque in the city. The implication is that this was the Djinguereber or Friday Mosque commissioned by Musa, which – though it is made from mud bricks – still stands today, the metamorphic slopes of its pyramidal minaret studded with wooden staves. These porcupinic pricks aren't structural but a kind of permanent scaffolding that facilitates the regular re-mudding of the mosque necessary to prevent it melting back into the desert sands. Al-Sahili's creation was the starting point for an entirely new Sahelian style of architecture, which reproduced Andalusian Islamic forms in the local mud-brick vernacular and led to the establishment of similar mosques in Malian towns like Gao and, most famously, Djenné, where the Great Mosque is the largest mud-brick building in the world.

But when Arab and European writers assert that al-Sahili introduced architecture to West Africa, we should listen out for the sound of grinding axes. Their histories buy into the mythologies of both Europeans and Arabocentrists, who cannot countenance the possibility of a local African tradition of building, and certainly cannot dignify any such tradition with the term architecture. Instead, there is the underlying assumption that Africans live in huts unchanging in their form since prehistory, and that their architecture – and history itself, for that matter – began only with Islamicisation or European colonisation. But it is incredible that one man could introduce architecture to a place, or even that he could single-handedly introduce Islamic styles, especially since mosques had previously existed in Mali, and other rulers had been to Mecca before Musa. It is doubly incredible since similar mud-brick stave-studded structures exist in local non-Islamic contexts, such as the Dogon culture of central Mali. And yet the myth persists.

The reason for all this mythologising is that monuments – whether intentional, such as the Taj Mahal, or unintentional, like the supposed hut of Romulus that stood on the Palatine Hill for centuries – mark the memories that nations and communities are built on. (The word monument comes from the Latin *moneo* – to remind – the German word, *Denkmal*, is more didactic: 'Have a think about it!') The meaning and physical substance of monuments are therefore well worth fighting for. Mali's heritage is still being disputed today, not just in academic journals but on the ground by Malians themselves: in 2012 Islamists attacked the Djinguereber Mosque, and in 2006 there was a riot in Djenné over the restoration of the mosque there.

Architectural monuments may seem to be eternal but they are as fugitive as memory itself: they can be damaged, destroyed, restored and given new meanings by their users, their significance changing as frequently as the discourse they mould in their turn. We have already come across several examples of monuments being contested as sites of memory: the fall of the Bastille and the preservation of its ruins is an archetypal instance of the complex push and pull of forgetting (in this case the absolutist past) and remembering (the vanquishing of the *ancien régime*); the icono-clastic retooling of Catholic churches in the Netherlands was just as complicated, since Spanish Catholic rule, represented by wall paintings, was literally whitewashed, while vacant niches have since proclaimed the absence of saintly idols. More permanent was the destruction of Nero's house and its burial beneath the public baths of a succeeding dynasty, but his colossal statue remained, re-identified with a halo as an image of the sun god and giving its name to the Colosseum that later filled the site of Nero's park.

In this chapter I will bring the memorial function of architec-ture to the fore, asking what monuments are for and who they serve. As Walter Benjamin fled a regime obsessed by monumen-tality, he wrote,

> Whoever has emerged victorious participates to this day in the triumphal procession in which the present rulers step over those who are lying prostrate. According to traditional practice, the spoils are carried along in the procession. They are called cultural treasures, and a historical materialist views them with cautious detachment. For without exception the cultural treas-ures he surveys have an origin which he cannot contemplate without horror.[5]

Monuments tend to be built by the victors of history, and they are often, as Benjamin says, 'documents of barbarism'. The triumphal Arch of Titus in the Roman forum, for example, the arch that served as a model for countless others around the world in the nineteenth century, including the Arc de Triomphe in Paris, commemorates the crushing of Jerusalem in AD 72. One of its panels shows the Menorah being carried away from the destroyed Temple as loot. But though monuments are necessarily built by the rich and powerful, they are often subjected to popular reconfigurations, which can give them, at least temporarily, a meaning quite unintended by their builders, such as the turf Mohican that crowned Churchill's head during the London May Day protests of 2000.

In the twentieth century photojournalism has meant that these messages can reach a wide audience and even attain a kind of permanence or iconic monumentality of their own. Not coincidentally, in the same period critics began to question the very idea of monumentality, idealising instead the lightness of nomadic ways of life. The surrealist Georges Bataille, for example, complained that 'great monuments rise up like dams, opposing a logic of majesty and authority to all unquiet elements; it is in the form of cathedrals and palaces that church and state speak to and impose silence upon the crowds',[6] and American polymath Lewis Mumford decried the dead weight of monuments: 'The very permanence of stone and brick, which enable them to defy time, cause them also ultimately to defy life.'[7] Since the Second World War there has even been a rash of 'counter-monuments' intended to undermine the petrifying, didactic tone of such structures, a movement pioneered unsurprisingly in Germany, a nation still coming to terms with bad memories. But as the recent riot over the Great Mosque in Djenné shows (the locals were reacting to interference by government and international bodies with their building), even grandiose official monuments can be imbued with meanings and memories that resist the intentions of the powerful. So can these 'documents of barbarism' be turned against the barbarians themselves?

The archetypal monuments – the Egyptian Pyramids – are African. The Step Pyramid of Djoser, built 4,600 years ago, is one of the oldest surviving masonry structures, and its architect Imhotep the first builder whose name has come down to us. The quantum leap in construction that this structure represents – the enormous investment in time, money and lives necessary to quarry, transport and erect these stones – speaks of a culture fixated on memory. The Greeks, who learned so much about building from the Egyptians, were evidently paying attention: another wonder of the ancient world, the tomb of King Mausolus of Halicarnassus (present-day Bodrum in Turkey), was crowned with an enormous step pyramid.

This monument to an incestuous marriage was completed by the wife – also the sister – of Mausolus after his death in 353 BC. The building, designed by a pair of Greek architects, was of an entirely new type: it was raised on a high plinth and surrounded by columns like a temple, but had no pediments or doors and was topped instead by the pyramid, which seemed, one Roman poet said, 'to hang in mid-air' over the deep shadows of the colonnade. We only know about the tomb from confusing ancient descriptions since it was destroyed, possibly by earthquakes, and its ruins quarried to build a crusader castle, but it lived on in copies and in name: the Emperor Augustus' dynastic tomb was called a mausoleum by the Romans.

These buildings were meant to perpetuate the memories of rulers in the minds of the living, providing focuses for posthumous cults where worship would transform kings into immortal gods. There was something in it for the worshippers too, of course: people came to these very tangible symbols of immortality to ask for the help of the deceased pharaoh or emperor, although some cults were less the focus of popular devotion than of manufactured allegiance to a regime or dynasty. Likewise, the periodic deface-ments or destructions that these self-aggrandising memorials attract are just as often directed by oppositional political forces as by the people. Nero's Golden House was buried by a succeeding dynasty, and although the toppling of Saddam's statue was cheered by some citizens of Baghdad, the event was carefully stage-managed for the cameras by the invaders – the square had been cordoned off by US marines and contained at most 150 people, including soldiers and journalists.[8]

As Saddam's statue testifies, the monumental deification of rulers isn't just some quirk of the ancients. The twentieth century saw the continuation of this practice on an epic scale, and the relics of Saddam's attempt to foster a personality cult pale in comparison with the grandiose mausoleums of Lenin and Mao (the former goes for an elemental step-pyramid look). People still queue for hours to see the decomposing inhabitants of these buildings encased in their Sleeping Beauty coffins, and maybe the mixture of ghoulish tourism and nationalist nostalgia that inspires contem-porary visitors to these shrines gives us some idea of what really motivated the adherents of ancient personality cults. More impor-tantly, the controversy and antagonism that these monuments provoke should remind us that no cult is ever without its critics. The majority of Russians now think Lenin's corpse should be buried, and his sarcophagus has been attacked several times over the years.

Perhaps the most controversial modern mausoleum is the Valle de los Caidos – Valley of the Fallen – outside Madrid. This massive complex, comprising a monastery and a subterranean basilica, and crowned with a 150-metre cross visible from twenty miles away, was built by Franco to commemorate the Spanish Civil War. When work began in 1940, he proclaimed,

The dimension of our crusade, the heroic sacrifices involved in the victory and the far-reaching significance which this epic has had for the future of Spain cannot be commemorated by the simple monuments by which the outstanding events of our history and the glorious deeds of Spain's sons are normally remembered in towns and villages. The stones that are to be erected must have the grandeur of the monuments of old, which defy time and forgetfulness.[9]

But if Franco was hoping to defy mortality with his monuments, his efforts were largely in vain: his statues were removed from every public place in mainland Spain under the Law of Historical Memory passed by the socialist government of 2004–11. During this period the Valley of the Fallen itself came under increasing scrutiny. Sympathisers have characterised the complex as a monument to national reconciliation, pointing out that the crypts are filled by the remains of those who fought on both sides. But it has become clear that the vast majority of the 34,000 people interred here were nationalists and fascists, and that republican corpses were added later as a sort of prophylactic against criticism, often in the dead of night and without the permission of their families. Not much of a reconciliatory gesture, particularly as at least fourteen of the republicans were forced labourers who died during construction. If there can be any doubt as to the purpose of this monument, the occupants of the two tombs behind the altar – the only ones in the complex – should dispel it: José Antonio, the founder of the Falangist movement, was interred here by Franco in 1959, and the Caudillo himself lies under a simple slab, garlanded daily with fresh flowers by the adherents of his cult.

The last century, with its ideological frenzies and global wars, was a good time to be a monument builder. Nietzsche may have criticised the nineteenth century's fixation with monumental history in 1874, and Viennese art historian Alois Riegl was already writing about the 'Modern Cult of Monuments' in 1903, but nothing could have prepared either of them for the monument mania of the coming decades. Communist, fascist and capitalist monuments to the nation, to liberation and to conquest, to leaders and workers, to battles lost and won, sprouted all over Europe and Asia. Many of these are less controversial than Franco's tomb – for example the mass graves of northern Europe built to commemorate the dead of the First World War. Lutyens' arch at Thiepval is the most architecturally distinguished of these, an enormous deconstructed structure that speaks not of victory, as a traditional triumphal arch would, but of loss. Appropriately for a building that marks an absence – it is for the 72,000 men whose bodies were never found after the Somme – its form suggests the crossing of a bombed-out cathedral, its great central arch being the nave and the two subsidiary arches the aisles of this ghostly structure. But even this monument passes over the suffering of civilians in silence; it is still a nationalistic, militaristic shrine.

It would take the Second World War to create a feeling of revulsion with the past so great that in Germany a wave of what James Young called counter-monuments were built, albeit belatedly. One of the most remarkable of these was the Monument Against Fascism, designed by artists Jochen and Escher Gerz for Harburg, a dismal suburb of Hamburg. Erected in 1986, the monument was a twelve-metre square black lead pillar which was lowered by stages into the ground. The artists invited visitors to add their names to the surface, with the intention that 'the counter-monument would not just commemorate the anti-fascist impulse but enact it, breaking down the hierarchical relationship between art object and its audience'.[10] Perhaps inevitably, the pillar was soon swarming with unruly graffiti, mainly of the 'Gertrud woz 'ere' variety but also with political statements both neo- and anti-Nazi in nature. The most provocative aspect of the programme was the fact that when the reachable portion was completely superscribed it would be buried, and eventually this self-effacing monument would completely erase itself, a truly counter-monumental gesture. What is more, because local dignitaries, press and members of the public assembled to applaud the increasing invisibility of their monument against fascism each time it sank a little further, the artists elicited from their audience an expression of relief at the recession of painful war memories. As Nietzsche had put it, 'It is always the same thing that makes happiness happiness: the ability to forget.'[11]

The auto-iconoclasm of counter-monuments is the product of a very particular place and time, informed by modernist critiques of monumentality and the political landscape of post-war Europe. But attacks on monuments have more often been, and continue to be, unsanctioned critiques of official culture. The Protestant destruction of images in Dutch churches in the sixteenth century was both politically and religiously inspired, intended to send a message to the Spanish rulers and their Catholic Church.

Faith continues to be a strong motivation for oppositional vandalism, as the damaged mosques of Mali attest. At the time of writing the political situation in that country – once the darling of neoliberals, aid agencies and Western sentimentalists alike – is a tangled mess. Following a military coup in 2012, Islamist groups and breakaway Tuareg nomads took control of much of northern Mali, using arms acquired after the collapse of Gaddafi's regime in Libya. As has been prominently reported, many Sufi shrines and tombs – by some estimates over half the shrines in the country – were destroyed during this period. These tombs are of great significance in Mali, where the majority of Muslims subscribe to the tenets of Sufism, which holds that particularly holy individuals or saints can have more intimate encounters with God than is permitted ordinary people, and that by visiting shrines or mausoleums dedicated to their memories these saints can be asked to intercede with God. Timbuktu – sometimes called the city of 333 saints – is richly provided with Sufi tombs, but during the violence of 2012 many of them were bulldozed, two of the mausoleums attached to Djinguereber Mosque being attacked with pickaxes.

The reaction of the foreign press has been fierce, as it was when the Taliban dynamited the Bamiyan Buddhas in Afghanistan, and wild accusations of al-Qaeda links have been made. In fact there are only very tenuous organisational connections between the iconoclasts of Afghanistan, the associates of Bin Laden (whose iconoclasm has been largely directed at the West, in any case) and the rebel forces of Mali. What they evidently share is a contempt for monuments. A person claiming to be a spokesman for Ansar Dine, the Islamist group which occupied Timbuktu during the unrest, was quoted as saying, 'There is no world heritage. It does not exist. Infidels must not get involved in our business.'[12] High-profile targets are partly selected in order to compensate for the relative weakness of the organisations, and the fact that their tactics succeed in attracting such attention confirms their implied critique: that Malian (or Afghanistani) lives are held to be of little conse-quence in comparison, thus revealing the hypocrisy of Western governments, which have shown little regard for Islamic architec-ture when bombing their countries, and the essential *in*humanism of the 'universal values' espoused by Western liberals, which are used to justify paternalistic interference by former colonial rulers.

But much more than sending a message to the West, the icono-clasm in Mali was intended to make a national political statement, both rallying sympathisers to the cause and attacking the corrupt Malian government from which the rebels are attempting to secede. In contrast the rebels profess to purvey a 'purified' Islam, but as historian Emily O'Dell has observed, 'In their destruction of these tombs and bodies as idols – and their redundant murder-ing of the already dead – Ansar Dine has betrayed their own message, for they have themselves traded in politics and religion with images.'[13]

Exploding cathedral: Christ the Saviour in Moscow was dynamited on the orders of Stalin in 1931

In recent years there has also been a great deal of iconoclasm directed against Muslim monuments from outside the faith, by Christians in the former Yugoslavia for instance, where nearly all the sixteenth-century Ottoman mosques were destroyed during the vicious wars of the 1990s, and by Hindus in India, who destroyed the 430 year-old Babri Mosque in 1992, an event which led to riots in which over 2,000 people died. By denying the Islamic histories of their own nations, these iconoclasts aimed to invalidate the rights of Muslims to live there in the present. Although faith often lies behind the destruction of monuments, in the twentieth century atheistic iconoclasm was also pursued on a massive scale by communist states in their attempts to effect a mass change in consciousness from faith to materialism. In 1931 Stalin blew up the biggest church in Russia, the Cathedral of Christ the Saviour in Moscow, to make way for a projected Palace of the Soviets. The nineteenth-century cathedral, which had been built to glorify the autocratic tsarist regime, was architecturally undistinguished – it was no patch on the deliriously domed St Basil's – and its demise was arguably no great loss, but it was undoubtedly a traumatic event for the Orthodox Church.

A series of high-profile international competitions was held to solicit designs for the cathedral's replacement, and the cream of international architects was encouraged to apply. Entries were submitted by Le Corbusier, Walter Gropius, Erich Mendelsohn and several Soviet modernists including Moisei Ginsburg and the Vesnin brothers, but in the end (and much to Le Corbusier's irritation) a gruesome neoclassical confection was designed instead by an official committee. This decision is often portrayed as the moment when modernism was symbolically crushed by Stalinist kitsch: the palace was to be a huge tower with a series of art deco setbacks, surmounted by a colossal statue of Lenin, his arm pointing skywards 'in the pose of a provincial actor', as one Russian visitor to the competition exhibition wrote in the comment book.[14]

The palace, which would have been just as monumental as the church it replaced, was never built – the foundations were poured and a steel frame begun, but the girders were recycled for the war effort. Nevertheless it continued to haunt the Soviet imagination into the early 1940s, exhibited at home and abroad in models, medals, murals, souvenir publications and even a documentary film. But in 1958 – two years after Kruschev's Secret Speech denouncing Stalin to the Politburo, and twenty-seven years after the cathedral had exploded – a swimming pool was begun on the site instead. Some might see this as a frivolous or populist replacement, but putting the world's largest open-air pool in the middle of an often freezing city where a grandiose monument to a personality cult was intended to stand appeals to me as a utopian democratic gesture, although perhaps people who aren't as keen on swimming would disagree. The heated circular pool steamed its way through the Moscow winters until 1995, when the mayor decided to rebuild the cathedral on the site. The restored Christ the Saviour is even more hideous than its predecessor, and it speaks volumes about the post-Soviet state's priorities – no more pools for people – and its rapprochement with the ultra-conservative Orthodox Church. Like Lenin's mausoleum, which clings on in the face of public indifference, the cathedral says a lot about what the Russian state wants to remember – and what it wants to forget – as it forges a new nationalist myth.

Restoration inevitably recreates the past as we want it to be. Sometimes this is done with flagrant disregard for historical accuracy, as was the case with Viollet-le-Duc's nineteenth-century gargoyles for Notre-Dame. A fierce debate over architectural restoration was raging in France and England at the time, stoked by the invention of photography – which meant that buildings could be documented more accurately – and struggles over the meaning of style and its inner relationship to the zeitgeist. John Ruskin saw architecture as an essential repository of memory – 'we may live without her and worship without her, but we cannot remember without her' – and urged the preservation of ancient monuments, 'true strong conquerors of the forgetfulness of men'. Yet he took a firm stand against restoring buildings, particularly Viollet-le-Duc's methods of scraping back the accretions and abrasions of time. Ruskin complained that restoration was

> the most total destruction which a building can suffer: a destruction out of which no remnants can be gathered; a destruction accompanied with false description of the thing destroyed . . . it is impossible, as impossible as to raise the dead, to restore anything

that has ever been great or beautiful in architecture . . . that spirit which is only given by the hand and eye of the workman, never can be recalled.[15]

His objection was based on the idea that a building is an authentic expression of a moment in a nation's history, and should be cherished as such in order to perpetuate the nation and its time-hallowed values, which are of course open to personal interpretation. In Ruskin's case this meant Gothic buildings and Christian socialism, which he pitted against the forces of industrial modernity. But though his 'anti-scrape' philosophy, which was picked up by William Morris when he established the Society for the Protection of Ancient Buildings in 1877, has become conservation orthodoxy, it does run into difficulties when the rights of old buildings conflict with those of living people. If buildings are preserved in aspic and set apart from modernity they are in danger of becoming irrelevant or even a burden, preventing people from improving their lives and their environments.

This tension between remembering and forgetting in architecture, between true and false memories, continues today, as with the resurrected Cathedral of Christ the Saviour in Moscow and the planned reconstruction of the eighteenth-century Berlin Palace, demolished by the DDR to make way for its own People's Palace after the war, which was in turn destroyed after reunification. The Great Mosque at Djenné is another mnemonic battlefield on which blood has recently been spilt.

In 2006 the Aga Khan Trust for Culture (the Aga Khan is the leader of the Nizari Ismailis, a Shia sect) sent a team to inspect the roof of the mud-brick building. The soluble structure is in constant danger of being washed away, so it is replastered every year by the townspeople in a celebration called the *fête de la crépissage*, when those wooden staves embedded in the facade come into play as

During the annual fête de la crépissage, *the people of Djenné come together to replaster the Great Mosque — and put on a show for the tourists who are one of the town's main sources of income*

foot- and handholds. Although this protects the building, over the years it had also added tonnes of extra mud to the roof and walls, transforming the originally crisp-lined mosque into a swollen biomorphic mass and endangering the structure's integrity. When the townspeople spotted the Aga Khan group investigating the roof of their mosque a huge riot broke out and the conservators were forced to flee. The rioters went on to destroy ventilators that had been installed by the US embassy as a bridge-building exercise during the Iraq War, and one person was killed during ensuing clashes with the police.

Before we conclude that this episode was simply a reaction to foreign interference in local heritage, it should be added that the offices of the prefect, the mayor and the central government's cultural mission, and even several cars belonging to the mosque's imam were also damaged. This comprehensive attack on authority figures speaks of an exasperation with the politics of heritage in general – and no wonder, since Djenné (and Mali as a whole) has been poked at relentlessly for decades, often without any obvious benefit to its people. Since 1988 the mosque and many historic houses in the town have been designated a UNESCO World Heritage Site, like the Djinguereber Mosque in Timbuktu, leading to an influx of money from aid agencies and tourists. But while authority figures grow rich from their heritage cash cows, ordinary people are forced to live in what they regard as substandard antiquated housing, as the UNESCO status of these buildings means that modernisation is forbidden. But as one local succinctly put it, 'Who wants to live in a house with a mud floor?'

Mahamame Bamoye Traoré, who heads the town's influential guild of masons, argues that 'if you want to help someone, you have to help him in a way that he wants; to force him to live in a certain way is not right'. Of one particularly tiny, windowless, mud-floored room, Traoré said, 'This is not a room. It might as well be a grave.'[16] His simile poignantly echoes modernist critiques of the mid-twentieth century, suggesting that we have learned little from Bataille's warning about architecture that 'smothers social life under a stone monument'. As the Malians have discovered, mud can smother too, and it is only preferred by people living far away, with their *nostalgie de la boue* – 'nostalgia for mud' – or the idealisation of supposedly unspoilt ways of life.

Undeterred by the violence that greeted its earlier visit, in 2009 the Aga Khan Trust returned to carry out restoration of the mosque. But what exactly were they restoring, and in accordance with whose memory? In fact the Great Mosque at Djenné may be a product of foreign dictations of Malian identity: the original thirteenth-century building was allowed to disintegrate by Seku Amadu, a puritanical theocrat in the nineteenth century. Amadu then built his own replacement, a much simpler mosque without any decoration. However, when the French conquered Mali at the end of the nineteenth century they wanted to promote a different, more accommodating kind of Islam, so they destroyed the ruins of the first mosque in order to create the present building in 1907. Whether it is 'authentically Malian' is a matter of heated debate: even at the time one French observer who had been familiar with the ruins of the original mosque called its replacement 'a cross between a hedgehog and a church organ', and said its conical towers made the building resemble 'a baroque temple dedicated to the god of suppositories'.[17] Critics continue to argue that its symmetrical monumentality is a European imposition, and indeed the three towers of the façade, the conical turrets of which are topped with ostrich eggs, do make it look rather like a Gothic cathedral. Could this be an example of the kind of monumental false-memory syndrome – specifically French again – that Ruskin had criticised in 1849, when he argued against Viollet-le-Duc's overenthusiastic restorations?

In any case, whether it is French-colonial or Malian, the Aga Khan Trust determined that the 1907 construction was the 'authentic' mosque, and proceeded to strip back the layers of accreted mud that had been added to the building over the last hundred years. They did this in order to protect the structure of the building, which was buckling under all the extra weight – one of the towers collapsed after heavy rains later that year – but they were also trying to rediscover the authentic essence of the building, which was supposedly hiding beneath the skin. But what if the essence *was* the skin: if the original mosque was created by the French, perhaps the most authentic thing about it is the gradual metamorphosis it has undergone since at the hands of the townspeople, whose bodies have left physical impressions on the mud?

The imam – pumped full of Saudi petrodollars – also has his qualms about the current mosque: he wants to give it a Middle

Eastern makeover by facing the exterior with green tiles and sticking gold minarets on top. However, UNESCO – working in concert with the central government's cultural mission – have stalled the imam's plans so far. Are these contradictory interventions from the West (UNESCO and the American embassy) and the East (the Aga Kahn Trust and the Imam's Saudi benefactors) just fresh instances of foreigners imposing their own visions on Mali and denying the authorship of African artists? Or is the idea of singular artistic authorship itself a foreign imposition? The Great Mosque was, after all, constructed by a community of local craftsmen who have handed down their expertise through the generations. If that is the case, then surely these buildings *must* be authentic, since oral, communal tradition is a more authentic expression of African identity than the myth of the lone artistic genius or the written history imposed by foreigners. You could say that this orality finds its analogue in the *fête de la crépissage*, when the people of Djenné hand on their knowledge of building practices from generation to generations, involving the whole community in the maintenance of their mosque.

But is orality really more 'authentically African', or is this just another romantic myth portraying Africa as an illiterate continent despite all the evidence to the contrary? After all, Timbuktu and Djenné were for centuries centres of learning and the nexuses of an international book trade. Today the region is still full of medieval manuscripts, the majority of them in private libraries despite international efforts to collect them in locations such as the Ahmed Baba Institute, a foundation funded and built by South Africans in Timbuktu in 2010. The reluctance of people to part with their books is understandable, since the French tried to steal their libraries too when they were in charge, and the precious leather-bound volumes are crucial links to the past for a battered nation. These books also came under attack during the recent conflict: like the Sufi tombs, they represent memories of an

Islamic history that the reformers wished to erase. Shortly before the rebels were forced out of Timbuktu by the French, the Ahmed Baba Institute was ransacked and several volumes were burned. Wisely, the majority had been hidden away by the centre's scholars – Malians have had a lot of experience of vandals. Just as these manuscripts give the lie to the myth of African orality, Mali's mosques are not fruits of some anonymous, inexpert or ahistorical tradition that rises magically out of the African 'mass': we know the name of the head mason of Djenné who rebuilt the mosque in 1907 – it was Ismaila Traoré – and the local architect who consulted on the Aga Khan's restoration, Abd El Kader Fofana, was trained in the USSR and speaks Russian and Chinese. The traditions of Malian building may be orally transmitted, but that doesn't stop them from changing with time, or mixing with international currents – as they have done since before the time of King Musa's hajj.

The carved tent-tomb of Victorian orientalist Richard Burton at Mortlake in South West London

Desiccation and deliquescence constantly threaten to return these Malian mosques to the formless desert sands. Their metamorphosis, and their need to be remade once a year by the caressing hands of their worshippers, may make them seem the opposite of the monuments criticised by modernists like Bataille or Mumford. The latter equated monumentality with permanent stone, but the mud-brick, possibly inauthentic but certainly hybrid Djenné Great Mosque is as permanent as the people who care for it; and just as Bataille and Mumford questioned the deadweight that monuments exert on society, the built heritage of Timbuktu and Djenné, set in stone by UNESCO, threatens to strangle the life of these towns. But the melting mud and the riots over the Great Mosque remind us that no monument is as fixed as we might imagine. Likewise the attacks by Islamists on the Sufi tombs of Mali tell us that not everyone shares the so-called universal values of world heritage that UNESCO espouses: the *Bilderverbot*, or image taboo, of the puritans makes these monuments heretical, not precious.

Many of the people who joined the recent Mali uprising were Tuaregs. Although these nomadic Saharan clans are traditionally followers of Sufism, many Tuaregs – especially those who have been agitating for decades for the establishment of a separate state named Azawad in the north of the country – have recently begun to ally with reforming Islamists, and joined in their destruction of Sufi shrines and books in Timbuktu. The nomadic way of life has been romanticised by Europeans and Arabs for centuries, and nomad tents have often been held up by critics of the monumental city as alternative dwellings that lie lighter on the land. Richard Burton, the nineteenth-century orientalist and explorer who managed to enter Mecca in disguise (he also published controversial unexpurgated versions of the *Thousand and One Nights* and the *Kama Sutra*), was buried outside London under a representation of a Bedouin tent carved from stone. It is a peculiarly permanent incarnation of this archetypically mobile structure that serves as a metaphor for the fleeting tent of skin of the human body and its inhabitant the soul's resurrection in the life eternal.

However, it would be an orientalist fantasy to portray the Tuareg people – who are in reality not a homogeneous mass but a cellular grouping of often antagonistic clans – as somehow essentially opposed to the city, its monuments and its memories: a Tuareg recently became prime minister of Mali, and many Tuaregs work in the cultural institutions of Timbuktu. Even so, in the twentieth century the nomad was imagined afresh as some new eternal, unchanging other, and the nomad's tent was also set to new metaphoric labours. Mumford wrote,

> the pastoral nomad spared himself the sacrifice of the living to the dead monument until he copied the ways of men in cities: he traveled light. Civilisation today, for different reasons, with different ends in view, must follow this example of the nomad: it must not merely travel light but settle light: it must be ready, not for merely physical movement in space, but for adaptation to new conditions of life, new industrial processes, new cultural advantages. Our cities must not be monuments, but self-renewing organisms.[18]

Hannes Meyer, the socialist director of the Bauhaus whom we came across at the end of the last chapter, also proposed a new nomadic way of life with a photograph entitled 'The dwelling: co-op interior 1926'. The image shows a mocked-up interior furnished with the bare essentials of mobile modern living: a camp bed, a gramophone on a stool and a folded chair hooked to the wall. The white modernist walls – *tabula rasa*, wiped clean of troubling memories – seem on closer inspection to be the draped skin of a tent. Meyer wrote, 'Because of the standardisation of his needs as regards housing, food and mental sustenance [the gramophone in the corner], the semi-nomad of our modern productive system has the benefit of freedom of movement, economies, simplification

Tent for modern nomads: Hannes Meyer's co-op interior, 1926

and relaxation, all of which are vitally important to him.'[19] Rootlessness wasn't just going to be economically and psychologically beneficial; it would also help to eradicate the nationalism that had led to the First World War and the bitter memories it had left behind: 'Our homes are more mobile than ever. Large blocks of flats, sleeping cars, house yachts and transatlantic liners undermine the local concept of the "homeland". The fatherland goes into a decline. We learn Esperanto. We become cosmopolitan.'[20]

Esperanto is now the faded pipe dream of long-dead cranks, and decades of globalisation have put paid to the idea that global capital is a pacific force – war is not eliminated by rootlessness, but the former often leads to the latter. Neither has globalisation done much for the livelihoods and psyches of the world's poor (there is an argument for brutalist monumentality as a counterweight to capitalism's solvent tendencies). Nor is the nomad's tent a peaceable kingdom. The Tuareg themselves are famed warriors and masters of the smooth space of the desert, whence some of them launch attacks on the cities of the south. And though the nomadic tent has been caricatured as an ahistoric zone – a kind of tonic for the nightmare of history from which modernists were desperate to awake – it is in fact just as permanent as mud or brick. Tuareg tents are built by women for their wedding days – in the Tuareg language the word for tent is both a metaphor for marriage and for the vagina – and they are carried around for a lifetime: not fixed perhaps, but not impermanent either, and just as suffused with memories – personal, family, social – as the grand monuments of Timbuktu and Djenné.

For sedentary Westerners too, the city can become a giant habitable madeleine, in which certain streets and certain corners are for ever marked by the incontinent dog of memory – for me a defaced street sign by a graveyard wall in Oxfordshire is a monument to a moment of teenage rebellion, and the view from Crystal Palace a monument to the end of a love affair. Architecture is full of these private memories, and even grandiose monuments to group memories are less than monolithic. In fact they are worm-eaten by individuals forgetting, misremembering and contesting interpretations of the past much more so than their builders would like. Every monument is made and remade like the melting mosques of Mali, and every monument can be a counter-monument superscribed by memories of our own.

4

Palazzo Rucellai, Florence
(1450)
Architecture and Business

I don't intend to build in order to have clients. I intend to have clients in order to build.

Ayn Rand, *The Fountainhead*[1]

A building is only as good as its client.

Norman Foster[2]

Giovanni Rucellai with his architectural projects

'There are two important things in life: procreation and building.' So wrote Giovanni Rucellai, fifteenth-century banker and patron of a remarkable group of buildings in his native city of Florence. A painting shows Giovanni, his beard as bushy as any biblical patriarch's, in front of a fictive huddle of his palace, church and tomb. It's a sort of family portrait, with Giovanni the proud father surrounded by his architectural babies. One of these, the Palazzo Rucellai (visible to the left), marked a watershed in domestic design. It dropped the gloomy heaviness of earlier palaces in favour of lightness and elegance and a brand-spanking-new classicism. The palazzo was a family home and, since family was inextricably entwined with business for Florentines, a corporate HQ: in this case, one as gleamingly new and impressive as any Shanghai skyscraper today. Giovanni's palace dresses its marmoreal permanence in cutting-edge garb, radiating both reliability *and* modernity – traits essential to a successful business. No wonder he thought building was as important as sex.

Rich men like Giovanni have always used architecture to promote themselves and their businesses, even – in the case of flamboyant developers such as Donald Trump – making building itself into an occupation. Architecture is, like any other art, a way of making money, and the priapic towers of developers like Trump expose the business of architecture at its most naked, pulsating with empurpled money lust. From the proto-capitalists who built Florence to the titanic developers of Manhattan, from the German inventors of corporate identity to the deracinated corporations parasitising contemporary London, corporate patrons have reconstructed the city in their own image. But business and architecture, client and designer, private interest and public good, are never as harmonious as the ordered stones of Giovanni's palace or the serenely soaring lines of Rockefeller Center contrive to suggest. Corporate builders tend to disregard the person in the street, when they aren't actively trying to pull the rug from beneath her feet. Their activities bring down economies, ruin neighbourhoods and, in some cases, kill. Countless attempts have been made to tame the business of architecture, but these are just pinpricks to leviathan: as we'll see, corporate builders have nothing to fear but their own success.

Giovanni Rucellai, born in 1403, came from a long line of Florentine cloth merchants, but lost his father at a young age and received only a modest inheritance. Like a preliminary sketch for the great capitalist myth of the self-made man, Giovanni, spurred on by a pushy mother, overcame these early setbacks to become a successful banker. He amassed a huge fortune in the process, becoming at one point the third richest man in the city. On his marriage to the daughter of Palla Strozzi, Florence's foremost citizen, his entry into the oligarchy that controlled the republic seemed assured – along with all the influence and opportunity that entailed – but his hopes were dashed when Palla joined forces with several of Florence's other leading families to kick Cosimo de' Medici out of the city. Cosimo had grown too big for his boots and was threatening to upset the balance of power, so the other oligarchs thought. Unfortunately for the conspirators Cosimo was soon back, and on his return in 1434 he was finally able to establish the Medici as the pre-eminent force in the republic.

This marked the beginning of a period of oligarchic consolidation and a terminal decline in the power of the relatively democratic guilds. More worryingly for Giovanni, it meant that his father-in-law and protector Palla was exiled for life. But despite this reversal in his fortunes Giovanni never abandoned Palla, though his loyalty cost him dearly. The Medici looked on friends of their enemies with suspicion, and after their rise to power Giovanni was excluded from public office for decades – as he complains in his diary, 'I have not been on good terms with the state, but rather under suspicion for 27 years.' This didn't put much of a dampener on Giovanni's business ventures, however, and in the end he managed to arrange a marriage between his son Bernardo and Nannina de' Medici. The marriage was loveless and unhappy, as Nannina's letters reveal, but it had the intended effect: the Medici forgot Giovanni Rucellai's connection to their old enemy. Giovanni could now take part in the government of the city, a role that had a grandeur pleasing to the proud old man but one whose responsibilities he didn't take very seriously.

Instead, Giovanni devoted his energy to architecture. This primitive bourgeois was no artist, and his notebooks reveal a brain untroubled by original ideas, yet in his hands the business of building became an art in itself. The fruits of his expensive hobby were his palazzo and the family portico or loggia across the way, the striking two-tone marble facade of Santa Maria Novella and a family chapel with an exquisite tomb shaped like the Holy Sepulchre in Jerusalem. None of these structures was particularly discreet when it came to its patron's identity: even the church – the kind of project usually accomplished with a degree of pious self-restraint – screams Giovanni's involvement. Rucellai family emblems cover the facade like a rash (there are also carved Medici diamond rings, boasting of the intermarriage of the families), and towards the top, inscribed in huge Roman capitals, is 'GIOVANNI RUCELLAI 1470'. It's the only Italian church to display its donor's name like a billboard, and references to the glory of God are conspicuous by their absence.

By tagging the first grand structure that visitors from the north would encounter (today, just across from the station, it is still the first sight that modern visitors see), Giovanni created a nice bit of advertising for his business, but why did the friars go along with this shameless self-promotion? The answer may be that they were keen to get the work done at any price. Marble facings didn't come cheap – they were so expensive in fact that Santa Maria Novella was the only Florentine church to have its facade completed in the course of the Renaissance. By comparison, the facade of the city's cathedral, the duomo, wasn't finished until the nineteenth century – when it got a fussy wedding cake confection plastered all over it – and even the Medici never got around to finishing the facade of their family church, San Lorenzo. So how did Giovanni manage it?

After his exile, Giovanni's father-in-law Palla Strozzi had sold him some valuable estates at knock-down prices in order to avoid the punitive taxes that had been levied on them under Medici pressure. By keeping them in the family, Palla hoped to maintain at least some influence over the disposal of his former properties, and his generosity was conditional on the income from some of them going to ecclesiastical works, which indeed they did: Giovanni used the money to pay for the facade of Santa Maria Novella. Meanwhile, Giovanni nominally transferred several of his new estates to the guild of bankers, of which he was a member, in order to avoid paying tax on them. (The city spotted some of these tax dodges, but not all.) So the great facade of Santa Maria Novella, one of the most striking and narcissistic of Florence's monuments, was built from the profits of tax evasion and the exploitation of Palla Strozzi's exile. The latter's name appears nowhere on the building, whereas Giovanni – his taste, his generosity, his vanity – is immortalised in marble.

Giovanni wasn't alone in his taste for self-promotion. Fifteenth-century Florence was a forest of logos and inscriptions, its markers of banking families and merchants as densely packed as neon on the Vegas strip. Giovanni's own logo was the wind-filled sail of fortune. It gave an old idea a new twist: instead of the medieval image of a blindfolded woman presiding implacably over the rise and fall of people on a wheel, now fortune was depicted as a force that could be harnessed for profit, like the trade winds that took Florentine goods around the world. The sail of fortune is carved all over Giovanni's projects and seems especially appropriate on Santa Maria Novella (it is an ill wind, after all . . .). Naming a massive structure ensured posterity of course, but it also demonstrated financial and social might. This was important because, in the modern Florentine economy, trust was everything: without it credit lines would snap and customers evaporate. One of the best ways to advertise creditworthiness, wealth and success was by building a formidable HQ; physical solidity has ever been a popular metaphor for financial soundness. Giovanni's own HQ, Palazzo Rucellai, expresses its builder's power in a new and sophisticated way, as a comparison to a slightly older house shows.

Palazzo Medici, begun around 1445, walks a tightrope between chameleonic camouflage and insidious co-option, taking on the tropes of local tradition and subtly modifying them to demonstrate the power of its owners. All the while it is careful to avoid bombastic statements that could offend the other oligarchs – the family had, after all, only returned from exile twenty years earlier, and they were keen not to tread on any toes. The story goes that Cosimo de' Medici rejected a much grander design by Brunelleschi, architect of the cathedral's dome, for this very reason. Nevertheless the twin windows of the Medici family home are strikingly like the *bifore* windows on the Palazzo Vecchio, home of the Florentine government. No previous building had had the balls to compare itself with this seat of power, and the Medici palace has balls in abundance: the *palle*, or balls, are a family emblem and appear on carved shields all over the building. Mirroring the *bifore* windows, the ground floor is divided into a row of wider-arched apertures originally housing shops, an important source of rental income. But after a new tax was levied on commercial space, ground-floor shops went out of fashion, and the ones on the Palazzo Medici were filled in.

The evolution of the building seems to confirm the Marxist idea that culture is determined by economics. But Engels rejected this as an oversimplified misreading of his friend's works, and as we go on we'll come across numerous cases when this supposed one-way street goes into reverse, and culture determines economics. Architecture is one of the most tangled nodes of this interaction, since it is both art and business, one of the most powerful drivers of economic growth and simultaneously one of its clearest expressions. However, these blind arches are clear enough: economics can shape the city as surely as any architect. Importantly, in this instance we are not looking at the work of the hidden hand of the market, but at government intervention via taxation. In another demonstration of the power of government over architecture, the ground floor is rusticated – that is, its stones are laboriously and expensively carved to make them appear roughly hewn. Although it may seem perverse to carve stone to make it look unfinished, rustication is a feature of many Florentine buildings and of countless later structures in the classical tradition. To many it has seemed a way of balancing the appearance of a structure, of giving it a heavy bottom, so to speak, so it doesn't look ready to topple over. But this reading is largely a product of our post-Romantic tendency to reduce art to aesthetics. In fact rustication was a response to local building regulations which stipulated that structures should be finished as richly as possible where they met the street in order to create a high-quality public space. Like the blind arches, rustication shows aesthetic decisions responding to other forces, and so points to my utopian leitmotif: though corporate builders bend and break the rules, it may be possible to channel their energies.

So what's new about Giovanni's house? It has those same *bifore* windows pioneered by Palazzo Medici, which was being constructed at the same time – perhaps in an attempt to borrow

Palazzo Rucellai: the facade sinks its teeth into the neighbouring house

some of the symbolic power the Medici had stolen from the Florentine government. Now, however, the facade is devoid of rustication and divided by a grid of flattened columns, or pilasters, looking for all the world as if the Colosseum had been unwound, inverted and turned into a house. This really was new. Apart from Roman ruins, Italians would only have come across columns in buildings of church and state, and the Rucellai Palace was the first to dress domesticity in these dignified vestments (every townhouse with its twin columns at the front door can be traced back to it). So what inspired this departure from tradition? It surely wasn't an idea of Giovanni's, whose notebooks are a soggy compost of received wisdom. Instead he sought out an architect capable of giving his house the appearance of modernity and dignity that he desired, an architect with a reputation for erudition and original-ity. In all probability this innovator was Leon Battista Alberti (although, due to a lack of firm documentary evidence, a conclu-sive attribution is impossible).

Architect, artist, theorist, antiquary, athlete, musician and horseman, author of the first treatises on sculpture, painting and architecture since antiquity, and codifier of the first Italian gram-mar, Alberti was the original Renaissance man. In an anonymous biography of himself he claimed that he could leap over the head of a man from a standing position and fling a coin up into the dome of the cathedral so that it rang off the stones. He boasted that 'he conquered himself by making a practice of looking at and handling the things he loathed, to the point that they ceased to offend him; and he thus offered an example to show that men can make anything of themselves, if they wish'[3] (the object of this self-mortifying exercise was garlic, of all things). With his Athenian learning, Spartan discipline and mercurial adaptability, Alberti was the perfect man to remake architecture for the modern age, not least because of his talent for self-promotion. From the papal curia to Florentine bankers, his writings spread his fame among

Italy's rulers. His texts are eelishly slippery, and his opinions difficult to pin down. This isn't an uncharacteristically modest
modulation of the authorial voice: by avoiding strident statements
of position, Alberti made himself amenable to all potential clients.
This was vital to his success because, although the Renaissance is
seen as the era when starchitects were born, designers were still the
servants of the money men who bought their expertise; Giovanni
Rucellai never names his architect in any of his writings. A contemporary of Alberti, architect Pietro Averlino, made an impassioned
plea for the recognition of his trade:

> The building is conceived in this manner. Since no one can conceive
> by himself without a woman, by another simile, the building
> cannot be conceived by one man alone. As it cannot be done with-
> out a woman, so he who wishes to build needs an architect. He
> conceives it with him and then the architect carries it. When the
> architect has given birth, he becomes the mother of the building . . .
> Building is nothing more than a voluptuous pleasure, like that of a
> man in love.[1]

Alberti was also deeply concerned with his professional status,
and his texts gave the architect a new presence in the public life of
Italy. We can see why Rucellai chose him: Alberti's talent for re-
invention, honed on himself, made him an ideal manipulator of
corporate identity. After falling out with his family, he renamed
himself Leon or Lion (a friend quipped after his death that
Chameleon would have been more appropriate), and besides
anonymously writing his own biography, he also designed a logo
for himself, a winged eye with grasping tentacles, and a motto,
Quid tum? – 'What next?' It's a pithy formulation of his restless
inquisitiveness, a love of novelty that was shared by the clients who
sought out his innovative designs.

In his book *On the Art of Building*, the first architectural treatise since Roman times, Alberti wrote that architects must observe the rules of decorum: a church (or temple, as he refers to it in his classicising idiom) should be the grandest building in a city, and all the other structures, each with its own appropriate degree of grandeur, should defer to it. He declares that 'there can be no project more pleasant or attractive than the representation of stone colonnading' for the design of walls, and his buildings demonstrate a subtle approach to the use of columns, taking into account the function and prestige of the structure they adorn.[5] The facade of Santa Maria Novella, for example, uses columns to create the impression of an ancient triumphal arch with a temple stuck on top, a cunning solution to the problem of designing a classical-looking Christian church. When it came to designing a house for his patron, temple fronts and triumphal arches would have been indecorously grandiose, so he turned instead to secular precedents such as the Colosseum. He borrowed the multi-storey arches and columns of that gigantic amphitheatre in order to create a dignified skin for Giovanni's house, but a skin is all it is: the structure beneath is a piecemeal accumulation of properties, and is totally unrelated to the exterior.

This is architecture as image (no wonder Rucellai chose master rebrander Alberti as his designer), and the image it creates is one of solidity, expense and permanence. Permanence because it borrows the essential element of ancient architecture, the column. But, as the great architectural historian Manfredo Tafuri wrote of another reworking of the classical tradition, it compromises 'the very symbol of order – and in its most authentically classical version – by using it in an everyday manner. The estrangement of the column became an allegory of urban estrangement.'[6] In Alberti's hands the column became a symbol of everyday financial rather than ecclesiastical power. This is a definite disenchantment, or rather a move to a different kind of mystification, one of bonds and derivatives rather than incense and rosaries. The columnar order no longer shores up religious institutions, but a newly confident banking class, unashamed to adopt the symbols of eternity. We can also read this, like Tafuri, as an allegory of urban estrangement. As the oligarchs cannibalised the public spaces of fifteenth-century Florence, they adopted the old signs of divine and state power. The column is no longer a possession of the republic, but of the individual.

Giovanni's house employs several other strategies in its struggle against the city. For a start, the architect cleverly exploited its constrained position to make the building seem bigger. The street on which the palace stands is far too narrow to allow a proper view of the facade, and via del Purgatorio, which approaches the building at an angle, is even narrower. As a result, the observer only glimpses the palazzo piecemeal, something that was almost certainly taken into account by Alberti. The end of the facade, which wraps around the corner of the building onto the via dei Palchetti, only extends as far as is necessary to create an impression of completion; visitors approaching from the west who don't inspect the structure too closely get an impression of a coherent cube clothed in the same facade on every side. If you approach down the via del Purgatorio, on the other hand, the facade, though narrow, fills your field of vision, the regularity of its pattern suggesting the possibility of infinite extension in either direction.

Tightening his clutch on the street, Giovanni convinced a relative who lived across the road – the area was riddled with Rucellais – to sell him his shop, which was then demolished to make room for a small triangular piazza. This allowed a better view of the house, and gave the Rucellai enclave a very visible heart. To reinforce this sense of ownership, Giovanni also built a family loggia – a columned and covered portico – on the other side of the piazza. By all accounts this was an anachronistic move: family loggias had been all the rage in the *fourteenth* century, when they were used for special occasions such as weddings. But loggias were also used for more everyday purposes, as Alberti advised: 'The presence of an elegant portico, under which the elders may stroll or sit, take a nap or negotiate business, will be an undoubted ornament to both crossroad and forum. Furthermore, the presence of elders will restrain the youth, as they play and sport in the open, and curb any misbehavior or buffoonery resulting from the immaturity of their years.'[7]

For Alberti, the loggia is a site of public life, of trade, relaxation, and of surveillance and social control. He probably had in mind Florence's ur-loggia, the Loggia dei Lanzi, which stands adjacent to the Palazzo Vecchio on the main square and now houses sculptures including Cellini's *Perseus*. This was used for all the purposes Alberti mentions, and also during state occasions as covered seating for members of the government. Loggias built by private patrons had a different significance: they were a way of creating an in-between space, neither wholly public nor entirely private, in which the owner could, by borrowing the architectural forms of state power, stake a claim to public life and display his personal power (the Rucellai loggia is, like the palazzo, covered in family emblems). They were the site of family celebrations, and it may be that the Rucellai loggia was erected as part of the spectacular wedding celebrations of Giovanni's son, for which the entire street was closed to the public and covered in a silk-draped platform for feasting and dancing.

But when Giovanni built his loggia in the mid-fifteenth century they had gone out of fashion, and many had been demolished or enclosed. The Medici had had one too, on a corner of their palazzo, but like the shops on the ground floor it was eventually bricked up, as was the Rucellai loggia itself. One reason for this might be that public life was being gradually strangled by the rise of the oligarchs. After the return of the Medici in 1434 there was a decline in guild power, and eventually the republic became a semi-monarchy, ruled at first implicitly and later explicitly by the Medici, who were crowned Grand Dukes of Tuscany in the sixteenth century. The top of the Loggia dei Lanzi was converted into an elevated viewing platform, so that the grand dukes could watch festivities on the piazza without mingling with the public. Meanwhile, the family loggias vanished, retreating into the interiors of the new palaces, where they became instead arcaded courtyards: absolutely privatised public space. The Medici were the first to build such a courtyard, the place where more privileged visitors could wait to bend the ear of the head of the family, safe from the democratic rabble of the street. At its centre stood Donatello's effete *David*, the tyrannicidal hero of the Florentine republic now imprisoned in a tyrant's house.

The palazzo meets the street with another incursion of private architecture into public space, a long stone bench that doubles as a podium for the structure. This may seem like the altruistic provision of a public amenity, and it still offers a welcome place for passers-by to rest, but it was emphatically the possession of the Rucellai family and was used, like the rest of the palace, to project their image to the world. The bench – a common feature of palaces at the time, including Palazzo Medici – was a place for petitioners to wait. In the clientelist states of Renaissance Italy visitors were a marker of status – of who was in and who was out in the volatile oligarchy. Chronicler Marco Parenti revealed just how important visitors were when he described the changing fortunes of the Medici and Pitti families. After Lorenzo de' Medici's death, he says, 'few frequented his house and they were men of little consequence', whereas Luca Pitti 'held court at his house, where a large part of the citizens went to consult on matters of government'.[8] After a while, however, the Medici star rose again, and Pitti 'remained cold and alone at home, and no one visited him to talk about political affairs – he who used to have his house full of every kind of person'.[9] Clearly, being visited was essential to one's social standing, and the number and quality of bums on your bench advertised your status to the world. Like the loggia and the piazza, it was a way of staking a claim to the street.

Today's corporations may have cast off their columnar exoskeletons in favour of sleek modernity, but their spatial strategies remain indebted to Rucellai and his ilk. From John D. Rockefeller Junior, pioneer of the city within a city, to Minoru Mori, who rebuilt an even larger district of Tokyo, businesses and developers have shaped the modern metropolis with the apparent inexorability of glaciers hollowing a valley. But these glaciers can melt, and the tectonic shifts of wealth that force edifices of steel into the city air can also bring mighty builders to their knees. Before I get to the moment of crisis, let's go back to the mists of industrial prehistory, where strange chimeras roam.

A weird mirage shimmers on the outskirts of Dresden: a huge domed mosque complete with minarets. This is no pipe dream out of the Arabian Nights; the truth is more outlandish. It was once a cigarette factory and its towers were chimneys. Like much corporate architecture from the turn of the twentieth century, it borrowed the trappings of antique splendour to project power and prestige, or, as in this case, to advertise a product which was, like the architecture, 'oriental'. The tobacco mosque, as it was once known – like the building itself, the phrase is a product of insensitive times – is outrageously inappropriate in its baroque surroundings, and caused quite a stink when it was completed in 1909 – the frisson of successful brand differentiation.

More popular among corporate builders of the time was the architecture of Renaissance Italy, an era that – famed for its mercantile spirit – must have seemed more appropriate for modern business than orientalist fantasy. The palazzo type was also an efficient 'machine to make the ground pay' – this was how Cass

Gilbert, designer of the 1912 Woolworth Building in New York, defined the skyscraper. The palazzo's cuboid form maximises floor space and thus rent, important considerations for corporate clients who were not just owner-occupiers but also speculative developers. (Like the Medici with their ground-floor shops, corporate builders let out much of their huge HQs.) But economics was not the only reason the titans of American business built high; indeed, like the palazzos before them, many of their taller structures were feeble generators of wealth. Perhaps it is more accurate to say these were machines to make the ground *speak*: they generated an intangible halo of charisma or corporate identity.

Once such corporate palazzo was built by the Metropolitan Life Insurance Company on Madison Square in New York. Beginning in 1890 with a block very much like a steroidal Florentine palace, complete with rustication, pilasters and a vertiginously overhanging cornice, the company expanded the site continuously up until 1909, when a vast fifty-storey tower based anachoristically on St Mark's Campanile in Venice was planted next door. Like most corporate towers, the Met Life campanile was not a big earner: due to the iron law of diminishing architectural returns, the higher up you build, the less rentable floor space you create, since more and more room is taken up by essential services such as lifts. Towers are also expensive to build, requiring sophisticated systems of structural support. But what it did provide, as the vice president of Met Life candidly remarked, was 'an advertisement that didn't stand the company a cent because the tenants footed the bill'.[10] And the company used the image of the tower remorselessly, on just about every piece of paper that passed through its office, on newspaper adverts and pins.

Architecture had clearly become central to corporate identity, to the point where the building now stood for the business. Perhaps this has something to do with the intangibility of the insurance trade. Insurers to this day strive to build the most recognisable homes – Lloyd's of London, for example, inhabits Richard Rogers' glorious eviscerated machine, naughtily flashing its inner workings as if transparency were its game, and Swiss Re commissioned Norman Foster's erotic gherkin. The latter might seem an abstract and perhaps arbitrary form, but Swiss Re has a different take on the building.

> From a distance, it looks like an imposing monument; from up close, it appears quite fragile. Far from being an intimidating landmark, it seems almost vulnerable, like a precious vase. Walking around the building, one becomes acutely aware of one's own physicality and body mass in relation to that of the tower. The building has an anthropomorphic quality. It symbolises man's exposure to the forces of nature as well as his ability to tame and articulate them ... Insurers try to mediate between these two poles – life and death. Even though they are ultimately as powerless as anyone else to prevent death, they have developed complex instruments for alleviating and absorbing its economic impact. This inner contradiction cannot be resolved, but architecture and art can be used to articulate such contradictions spatially.[11]

Bloated with money-mysticism, this pseudery reveals that even after dispensing with columns and pediments, business architecture continues to reiterate the message of its ecclesiastical predecessors: triumph over death, with the aid of a life insurance policy instead of the Nicene Creed.

The ultimate expression of corporate architecture's religious pretensions can be found in a grimy industrial suburb of Berlin. Though Moabit doesn't much resemble the Acropolis, it does have a factory, built in 1909 (the same year as those other capitalist temples, the tobacco mosque and the Met Life campanile) for massive electrical firm AEG, that looks for all the world like an up-to-date edition of the Parthenon, complete with concrete pillars

Napoleon Le Brun and sons, Met Life Building (1909)

and a pediment. But the pillars no longer support the roof; instead, an exposed steel frame of girder-columns does the donkey work. The architect has opened a little gap at the foot of each column to let us know that there is some ambiguity vis-à-vis the structure and its relationship to the past, and on the front of the building, where the gods would go if this really were a Greek temple, is the company logo: a subdivided hexagon redolent of busy bees and chemical structures. This is the ideal expression of the reform-minded capitalism then fashionable among architects and industrialists in Germany, many of whom came together in an organisation called the Werkbund to promote modern design.

The Werkbund's members were a diverse bunch, coming from many professions and all extremes of the political spectrum, but they were united by the aim of reforming the community, fractured – they thought – by the industrial age. Peter Behrens, architect of the AEG factory and founder member of the Werkbund, shared this ideal of fostering social unity through design. Apart from the company's buildings, Behrens also designed AEG's logo and many of its products. He has been called the first industrial designer, and while this is not quite true, he did create an unprecedentedly unified look for AEG that almost realised the Werkbund's slogan, 'From sofa cushion to town planning.' In other words, he pioneered what we have come to call corporate identity.

It is no paradox that Behrens' reformist project – inspired by the fear of proletarian revolution – led to the seamless consumerist spectacle of the present, and it should perhaps be no surprise that Behrens, whose architecture Hitler and Speer admired, was an early member of the Nazi party, another group with a fixation on

Peter Behren's 1909 Turbine Factory in Berlin: a temple of industrial production

the community and corporate identity. The AEG temple may aspire to a reunification of the community, but it is also just as much an advertising gimmick as the tobacco mosque outside Dresden, albeit a vastly more sophisticated one – its pioneering expanses of glass are precursors of today's corporate taste for transparency. But although the turbine factory transforms historic forms for the modern age, with its prostration before machines instead of gods, it is still recognisably an existing building type. Soon, however, Behrens' students, including future Bauhaus heads Walter Gropius and Mies van der Rohe, and Swiss architect Le Corbusier, would – looking across the Atlantic to the 'vernacular' industrial architecture of grain silos and the like – develop new types for the New World's corporations which seemed to cast off the raiment of antiquity.

But the architecture of Manhattan had begun to change long before the German invasion. By the 1920s the blocky palazzos of the 1900s had shed their columns and grown as jagged as the step pyramids of Peru. Ayn Rand rhapsodises over these ziggurats in her Benzedrine-fuelled doorstop *The Fountainhead*:

> The building stood on the shore of the east river, a structure as rapt as raised arms. The rock crystal forms mounted in such eloquent steps that the building did not seem stationary, but moving upward in a continuous flow – until one realized that it was only the movement of one's glance and that one's glance was forced to move in that particular rhythm. The walls of pale grey limestone looked silver against the sky, with the clean, dulled luster of metal, but a metal that had become a warm, living substance, carved by the most cutting of all instruments – a purposeful human will.[12]

Rand prostrates herself before these crystallisations of cash, believing as fervently as any steppe-bound babushka in the magic forces behind her graven images. However, the force that moulded these striking forms and drew Rand's gaze heavenward was not the excitingly fascistic Iron Will of the Individual, but rather the impersonal rule of government. The ziggurat setbacks were – like the rustication on Florentine palaces – the direct result of planning regulations. This legislation was largely a response to one enormous palazzo-style structure, the Equitable Building on Broadway. So vast was this man-made mountain, which contained 1.2 million square feet of rentable space on forty storeys, that all surrounding buildings were literally overshadowed by its bulk. Responses were so unanimously negative that the city government responded with zoning laws that would fundamentally alter the concept of buildable space.

An Italian jurist in the thirteenth century named Accursius had written, 'whoever owns the soil, it is theirs up to Heaven and down to Hell': the origin of the legal notion of air rights. Now, however, NYC whittled air rights down into a pyramidal envelope in order to allow sunlight to penetrate the concrete canyons of the city, and in order to create the maximum floor space within the zoning pyramid, builders simply stacked ever-narrower boxes on top of one another, thus creating the setback. Some did this with more grace than others: the Chrysler and Empire State Buildings are both expressions of the 1916 code; the former, with decorations shaped like hub caps and radiator grilles, also alludes to the source of Chrysler's wealth. These buildings were products of the intense boom that occurred in the gilded 1920s, and like many other setback skyscrapers, they were completed as the bottom fell out of the rental market. After the 1929 crash demand went limp, and the Empire State Building was soon nicknamed the Empty State Building (it didn't reach full occupancy until after the war, and only turned a profit in 1950). Speculative building was also partly responsible for the boom that led to the Wall Street Crash, when Manhattan became a white elephants' graveyard filled with empty monuments to the folly of market exuberance. The crash crippled the world economy, and would soon lead to war. So while zoning changed the face of the city, it did nothing to curb the most dangerous aspects of architecture as business; in fact it stoked the overdevelopment of 'hot' areas. Zoning did not go far enough.

While building sites around the world ground to a halt, one spot in Manhattan's Midtown remained a hive of activity throughout the Depression. Bankrolled by one of the richest men in the world, Rockefeller Center – a mammoth twenty-two-acre development covering three city blocks – was the first attempt by business to recreate the city, and not just the edifice, in its own image. Earlier skyscrapers had simply plunged into the ground, and their increasingly elephantine footprints filled entire blocks, creating uniform impenetrability where city life actually takes place. Now the developers turned their hand to the problem of the street, creating the famous piazza and roof gardens of the Rock, both of which were meant to be 'public' spaces. Of course this was no altruistic gesture. Raymond Hood, chief architect of the project, advocated the inclusion of features like the 'hanging gardens' (as he called them) because each one 'stimulates public interest and admiration, is accepted as a genuine contribution to architecture, enhances the value of the property and is profitable to the owner in the same manner as are other forms of legitimate advertising'.[13]

Rockefeller Center was, like the Met Life tower, architecture as advertising, but it dispensed with the instantly recognisable crowns and spires of previous skyscrapers in favour of flat tops and severe linearity. Instead, the Center's USP is its faux-public amenities. But the plaza is no more public than the towers themselves. Like the benches and loggias of Renaissance Florence, it is a privatised space, allowing corporate control over messy public life. Today that means the exclusion of the economically inactive (the poor, jobless and homeless, who can't realise the capital investment of the space by shopping, working or eating at smart restaurants); the arbitrary regulation of photography (characterised as a prelude to terrorism or paedophilia); and the banning of assembly or protest (this would disrupt the economic activity of good visitors). The Center's art gives the lie to the Rock's publicness: the aquiline *Prometheus* swooping over the skaters and the bronze *Atlas* with his constipated brow are indistinguishable from the lumpish neoclassicism being churned out by Nazi Germany at the same time. (Bizarrely, communist artist Diego Rivera was also commissioned to contribute work to the Center, but when he included a portrait of Lenin in his mural the painting was destroyed.) Like Ayn Rand's equally poorly drawn characters, these sculptures are gargoyles of psychopathic individualism, and the space they guard, purged of civil rights, is sanitised for optimal monetisation.

© Ezra Stoller / Esto

The Seagram Building and its plaza

Inspired by Rockefeller Center's success, other corporate builders began to provide pseudo-public spaces as publicity for their
developments. One of the first was the Seagram Building of 1958,
designed by ex-Bauhaus director Mies van der Rohe. Mies, having
tried and failed to win commissions from the Nazis, became
preeminent among that generation of transplanted German
modernists who transformed the face of corporate America. His
design for the Seagram Building in New York seems to go even
further than Rockefeller Center in its quest for perfect anonymity,
and yet this smoked-glass monolith, apparently abstract and
devoid of historic references, still harks back to the prestigious
buildings of antiquity.

The I-beam girders running from the base to the crown reinforce the visual impression of verticality but have absolutely no
structural function. Instead, by transforming the basic unit of the
building's frame into a purely decorative flourish, they refer to
the flattened columns of the Colosseum and Giovanni's palace.
The girder – recast in bronze, no less – has become a twentieth-
century pilaster. By using a mass-produced building material as
a symbol of prestige, Mies – who studied under Peter Behrens in
Berlin – continues in the tradition of the tobacco mosque and the
Parthenon factory: all three are attempts to remystify the industrial age. Unlike Behren's AEG factory, however, his edifice is
not an attempt to create a communally minded reform capitalism. Seagram & Co. was not motivated by social concerns; it was
a whiskey distiller born during Prohibition. Dogged by associations with corruption and mob violence, the company did not
come out well from the 1950–1 Kefauver Committee investigation into organised crime. The building was thus an enormously
expensive whitewash, intended to convey an impression of
propriety and affluence.

This is confirmed at ground level. Seagram Plaza is as spare as
the tower, its rigid symmetry unsullied by seats. By leaving the

space as a void, Seagram demonstrated its immense wealth – this is, after all, prime real estate in the heart of Manhattan. But the barren space is a popular spot, always full of people eating, sitting and socialising. The inadvertent success of the plaza inspired a reformulation of NYC's zoning laws in 1961, allowing builders to go higher if they provided open space at street level. However, as researcher William H. Whyte found, the resulting plazas were often cold and empty, seeming to deliberately exclude street life. As part of his research Whyte made a film called *The Social Life of Small Urban Spaces*, in which he carried out an ethnological investigation into behaviour on Seagram Plaza.

His cameras observe couples *trysting*, men eyeing women, and children splashing in the fountains. Asking why the plaza is so successful, he concludes this is down to a number of factors, including the availability of 'sittable space' – the marble ledges, walls and steps. This behaviour was not built into the design, and Mies was apparently surprised by the way people used his landscaping.

In contrast, the palaces of Florence assiduously courted sitters with the benches on their facades. But before we mourn the passing of a more altruistic civic-minded age, we should remember that Florentine benches were billboards advertising the popularity of their owners, and thus a monetisation of public space. Likewise, their loggias were an appropriation of public architecture intended to demonstrate their builders' power. The corporate plazas of NYC play a similar game, and so it shouldn't be too surprising that, when it came to publicness, they talked the talk but didn't walk the walk, adopting a variety of tactics to keep people out. Whyte castigates the later plazas for their unsittable spaces: most of the benches provided by corporations, he says, 'are artefacts the purpose of which is to punctuate architectural photographs. They're not so good for sitting.' Worse still are narrow walls, spiked ledges and what Americans quaintly call 'bumproof' seats. These torture devices have been adopted around the world in order to dissuade 'loiterers', the homeless and the jobless: in other words, those who are not using the city to make money for someone else. And if discomfort is not enough, zealous security guards are on hand to expel undesirables from these corporate Edens. But, as Whyte pointed out, these spaces had been 'provided by the public, through its zoning and planning machinery. The public's right in urban plazas would seem clear.'[14]

The Seagram Building took a step back from the full-scale re-creation of the city grid proposed by Rockefeller Center. Nevertheless, it learned from Rockefeller's success by incorporating its most novel element, the plaza. With this space the individual architectural object falsely assumes an attribute of the wider city, transforming the plaza into a fig leaf of publicness pinned over the obscenity of corporate power, which in Seagram's case originated in true gangsterism. The most extraordinary part of Seagram's architectural PR campaign, however, never got off the drawing board. This was a nuclear bunker below the building, an interiorised, securitised plaza, the ideal of a neoconservative 'public' space. Conceived as a publicity device tapping into the extreme paranoia of the Cold War, the idea was received favourably by the authorities, but in the end Seagram decided not to build its corporate bomb shelter.

However, as the Cold War has morphed into the War on Terror, paranoia has grown increasingly important in corporate architecture, and structures like the Burj Khalifa in Dubai and the Shard in London have attempted to bring the piazza into the palazzo in a repetition of the enfolding of semi-public loggias into the totally private courtyards of Renaissance Florence. These gigantic skyscrapers are all divorced from their urban settings by their vaunted self-sufficiency. The Shard, for example – which its developer calls a 'virtual town' – houses offices, shops, a hotel, ten apartments offered for sale at between thirty and fifty million pounds, Michelin-starred restaurants and a spa, and is plugged directly into London Bridge Station so that commuters don't have to engage with the city in their journey to and from the suburbs.

This kind of anti-urban urbanism was given its most extreme formulation by Marvel Comics in the form of superhero Iron Man, another Cold War baby. Iron Man is the alter ego of billionaire arms manufacturer Tony Stark, who devises a high-tech metal suit in which to fight international communism and promote the American Way. Stark/Iron Man – a techno-fascist fusion of man and machine – constructs an enormous HQ in New York, which in the 2012 film *The Avengers* is depicted clinging to the top of the MetLife Building like a parasitic orchid. Stark Tower is simultaneously playboy shag pad, high-tech launch pad and survivalist bunker with an integral reactor that makes it independent of the city grid. This is a kind of futuristic update of Ayn Rand's individualistic architecture of the will, both within the city and yet totally independent of it. It may seem like autistic fantasy, and yet a real-life super-developer created something very similar in Tokyo in 2003.

Minoru Mori's self-named Mori Tower is the centrepiece of an enormous development called Roppongi Hills. Attaining an unprecedented degree of self-sufficiency, the twenty-seven-acre site incorporates offices, apartments, restaurants, shops, cafes, cinemas, a museum, a hotel and a TV studio. Like Stark's HQ, the beating heart of Mori Tower is the generator in its basement, which makes it theoretically independent of the city, able to survive natural disaster or social breakdown. The company's crisis-fixated mission statement opens with an assertion of arresting hubris: 'In the creation of cities, Mori Building always pursues . . . communities that people will seek refuge in, not run away from in times of disaster.'[15] Like many anti-urban developments, Roppongi Hills also claims to be improving the neighbourhood around it and the city at large.

This argument, beloved of urban regenerators and erectors of icons, is as old as the palazzos, whose builders insisted that their architectural extravagance was for the good of Florence. It's also a lie, as shown by the example of London's Docklands, which, like so many other regenerative developments, is a desert island of international finance in a dead sea of poverty. There is no trickle-down of wealth here, only the creation of ghettos. Mori Tower unmasks the 'altruism' of the developer once and for all. It is no haven but a Waco in the megalopolis, and its sociopathy has already had its consequences. Despite Mori's ostensible aim of providing a 'safer and more secure city' through the marvels of high-tech hardware, in 2004 a six-year-old boy was crushed to death when his head was caught in the tower's revolving door. This was no accident: a judicial investigation revealed that thirty-two other people including several children had been injured by doors in Roppongi Hills. The developers had, despite previous incidents, deliberately chosen not to install sensors below a certain height, or even to put up safety barriers, because they wanted to preserve the aesthetic integrity of the tower and hence its marketability.

In the last hundred years corporate architecture has become ravenous, with super-developments like Rockefeller Center and Roppongi Hills devouring huge swathes of the city. Palazzo Rucellai took one of the first bites: apart from chewing off parts of the street with its loggia and piazza, the facade's jagged edge sinks its teeth into the building next door. This spectre of a cannibal house lurks in the shadows of the Renaissance, imagined as an era of reborn rationality and classical allusion. But this blood-lust is structural, not some monstrous offspring of the sleep of reason: as the palazzo threatens its surroundings with the unremitting logic of its exquisitely ordered facade, those crisply carved lines become, at their cutting edge, carious fangs.

Giovanni's development strategy was equally predatory. He pressured his neighbours to sell their properties to him one by one, slowly making, as he noted in his diary, 'one house out of eight', building the first stretch of the facade across the two houses facing the street. Here he paused a while, waiting for his neighbour on via della Vigna Nuova, who had resisted offers on his house for many years, to die. Giovanni then bought the property (at a grossly inflated price) and extended his facade yet further. But the resulting unbalanced, saw-toothed composition suggests that Giovanni had even grander ambitions. His plainly unfinished palazzo sends a threat to his new neighbour: my home won't be complete until it has devoured yours too. Ironically it also stands as a warning to builders. The neighbour would not give in, and Giovanni's insatiable acquisitiveness resulted in an imperfect structure. He had bitten off more than he could chew – in business as in architecture – for in his later years Giovanni went completely bust, cleaned out by shady dealings in his Pisan office. The sails carved all over his house, loggia and church must now have seemed bitterly ironic emblems of fortune's infidelity: no longer blowing his ship to the promised land but hollow as an empty purse.

This may be our only hope: that corporate architecture will eat itself. Governments can mould it, as the rustications of Florence and the setbacks of New York show, but these interventions are largely cosmetic, and powerful patrons can easily circumvent planning regulations – as in the case of New York's uninhabitable plazas. Timid intervention can even be disastrously counterproductive, like the 1916 zoning laws that stoked the fires of property speculation in New York. This contributed to the skyscraper boom of the 1920s and eventually to a crash, like every property bubble before and since. As Marshall Berman put it, quoting Marx,

> The pathos of all bourgeois monuments is that their material strength and solidity actually count for nothing and carry no weight at all, that they are blown away like frail reeds by the very forces of capitalist development that they celebrate. Even the most beautiful and impressive bourgeois buildings and public

works are disposable, capitalized for fast depreciation and planned to be obsolete, closer in their social functions to tents and encampments than to 'Egyptian pyramids, Roman aqueducts, Gothic cathedrals'.[16]

In fact the ever-worsening cycles of boom and bust can be charted – even predicted – by clusters of enormous buildings, as economist Andrew Lawrence has shown. Lawrence's Skyscraper Index proposes that economic exuberance always results in surplus capital investment, creating skyscrapers that reach completion just as the boom inevitably turns to bust and recession sets in. Several of the buildings I have discussed in this chapter can be mapped on the Skyscraper Index: the Met Life campanile, which marked the US economic crisis of 1907–10, and the Chrysler and Empire State Buildings, completed shortly after the Wall Street Crash. To these can be added the World Trade Center and Sears Tower, harbingers of the mid-1970s slump, Canary Wharf, which presided over the early-1990s recession, the Petronas Towers and many other baubles erected by Asian tigers shortly before their mangy demise, and most recently, the Burj Khalifa in Dubai, dogged by financial problems and emblem of the current crisis. None of these buildings are mere metastases of some deeper cancer; they are the cancer itself. The Skyscraper Index is fascinating because it reverses the traditional causal vector of art history: instead of culture being some surface manifestation of economic or political or historical change, culture – architecture – drives the motor of history, to the point that art can predict economics. So when business starts building high, it's time to watch out. But disaster clears the ground for new beginnings, and perhaps one day soon the crash will come that sparks a real revolution in building.

The Garden of Perfect Brightness, Beijing
(1709–1860)
Architecture and Colonialism

And you would walk out with me to the western corner of the castle,
To the dynastic temple, with water about it clear as blue jade,
With boats floating, and the sound of mouth-organs and drums,
With ripples like dragon-scales, going glass green on the water . . .
And all this comes to an end.
And is not again to be met with.

    Li Bai, *Exile's Letter* (eighth century), translated by Ezra Pound,

1915[1]

We Europeans are civilised, and for us, the Chinese are barbarians; here is what civilisation has done to barbarity!

Victor Hugo, 1861

The ruins of the European Pavilions

In a dusty northern suburb of Beijing there is an expanse of park generally known to the few Western visitors who venture there as the Old Summer Palace, where scrub borders wide stretches of water, and broken pillars are the only trace of former habitation. (Before you drift into a reverie of romantic desolation, however, I should add that the site has been embellished in recent years with noisy fun-park rides, a paintball range and a go-kart track.) The stony fragments, much lamented by Chinese officialdom, are all that remain of one of the greatest palaces ever built: the Yuanming Yuan or Garden of Perfect Brightness. Constructed over a period of one hundred and fifty years by the Qing, China's last dynastic rulers, this wasn't in fact a summer retreat but the principal residence of five successive emperors, and the repository of a vast collection of paintings, books and other artefacts. To get some impression of its significance, imagine Versailles, the Louvre, and the Bibliothèque nationale de France rolled into one. (I've chosen French examples since Buckingham Palace, the National Gallery and the British Library are sadly frumpish in comparison.) The 1.3 square miles of garden were packed with structures – grand audience halls, pavilions, temples, libraries, studios, administrative offices and even a model village where the imperial family could play at being commoners among eunuchs posing as shopkeepers. Early European travellers wondered at such strange magnificence.

As for the Pleasure-houses, they are really charming. They stand in a vast Compass of Ground. They have raised Hills, from 20 to 60

Foot high; which form a great Number of little Valleys between them . . . In each of these Valleys, there are Houses about the Banks of the Water; very well disposed: with their different Courts, open and closed Porticos, Parterres, Gardens, and Cascades: which, when view'd all together, have an admirable Effect upon the Eye.[2]

So wrote a French priest residing at the court named Jean Denis Attiret in 1743. But all this was wiped out in a few days in October 1860 when, at the close of the Second Opium War, British forces, having thoroughly looted its treasures, burned the place to the ground. It is ironic then that the only surviving structures – those broken pillars and baroque curlicues – should be the remains of Western buildings designed by Jesuit missionaries. The story of these buildings is marked by such wild reversals of cultural interaction as characterise the history of architecture and colonialism. It is usually, and quite rightly, 'the West' that is portrayed as the villainous imperial force in these tales, but there is a concomitant tendency – one that I want to redress – to underplay the agency of those 'benighted lands' that were unfortunate enough to end up on the receiving end of European expansion. For although it was Western colonialists who burned the Garden of Perfect Brightness, it was Chinese – or rather Manchu – colonialists who constructed it.

The Qing dynasty rulers who built the Garden of Perfect Brightness were not ethnic Han Chinese, but Manchu invaders from beyond the Great Wall. These 'barbarians' (by Han standards) descended on the capital on horseback in 1644 after the last Ming emperor quietly hanged himself from a tree behind the Forbidden City. The conquerors brought with them strange practices, such as the ponytail worn by male Manchus, the imposition of which met with fierce and bloody resistance. The success of their invasion depended not on forceful impositions of Manchu culture, however, but on the skilful way they courted the Chinese gentry, maintained the traditions of the preceding dynasty, and to a certain extent assimilated the mores of their new subjects. The Qing dynasty's multiculturalism was the conscious policy of its greatest rulers, the Kangxi, Yongzheng and Qianlong emperors, who governed in an unbroken period of imperial expansion and autocratic centralisation from 1662 to 1795, a period known in China as the Prosperous Age. During this era China was the richest and most powerful nation on earth, the early leader in the expansionist struggle for central Asia that would later become the so-called Great Game. As the Qing pushed the borders of the empire westwards to incorporate huge tracts of Muslim-ruled desert and the mountain kingdom of the Dalai Lama, creating in the process a nation larger than present-day China, they carefully imported the culture of these new subjects into courtly life – taking Muslim concubines and making ostentatious displays of Tibetan Buddhist devotion, for example.

The architecture of the Yuanming Yuan was a particularly important locus for this strategy. The Qing emperors for the most part despised the Forbidden City in Beijing – one called the traditional seat of the Ming dynasty 'that dank ditch of a place with its vermilion walls and tiled roofs'. Instead they preferred to live a semi-rusticated life amid spacious gardens, lake and mountain landscapes, and hunting grounds. However, their 'forbidden garden', though a day's journey north of the capital, was carefully set-dressed in order to avoid any accusations of absentee-landlordism. Yongzheng was the first Qing emperor to permanently move the court there from Beijing, and he was highly sensitive to the charge of laziness. He constructed a scaled-down replica of the Forbidden City's Hall of Supreme Harmony just inside the main gate, and when the court visited he would conduct state business here seated on a mahogany throne. Like anyone arguing the case for working from home, he insisted that he would be more productive in relaxed surroundings. His ministers, however, lacked his discipline and relaxed just a little too much: on one occasion in 1726 at the appointed audience hour Yongzheng sat on his throne in the Court of Diligence awaiting the reports of his courtiers – in vain. No one turned up. He reprimanded his ministers and hung the characters *wu yi* behind his throne: 'Don't indulge in pleasure.'

Yongzheng was something of a workaholic, keeping the kind of office hours that bureaucrats were only used to working during wartime – 5 a.m. to midnight most days. He was a hard-nosed, efficient ruler, rooting out corrupt officials, attempting to impose a standardised form of Chinese – a forerunner of today's Mandarin – on his linguistically diverse subjects and banning the smoking of opium, which the British were just beginning to import, to the great physical and financial cost of the Chinese. He also established a model farm and silk wormery in the Yuanming Yuan, personally overseeing the eunuchs who worked the paddy fields as if they were common farmers. Unlike Marie Antoinette in her coquettish shepherdess's outfit, however, Yongzheng was no decadent slumming it in an ornamental farmyard. The Chinese aristocratic garden had traditionally been a source of income for its owner, and although the mini-farm in the Garden of Perfect Brightness could in no way pay for all that perfection and brightness (one estimate puts the cost of running the palace at $800,000 per year), it helped – like a sort of fig leaf of functionality – to justify the emperor's earthly paradise. As art historian Craig Clunas put it, the Chinese garden was 'a way of making money look natural'.[3]

Yongzheng's unease over perceptions of his garden existence was understandable given the precarious path he was treading between two cultures: the imperial authority represented by the replica of the Forbidden City's Hall of Supreme Harmony and the leisured retreat of its bucolic hinterland. The contrast between the two spaces had deep symbolic significance, since according to the ancient Confucian classic *The Rites of Zhou*, 'It is the sovereign alone who establishes the state of the city, gives to the four quarters their proper positions, gives to the capital its form and to the fields their proper divisions. He creates the offices and apportions their functions in order to form a centre to which the people may look.'⁴

So the axial symmetry of the Forbidden City and the grid layout of the capital beyond it were expressions of the power and centrality of the emperor. His personal charisma flowed out in regular channels which permeated and regulated the land, so that every provincial mansion, no matter how far-flung or unimportant, was aligned with his rule – most significant buildings looked south, the direction the emperor faced when enthroned. The regularity and symmetrical arrangement of the administrative buildings in the Yuanming Yuan reflected this organising principle, demonstrating that, though outside the capital, the emperor's status was unchanged, and so the rigorously hierarchical structure of Chinese society was maintained. The asymmetrical disposition of the buildings in the garden, on the other hand, and the site's undulating terrain divided by meandering paths and streams, encouraged a very different sort of existence: one of contemplation not action, of informality rather than rigid hierarchy.

By the mid-eighteenth century this kind of relaxed garden-dwelling lifestyle had become de rigueur among that peculiarly Chinese class, the retired scholar. In China advancement in the vast and complex government bureaucracy was based – in theory – on merit. All young men, or at least those with the cash to devote themselves to study, could compete in the imperial exams in order to gain a foothold on the bureaucratic ladder. Success in these exams was rewarded with financial gain, social prestige and great power, but the way down was equally precipitous, and disappointed scholars became a fixture of provincial life. This was especially the case for educated Han Chinese, many of whom felt disenfranchised by the new regime. Such men were legion in the cultural heartlands of the former Ming dynasty: cities south of the Yangzi like Suzhou, Nanjing and Hangzhou. Ostentatiously retreating from Qing-dominated politics while maintaining a firm grip on local affairs, the Han literati would, in Voltaire's words, 'cultivate their gardens' – devoting their time to literature, wine drinking, calligraphy and patronage. One retired official named Zhao Yi wrote,

> Possessing a gifted writing brush that can render flowering words
>   and a heart
> filled with ideas as fresh as snow,
> You commit yourself to worldly drudgery
> Is this not a waste of all your gifts?
> I prefer to have a thousand books in my study,
> And to meet the ancients in their pages every day.[5]

These activities typically took place in walled estates located within city limits, so avoiding the inconvenience, discomfort and isolation of a genuine hermit's cave. Today the most famous of these gardens is the Unsuccessful Politician's Garden (also known as the Humble Administrator's Garden) in Suzhou. Founded in the sixteenth century, the garden as it stands is a late Qing confection of white walls topped by rippling tiles, polygonal windows and miniature mountain landscapes of contorted 'scholar rocks'. Pavilions and halls dot the grounds, which are punctuated with ponds criss-crossed by zigzag bridges. By cramming such variety into a relatively modest space the Unsuccessful Politician's Garden, and Chinese gardens in general, miniaturise the world to comprehensible, pocketable, *possessible* dimensions – they were, after all, commodities, and a good way of passing on wealth to the next generation. They also seemed to possess their owners, becoming such an integral part of the literati lifestyle that many scholars named themselves after their gardens. One writer went so far as to claim that 'a garden is like a portrait of its owner: its every flower, tree, and every stone, put in their appropriate places, reveal their owner's manner and expression'. Just as the Chinese emperor was identified with his lands, these gardens became a sort of mini-empire to their landed rulers, as *The Dream of the Red Chamber*, China's greatest novel, illustrates.

In this book, written by Cao Xueqin, descendant of a powerful Han family that went into steep decline under Qing rule, an aristocratic clan cavorts in a luxurious garden setting. But although they spend a great deal of time flirting, drinking and poetising, there is a strong undercurrent of darkness to the tale. The scion of the family is weak and aesthetic, the matriarch is tormented by the reprehensible behaviour of younger family members, and there are dodgy financial dealings in the background that threaten to bring the whole edifice of carved wood and cultured soirées crashing to the ground. In short, the 'Grand View Garden' of the novel is a bonsai version of the Qing empire, with all its superficial splendours and substantial failings. Similarly, although without any critical intent, Emperor Yongzheng turned the Yuanming Yuan into a rather literal-minded miniaturisation of his empire. Behind the main administrative area he established a royal residence, a collection of palaces on nine islands hugging the shores of a wide lake. These islands, linked to the shore and to each other by zigzag causeways and hump-backed bridges, he named the Nine Continents after the nine regions of the world in ancient Chinese cosmology. By gathering the world around his person as a private residence, the emperor was clearly proclaiming that, as ruler of the Middle Kingdom, he was rightful monarch of the entire globe. (This kind of hubris hasn't gone out of fashion, as Sheikh Muhammad's creation of the artificial island resort 'The World' off the coast of Dubai demonstrates.) Yongzheng was also reaffirming the colonial mastery of the Qing dynasty over the Chinese landscape.

Although Yongzheng made numerous contributions to the garden and its buildings, the Yuanming Yuan reached its pinnacle of luxury – one might say extravagance – under the rule of his son Qianlong. The lives of the three great Qing emperors describe a Buddenbrooksian arc of ascendancy magnificence, and decline. Between Kangxi's martial and intellectual brilliance and his son Yongzheng's shrewd management, the Qing empire had attained a scope and glory not seen before in Chinese history. Qianlong continued these successes but took them, perhaps, too far. The new empire, incorporating Mongolia as well as the vast western Muslim region of Xinjiang, was simply too huge and costly to sustain. And one senses in Qianlong's character, despite his unquestionable successes and frenetic activity, a creeping self-satisfaction, an attenuation of force, until finally the unmistakable odour of corruption taints the close of his sixty-year reign. In his last decade as emperor a eunuch named Heshen, Qianlong's favourite (and, some said, lover), amassed a huge personal fortune through bribery and extortion. Meanwhile the imperial accounts went into the red, depleted by a protracted war against insurgents known as the White Lotus Society.

This combination of over-expansion, corruption and revolt sent the Qing dynasty into a downward spiral from which it never really recovered, allowing Western barbarians to burn down the buildings of the Garden of Perfect Brightness sixty years later. Many of the structures that the British destroyed had been constructed by Qianlong, who never tired of demonstrating his exquisite aesthetic sensibility. His additions to the palace were vast: like his father and grandfather before him, he employed a family of architects and landscapers named Lei, who lived in the gardens themselves, to construct grand buildings, and expanded the site's area to 1.3 square miles by adding two subsidiary gardens, the Garden of Elegant Spring and the Garden of Eternal Spring.

Qianlong's many building projects included a series of grand libraries. The Chinese garden was a very literary landscape, always the site of composition, of reading – to oneself and to others – and of text itself, and the Yuanming Yuan was no exception. The model for its Library of Literary Sources was the famous Single Heaven Library in the southern city of Ningbo, which belonged to the venerable Fan family and was over 200 years old. But mere emulation wouldn't do for the imperial taste; Qianlong's library was more than twice the size of the twenty-three-metre-wide original, and three storeys tall. Its sections were colour-coded green, white, red and black according to the category of book held there: Confucian classics, philosophy, history and literature.

Taking pride of place was a copy of the 36,000-volume *Complete Collection of Four Treasures*, another example of the emperor's gigantism and a very physical demonstration of his mastery of Han culture. This anthology of classical Chinese writings was commissioned by Qianlong in 1722 and completed over twenty years later by a team of around four hundred scholars. The project was a cunning way of killing several birds with one stone: it loudly proclaimed the emperor's concern for traditional Chinese learning while conveniently busying exactly the class of Han scholar that might have harboured less than affectionate feelings towards Qing rule. Furthermore, in the process of compiling the 3,461 titles that comprised the encyclopedia, the editorial board was commanded to compile an almost equally lengthy catalogue of banned books. These works were then burned, consigned to the flames because they either questioned the legitimacy of the Qing or committed some other breach of protocol deemed unacceptable by the emperor. Carefully whitewashed by the anthologising exercise of which it was an ostensible by-product, Qianlong's literary inquisition acquired the status of an heroic act of literary connoisseurship. But his vandalism was not as barbarically indiscriminate as that of the Europeans: when the garden burned in 1860, its books – including Qianlong's encyclopedia – burned too.

The swastika-shaped Pavilion of Universal Peace, in one of Qianlong's
Forty Views of the Yuanming Yuan

As well as being a place for reading, the garden was also a site of writing. Qianlong, who emulated the literati lifestyle to a fault, loved to gaze moonily at peonies, starlight and lake views, recording his musings in torrents of verse. He completed around 40,000 poems in his lifetime, many of them on the topics of his gardens and its palaces. This may seem an incredible feat, and one that in the words of one exasperated Sinologist could only result in 'a prodigious output of utterly worthless rhymes', but this imperial pastime is better understood as a social practice than as the production of Works with a capital W.[6] It was performative in the sense that Pierre Bourdieu accords to photography: an occasional activity that reinforces the social bonds of its practitioners. Like a snapshot, the end result of Qianlong's poetising was not as important as the declaration, 'I was here.' And because the subject of that declaration was always the emperor, like the leader of the pack marking every tree in his territory, it reinforced his authority and ownership.

Besides being written *in*, the Yuanming Yuan was also written *on*: Yongzheng constructed the swastika-shaped Pavilion of Universal Peace on an island to the west of the Nine Continents. 卍 is a Chinese character meaning Buddha's heart, and this building is also a pun. The character is pronounced 'wan', which sounds like the character 万, meaning ten thousand and implying everywhere: hence the building was an expression of the omnipresence of the Buddha's compassion. (The emperor loved to sit here and contemplate universal peace while his generals were off suppressing the western provinces.) It wasn't the only structure in the garden with symbolic form: there were also pavilions shaped like the character 田 (pronounced 'tian' meaning field), called the Pavilion of Still Waters; the character 工 ('gong' – work), called the Studio of Summer Coolness; and a pavilion shaped like the character 口 ('kou' – mouth), called the Pavilion Containing Autumn.

Writing was also present on a less monumental scale, for the garden was filled with inscriptions. The Chinese garden, as well as being a literary site, was also closely related to the art of landscape painting, and groups of rocks, trees, water and buildings were given titles as if they were pictures in an album. In the Yuanming Yuan these titles were often taken from the emperor's poetry and engraved in the style of his own calligraphy on rocks or boards like captions on a painting. Indeed, Qianlong's inscriptions – another manifestation of his graphomania – still litter the Chinese landscape, their frequency only matched by those of Mao Zedong, who continued this imperial practice. (Mao also wrote poems. The great Sinologist Arthur Waley thought them better than Hitler's paintings but not as good as Churchill's.) The importance of inscription was widely recognised in Chinese society: one character in *The Dream of the Red Chamber* remarks of his garden, 'All those prospects and pavilions – even the rocks and trees and flowers will seem somehow incomplete without that touch of poetry which only the written word can lend a scene.'[7]

The chapter from which this quotation comes demonstrates how complex the game of naming could be. In it paterfamilias Jia Zheng leads a group around the Grand View Garden before its official opening. The garden is to be the home of his daughter, recently elevated to the status of imperial concubine, and the various scenes and structures require suitably prestigious names. But in an unconventional twist he allows, with much mock protestation, his wayward and effeminate son Baoyu to choose the names. The author is at pains to explain why this was permitted: the Jias, he reassures us, were 'a scholarly family all of whose friends and protégés were men of parts', by no means 'like nouveaux riches who throw money about like dirt and, having painted their mansion crimson, put up huge inscriptions such as "Green willows with golden locks before the gate, blue hills like embroidered screens behind the house", fancying these the height of elegance'.[8] Instead the process of naming is a means for Jia Zheng to test and educate his boy, and thereby to reaffirm the order of things.

Suddenly raising his head, Jia Zheng saw a white rock polished as smooth as a mirror, obviously intended for the first inscription. 'See, gentlemen!' he called over his shoulder, smiling. 'What would be a suitable name for this spot?' 'Heaped verdure', said one. 'Embroidery Ridge,' said another. 'The Censer.' 'A miniature Zhongnan Mountain.' Dozens of suggestions were made, all of them clichés, for Jia Zheng's secretaries were well aware that he meant to test his son's ability. Baoyu understood this too. Now his father called on him to propose a name. Baoyu said, 'I've heard that the ancients said, "An old quotation beats an original saying; to recut an old text is better than to engrave a new one." As this is not the main prominence or one of the chief sights, it only needs an inscription because it is the first step leading to the rest. So why not use that line from an old poem: "A winding path leads to a secluded retreat." A name like that would be more dignified.' 'Excellent!' cried the secretaries. 'Our young master is far more brilliant and talented than dull pedants like ourselves.' 'You mustn't flatter the boy,' protested Jia Zheng with a smile. 'He's simply making a ridiculous parade of his very limited knowledge. We can think of a better name later.'[9]

It was this very erudite practice that Qianlong adopted when he identified forty principal scenes in the garden (he had a mania for lists), giving them names such as (4) Engraved Moon and Unfolding Clouds, (8) Heavenly Light Above and Below, (11) Harmony of the Present with the Past, and (17) Vast Compassion and Eternal Blessing. He had these scenes painted by his court artists, and the resulting album was displayed in the palace accompanied by the emperor's own poetic commentaries. (It was looted by the French in 1860 and is now in the Bibliothèque nationale.) But the emperor didn't just emulate scholarly garden activities; he also imported the literati garden wholesale into his palace grounds. This was not so much acculturation as colonisation.

Reinstating a habit of his grandfather's, he made several grandiose ceremonial tours of the Yangzi delta, heartland of Han culture and source of much of the nation's wealth, where he attempted to woo and awe his subjects into submission with a combination of cultivation and might. These excursions were ruinously expensive for his hosts: before one visit to the famously scenic city of Yangzhou, the residents were compelled to rebuild massive chunks of the place just so that it would live up to the emperor's expectations. Unsurprisingly this was deeply unpopular with just the sort of people that the emperor needed to please, but where charm failed force prevailed: one southern official wrote an open letter pleading with the emperor to cancel a visit, and was consequently sentenced to the death of a thousand cuts. In this gruesome execution the victim was tied to a stake in a public place and small pieces of his body were cut away with exquisitely sharp knifes, prolonging the moment of death as long as possible. In case this didn't get the message across, over a thousand of the official's family and associates were beheaded or exiled too.

Apart from a big stick, Qianlong took draughtsmen with him on these travels. Their task was to record the famous sights of the south so that he could re-create them in his northern garden. One such scene was borrowed from a monastery in Hangzhou. Called *Fish in the Stream*, the original was a place where devotees could release captive fish into running water, a practice symbolising compassion for all creatures that still takes place in many Buddhist temples today. Recreated in the Garden of Perfect Brightness, however, it was transformed into a metaphor for imperial benevolence – and, by comparing the emperor to the Buddha, irreligious hubris.

Beyond the reproduction of isolated scenes, five southern gardens from cities such as Suzhou and Nanjing were recreated in their entirety for the emperor's pleasure. It was a demonstration of his cultivated appreciation of the classical garden tradition, but it also sent an unmistakable message that these ostensibly private, apolitical domains were incorporated into his all-encompassing sphere of influence. Like his father, who built his garden residence on an archipelago representing the nine continents of the known world, Qianlong was symbolically incorporating the cultural topography of Han China into his own private garden, but unlike Yongzheng he did not fear accusations of decadence, of slipping from Manchu martial prowess into effeminate Han bookishness.

Qianlong was comfortable playing the role of Han scholar, even though that role was traditionally opposed to Qing rule, because it was transformed by his majesty into something quite different: a confirmation of the legitimacy and magnificence of the dynasty. Looking with satisfaction over his handiwork he asked imperiously, 'Why should I miss the south again?'

Qianlong's most substantial addition to the garden was a 1,059-acre eastwards extension that nearly doubled the size of the site. This was to be his residence when he retired, for he had announced with a characteristic combination of Confucian piety and theatricality that he would step down rather than exceed his grandfather Kangxi's sixty-one-year reign. (In the event he continued to pull the strings until his own death four years later.) Qianlong's new addition was optimistically named the Garden of Eternal Spring, and being meant for retirement was even less formal than the Yuanming Yuan itself. It was laid out around a series of lakes – it was in fact more lake than land, and on the islands that dotted the watery scene were a series of fantastic buildings, including a multi-level circular structure like the Temple of Heaven in Beijing on the strikingly named Mind Opening Isle.

One of this garden's most famous features today is the Xiyang Lou, the 'Western-style Buildings', whose ruins are the most visible remains of the garden complex; the rest of the palaces, being made chiefly of wood, burned rather more easily. The genesis of their construction is highly revealing of Qing attitudes to foreigners. We tend to imagine that cultural exchange occurred in only one direction during the eighteenth century – from east to west – and indeed the European craze for chinoiserie, whether in the form of porcelain, silk or furniture, was certainly more widespread than its Chinese counterpart: what one might call Europhilia. But this phenomenon did exist, and one of the main sources of Western culture in China was the group of Jesuit missionaries hosted by the court since the Ming dynasty, whose aim was the conversion of the most populous nation on earth. One of the ways they hoped to achieve this was by demonstrating the superiority of 'Christian' arts and sciences.

Attitudes to the Jesuits varied from ruler to ruler: Qianlong's grandfather Kangxi was an inquisitive man who was fascinated by Western science, and he loved to demonstrate his personal mastery of Jesuit-imported knowledge to his court. Qianlong retained a Jesuit presence in his retinue but was more interested in using exotic modes of representation as a mirror of his majesty. The Milanese painter Giuseppe Castiglione, called in Chinese Lang Shining, was a resident of the Qing court throughout the reign of its three greatest rulers, and he painted portraits of each. These pictures occupy a curious middle ground between Western perspective and traditional Chinese painting. Qianlong expressly forbade the use of shadow in his portraits, and Castiglione's pictures of him have a kind of hieratic planarity, despite employing spatial recession.

While Kangxi had taken an interest in technology, his son had a disregard for foreign science beyond its novelty value. This attitude coincided with the slipping of the Qing empire – once the greatest, richest, and most powerful force on the planet – behind European upstarts such as the British: ballistics, after all, depended on the same scientific conception of space that had led to the development of linear perspective. It was Qianlong's interest in the more spectacular fruits of Western science, however, that led to his commissioning of Western buildings. On seeing an engraving of baroque fountains, he decided he had to have some of his own. The Garden of Perfect Brightness was a microcosm of the world under Chinese rule, and since the Middle Kingdom regarded all other nations, especially those beyond its immediate borders, as potential vassal states, it would not be complete without these barbaric European structures. Although Qing imperial residences included examples of other Asian architectures, including a huge replica of the Dalai Lama's

Potala Palace in the northern summer retreat of Chengde, this was quite a novel approach to architectural exoticism. According to the Jesuit Father Attiret, Chinese attitudes to European building had traditionally been quite different:

> Their Eyes are so accustom'd to their own Architecture, that they have very little Taste for ours. May I tell you what they say when they speak of it, or when they are looking over the Prints of some of our most celebrated Buildings? The Height and Thickness of our Palaces amazes them. They look upon our Streets, as so many Ways hollowed into terrible Mountains; and upon our Houses, as Rocks pointing up in the Air, and full of Holes like Dens of Bears and other wild Beasts. Above all, our different Stories, piled up so high one above another, seem quite intolerable to them: and they cannot conceive, how we can bear to run the Risk of breaking our Necks, so commonly, in going up such a Number of Steps as is necessary to climb up to the Fourth and Fifth Floors. 'Undoubtedly, (said the Emperor Kangxi, while he was looking over some Plans of our *European* Houses,) this *Europe* must be a very small and pitiful Country; since the Inhabitants cannot find Ground enough to spread out their Towns, but are obliged to live up this high in the Air.'[10]

(Attiret adds, somewhat sniffily: 'As for us, we think otherwise; and have Reason to do so'). In the end a large number of Sino-baroque stone structures were erected in the Yuanming Yuan, including palaces, belvederes, terraces, fountains, an aviary and a maze. These were clumsily designed by contemporary European standards, but they had a sort of impressive weirdness, as the remains show. We can also get quite an accurate impression of how they looked from a series of engravings of the buildings commissioned from a Chinese court artist who had apparently been trained by the Jesuits. The pilasters, arches, balustrades and

– unusual for China – glazed windows are clearly visible, as are the *echt* Chinese eaves that curl incongruously above them. Appropriately enough, these prints combine Western technology (copperplate engraving and linear perspective) with more Chinese representational traditions. The results are fantastic, the distortions in perspectival recession not the result of cack-handedness but a deliberate adaptation of Western technology to suit Chinese purposes. It has been suggested that the multiplicity of vanishing points is an attempt to portray the subject from the all-seeing imperial perspective. For example, an additional eyeline in the image of the Grand Fountain corresponds to the viewpoint from an outdoor throne located opposite the subject.

Yi Lantai, The European Pavilions at the Garden
of Perfect Brightness *(1783–6)*

These buildings, it seems, were used by Qianlong only to display his collections of Western curios – he had a particular fondness for clocks – and as a backdrop for ceremonial spectaculars of fountains and fireworks. But they did have at least one resident, an imperial consort known to legend as the Fragrant

Concubine from the newly conquered region of Xinjiang. Many romantic myths have grown up about this woman: that she was captured from a Muslim tribe; that Qianlong fell hopelessly in love with her but she refused his attentions, devoting herself instead to a life of secluded piety; and that, overcome with melancholy, she eventually took her own life. The facts are of course more prosaic: the concubine's tale is a commonplace account of sexual realpolitik. The woman in question belonged to a Turkic tribe that had allied themselves with the Qing, so helping the latter to conquer Xinjiang. In order to cement this alliance, the chief's daughter was given to Qianlong in marriage, and she eventually produced a child. It is possible, however, that one of the European-style buildings she occupied was used as a mosque, for the Qing empire was generally tolerant of religious freedoms, although not of aggressive Christian proselytising: Yongzheng forbade missionary work outside the capital. This combination of sexual and architectural conquest (of Turkic and European others, respectively) is a revealingly graduated demonstration of the symbolic order of the Garden of Perfect Brightness in its role of imperial microcosm.

Very shortly afterwards the garden also became symbolic of imperial decline as, in the last decade of his reign, Qianlong's judgment faltered and the empire weakened. Lord Macartney, leader of a British mission to Qianlong's court on the occasion of the emperor's eightieth birthday, observed,

> The Empire of China is an old, crazy, first-rate Man of War, which a fortunate succession of able and vigilant officers have contrived to keep afloat for these hundred and fifty years past, and to over-awe their neighbours merely by her bulk and appearance. But whenever an insufficient man happens to have the command on deck, adieu to the discipline and safety of the ship. She may, perhaps, not sink outright; she may drift some time as a wreck, and

will then be dashed to pieces on the shore; but she can never be rebuilt on the old bottom.[11]

Qianlong's birthday was celebrated that year by a spectacular ceremony in the garden which included a display of the Western-style fountains. But the pumping mechanism for these had broken down some time before and, with the Jesuits no longer around to fix them, their order having been dissolved by the pope in 1773, Qianlong had to order the immense reservoirs to be filled by hand – specifically by eunuchs carrying buckets, a laborious and time-consuming task. Undeniably grand on the surface, but fundamentally and hopelessly dysfunctional: the consequences for the Qing were, perhaps inevitable.

By the evening of the 19th October [1860], the summer palaces had ceased to exist, and in their immediate vicinity the face of nature had changed: some blackened gables and piles of burned timbers alone indicating where the royal palaces had stood. In many places the inflammable pine trees near the buildings had been consumed with them, leaving nothing but their charred trunks to mark the site. When we first entered the gardens they reminded one of those magic grounds described in fairy tales; we marched from them on the 19th October, leaving them a dreary waste of ruined nothings.[12]

So wrote British officer Garnet (later Viscount) Wolseley shortly after his victorious return from the Second Opium War (1856–60). This war – fought in order to force a sovereign nation to legalise a pernicious drug trade – had all but been concluded, and peace had been declared when Anglo-French troops forced their way into the deserted Yuanming Yuan, Emperor Xianfeng having fled to his northern resort of Chengde.

The invaders were astounded by the paradise they discovered

there, an impression unmarred by the suicide of the garden's superintendent, whose body was floating face down in a lake. Among the emperor's many possessions they found three luxurious coaches made by John Hatchett of Longacre, unused because the arrangement whereby the coachman sat with his back to the passenger broke imperial protocol, and a number of English cannon, equally unused – gifts, ironically, of an earlier mission. Their astonishment soon turned to greed, however, and participants in the subsequent looting later reported incredible scenes of soldiers running about dressed in mandarin robes and smashing priceless vases, much of the rest being shipped off to London and Paris. The British Museum still holds a great deal of the loot, including one of the most famous of all Chinese paintings, the eighth-century *Admonitions Scroll* after Gu Kaizhi.

The representatives of the emperor had understandably dragged their feet over the ratification of the peace treaty, since its conditions included signing over large areas of China to foreign rule and the legalisation of the opium trade. But when eighteen European envoys who had been sent to discuss terms were returned in boxes having been tortured to death, the reaction was, perhaps equally understandably, furious. The leader of the British, Lord Elgin, son of the Elgin who took the Parthenon marbles, decided unilaterally to burn down the emperor's favourite residence as 'punishment' (the French washed their hands at this point, calling the arson an act of 'Goth-like barbarism'). Elgin justified his retaliation by saying that it was a way of striking back at the emperor directly without harming the Chinese people. He was a great fan of such rationalisations, writing after the looting,

I have just returned from the Summer Palace. It is really a fine thing, like an English park – numberless buildings with handsome rooms, and filled with Chinese curios, and handsome clocks, bronzes, etc. But, alas! Such a scene of desolation . . . There was not a room I saw in which half the things had not been taken away or broken in pieces . . . War is a hateful business. The more one sees of it, the more one detests it.[13]

He ordered the palace to be torched shortly afterwards. It is characteristic of the British that they should water the ashes with crocodile tears: such laments form a constant counterpoint to the rhetoric of the 'white man's burden'. What Simon Schama has called the Empire of Good Intentions could more honestly be called an Empire of Bad Faith. Elgin himself was an international hand wringer with a seemingly bottomless capacity for self-abnegation surpassed only by his ruthlessness. He presided over imperialist wars in Canada, India and China, leaving a trail of destruction and self-pity wherever he went. On his way to bombard Canton he read an account of the suppression of the Indian 'Mutiny' and wondered, 'Can I do anything to prevent England from calling down on herself God's curse for brutalities committed on another feeble Oriental race? Or are all my exertions to result only in the extension of the area over which Englishmen are to exhibit how hollow and superficial are both their civilisation and their Christianity?'[14] This and the numerous other guilt-ridden exclamations that punctuate his diaries remind one of Lewis Carroll's oyster-eating walrus.

> 'I weep for you,' the Walrus said:
> 'I deeply sympathize.'
> With sobs and tears he sorted out
> Those of the largest size,
> Holding his pocket-handkerchief
> Before his streaming eyes.

Hypocritical self-exoneration was not only practised by the vanguard of European imperialism; it affected even the most famous critic of the sack of the Yuanming Yuan. Victor Hugo – whose lament 'Here is what Civilization has done to Barbarity!' has been quoted approvingly by numerous Chinese historians over the years – possessed a substantial quantity of the finest Chinese silk, which had been looted from the Garden of Perfect Brightness by French soldiers. He bought it a mere five years after the sack, by which time his *bien pensant* outrage had evidently abated.

For all his hand wringing, Elgin's imperial arrogance comes through loud and clear in his estimation of the artefacts he destroyed:

> I do not think in matters of art we have much to learn from that country . . . the most cynical representations of the grotesque have been the principal products of Chinese conceptions of the sublime and beautiful. Nevertheless I am disposed to believe that under this mass of abortions and rubbish there lie some hidden sparks of a divine fire, which the genius of my countrymen may gather and nurse into a flame.[15]

His chief regret seems to have been, typically for a son of this nation of shopkeepers, that the objects destroyed were extraordinarily valuable. 'Plundering and devastating a place like this is bad enough, but what is much worse is the waste and breakage. Out of £1,000,000 worth of property, I dare say £50,000 will not be realized.'[16] There has clearly been a massive reversal in attitudes to Chinese culture since the eighteenth century, when the craze for Chinese art resulted in William Chambers' 1761 Pagoda at Kew. Chambers, who also built the very un-Chinese Somerset House, had actually visited China, and his knowledge of its architecture was unusually accurate. Frederick the Great's more fantastic Chinese House was built at the same time in Potsdam. By the mid-nineteenth century, however, Europe was on the rise, and the admiration of Enlightenment figures such as Voltaire for

Confucian values had been replaced by a Smithian laissez-faire approach that saw Chinese society as fatally static and authoritarian. Marx described the moment of this change with characteristic pithiness in a *New York Daily Tribune* article dated 20 September 1858.

> That a giant empire, containing almost one-third of the human race, vegetating in the teeth of time, insulated by the forced exclusion of general intercourse, and thus contriving to dupe itself with delusions of Celestial perfection – that such an empire should at last be overtaken by fate on [the] occasion of a deadly duel, in which the representative of the antiquated world appears prompted by ethical motives, while the representative of overwhelming modern society fights for the privilege of buying in the cheapest and selling in the dearest markets – this, indeed, is a sort of tragical couplet stranger than any poet would ever have dared to fancy.

The newfound supremacy of the West translated into contempt for Chinese culture, as we have seen, but also for Chinese lives. When the Anglo-French forces occupied the town of Beitang they demolished extensive parts of it in the process, and one of Elgin's men later mused with sinister naivety that the town had had 20,000 inhabitants, but 'what became of a large majority of that population we never could ascertain'.[17] As Heinrich Heine had written earlier that century, where men burn books they will also burn people.

Today the Garden of Perfect Brightness is maintained as a sort of national monument to wounded feelings. The site is heavily garlanded with slogans like 'Never forget the humiliation of the nation', and the ruins themselves are covered in recent graffiti berating the British and French. Since the end of the Cultural Revolution there has been a gradual reoccupation of imperial

history by a Chinese government that has discarded the legiti-
mising narrative of communism. Instead, China watchers will be
familiar with the rhetoric of 'national harmony' and 'historical
continuity' spouted by its leaders, who relentlessly invoke the
country's '5,000 years of continuous civilisation' to justify their
rule, as if ruptures like the Qing colonisation, or indeed their
own communist revolution, had never happened. The ruins of
the Yuanming Yuan – largely ignored if not viewed with suspicion as remnants of a feudal past between 1949 and 1978 – are
now used to whip up nationalist, and sometimes xenophobic,
sentiment, in order to forge a nation state based on those very
nineteenth-century European ideals that led to the destruction of
the palace in the first place.

The cruel irony that the most visible of its remains are Western
buildings has not been lost on Chinese observers, although the
possibility that they might be inappropriate touchstones for a
supposedly socialist country is very rarely suggested. And today,
Beijing, Shanghai and the other mega-cities of China are filled
with modern buildings that meld Western and Chinese character-
istics. The so-called Bird's Nest stadium in Beijing, for example,
was the result of a collaboration between Swiss architects Herzog
& de Meuron and Chinese artist Ai Wei Wei. Like the Olympic
opening ceremony that took place there in 2008, it's a bizarre
confection of Soviet and consumerist spectacle. Similarly, the new
HQ of the Chinese national broadcaster, a heavily censored propaganda outlet going by the sinister acronym of CCTV, was designed
by erstwhile enfant terrible Rem Koolhaas as a kind of gigantic
character □ (pronounced 'kou' meaning mouth – of the party?)
pierced by walkways to permit, in the architect's own disingenuous estimation, public penetration of an utterly impenetrable
organisation. (Although the building was completed in 2012, the
public walkways remain closed.) Perhaps the real tragedy is that
– in a dialectical move towards both Chinese feudalism and

Western capitalism – such Sino-European structures are once again being built by an autocratic empire in order to create an impression of might. The West, needless to say, hasn't improved much either: we are still using force to dictate the policies of sovereign states for our own financial gain, and still mindlessly destroying other people's architectural history – and lives – in the process.

Creative Commons

OMA, CCTV headquarters, Beijing

Festival Theatre, Bayreuth, Germany
(1876)
Architecture and Entertainment

Buildings are used as a popular stage. They are all divided into innumerable, simultaneously animated theatres. Balcony, court-yard, window, gateway, staircase, roof, are at the same time stage and boxes.

Walter Benjamin and Asja Lacis, *Naples*[1]

Broadway's turning into Coney.
Richard Rodgers and Lorenz Hart, 'Give it back to the Indians'

Wagner Festival Theatre, Bayreuth

One of my most vivid architectural memories, formed when I was perhaps sixteen years old, is of walking slowly down a narrow stone corridor in my home. The passage twisted like sheep guts, as the Chinese say, and I couldn't see more than a few feet ahead of me at any time, but strange grunts echoing from around each corner gave me some intimation of what lay ahead. Unnerved, I continued inching forward. Suddenly a figure burst from the darkness, a grotesque pig-man with a Mohawk of bristles, curving tusks and a pair of sunglasses on its snout, running towards me at full tilt. Overcoming my fearful paralysis, I raised my gun and – just in time – shot the creature dead.

Perhaps you have a similar memory: the game was a popular one. Released in 1996, *Duke Nukem 3D* was one of the most successful (and controversial) first-generation three-D shoot 'em ups, and I found it powerfully addictive. In retrospect, perhaps what appealed most was the atmosphere of suspense and dread conjured by the fictive architecture of passageways, caverns and desolate industrial installations. By today's standards the animation is primitive and pixilated, but when I look at the screenshots, the emptiness of the game's spaces – punctuated by the gun-filled hands at the lower edge of the screen reminding me that this is *my* field of vision, *my* experience – retains a dim frisson of horror. The intensity of my emotional engagement, apart from being the natural state for a sixteen-year-old, may have had something to do with the fact that the screen of the computer was a portal between the familiar world of home and a disturbing elsewhere, and unlike the fictions on the TV, I was the protagonist of this narrative. Sometimes when

I went to bed late at night after playing I would continue walking those corridors in my dreams.

I suppose that many people of my generation have similarly intense memories of virtual architecture. And although the medium of computer games is new, the architecture of entertainment has long held an important role in people's lives, from the amphitheatres of ancient Greece to the picture palaces of 1920s America. Entertainment is far more than a frivolous means of passing the time, it is a central social experience. The architecture of (and in) entertainment is embedded in our collective and individual imaginations: the darkened cinema, for example, has an intense erotic charge for many people who experienced their first kisses there, and the architecture onscreen, whether inhabited by Cary Grant or conjured by Hitchcock, burns a powerful spatial memory – the camera roving through space puts the viewer deep in the picture. In this chapter I will trace some of the transformations the architecture of entertainment has undergone on its way from amphitheatre to computer screen, beginning with a pivotal episode of mingled silliness and significance, the opening of Richard Wagner's Festspielhaus – Festival Theatre – in 1876.

To those unfamiliar with his music, Wagner's name may conjure images of globular sopranos in horned helmets, interminable operas about magic rings and associations with the Nazis – he was indeed one of Hitler's favourite composers and a terrible anti-Semite. But recall one of the greatest scenes in cinema, when in *Apocalypse Now* American helicopters swoop low across the waves towards a Vietnamese village with the 'Ride of the Valkyries' blaring from loudspeakers, and one realises the enduring power – and moral ambiguity – of Wagner's music. His work scandalised his contemporaries, who divided into Wagnerians and anti-Wagnerians; sometimes it even divided individuals, as in the case of Thomas Mann, who was exiled from Germany after giving a lecture on Wagner's 'diseased brand of heroism' in 1933,[2] or Mark Twain, who wrote, 'I have witnessed and greatly enjoyed the first act of everything which Wagner created, but the effect on me has always been so powerful that one act was quite sufficient; whenever I have witnessed two acts I have gone away physically exhausted; and whenever I have ventured an entire opera the result has been the next thing to suicide.'[3] Friedrich Nietzsche, who was briefly friends with the composer, famously switched from admirer to critic, and Marxist theorist Theodor Adorno combined the two positions – dialectically. Others were less ambivalent. Ludwig II of Bavaria, Charles Baudelaire, George Bernard Shaw, W. H. Auden, T. S. Eliot, Salvador Dali and Oscar Wilde were all devotees of Wagner's morbid eroticism and unsettling chords. His dissonances ushered in the avant-garde compositions of Mahler and Schoenberg and influenced countless Hollywood scores, such as Bernard Hermann's unforgettable music for *Vertigo*; and his concept of *Gesamtkunstwerk* – a 'total work of art' unifying poetry, music and drama – had an enormous impact on *fin de siècle* art and, later, modernism. Adorno even argued that with the *Gesamtkunstwerk*, Wagner invented cinema.

Wagner's opera house – or rather theatre (he called his productions 'music dramas' in order to distinguish them from operas) – was as distinctive as his music. Built solely for the production of his works, a role that it still performs each summer, the theatre stands on a little hill surrounded by fields above the small Bavarian town of Bayreuth. The structure is imposing because of its site, but it isn't particularly grand: originally made with a timber frame (recently replaced with reinforced concrete) filled in with red brick, its vernacular *Volk*iness was meant as a riposte to the grand classical opera houses of the nineteenth century.

This tradition had culminated in the Paris opera designed by Charles Garnier, which opened the year before Wagner's theatre. Palais Garnier is an elephantine building wallowing in the gilded slurry of the classical tradition, standing at the confluence of several boulevards in Hausmann's reconfigured city. Gewgaws from nearly every period are slathered over every available surface. Its interior is just as elaborate, with such a grand foyer that architectural reformer and Gothic revivalist Viollet-le-Duc observed that 'the hall seems made for the stairway, and not the stairway for the hall'. This was partly sour grapes, since he had lost out in the competition to design the building, but he wasn't far wrong: in the Paris of the Second Empire the bourgeoisie had invaded the stage of public life. Theatres were sites of their mutual exhibitionism, with the performance a pretext for seeing and being seen. Although this had been the case to some extent for centuries, Garnier's opera was unlike earlier theatres – and those in more backwards countries like England – which aristocrats entered through private portals while lesser mortals tramped through undistinguished side doors. Instead, in bourgeois Paris everyone – everyone, that is, who could afford a ticket – was funnelled up the grand stair, mingling in a way that struck foreign visitors as shockingly improper.

Meanwhile, German opera continued trundling along in a feudal tradition stretching back over two hundred years. Until its unification in 1871 Germany was divided into a number of large and small states, each regional court having a theatre of its own patronised by the local ruler. One of these was the court opera in Dresden, the glittering capital of the kingdom of Saxony and a byword for opulence and high culture. In 1848 the city was also a hive of subversive activity. During that 'year of revolutions', when the whole of Europe seemed ready to explode, Dresden's residents included the father of anarchism Mikhail Bakunin, court architect Gottfried Semper, whom we encountered looking at a 'Caraib cottage' in the introduction, and Richard Wagner, director of the state orchestra.

These three often met to debate the possibility of revolution, national unification and constitutional reform, although Bakunin was far more radical than Semper and Wagner, who naively petitioned the king to declare a republic and seemed almost not to realise that their political activities had forfeited their state

JOHN KELLERMAN / Alamy

The Grand Stairway of Opera Garnier puts the audience on stage

appointments and possibly their lives. However, the perpetually vacillating king ignored calls for reform, and when soldiers opened fire on the populace of Dresden in May 1849 barricades went up all over the city. Wagner, who was elated by this turn of events, advised Semper to turn his architectural talents, formerly employed in the production of royal operas, to revolutionary purposes. The resulting 'Semper barricade' was a miniature fortress of one storey, erected – as Wagner somewhat mockingly put it – 'with all the conscientiousness of a Michelangelo or Leonardo da Vinci', both of whom had worked as military engineers in their day. Semper personally manned his barricade for three days, while Wagner paraded the streets making blood-curdling threats to burn down the palace – and indeed the old opera was torched. However, when the Prussian army descended on Dresden, Wagner and Semper saw the game was up and fled. Semper ended up in London, where he found it hard to get work and spent most of his time writing about architecture in the British Library (Karl Marx, another exile of 1848, was sitting nearby); meanwhile, Wagner made his way to Switzerland, instructing his wife to follow with their pet parrot.

In his Zurich exile Wagner published several essays including 'The Artwork of the Future' and 'Art and Revolution' (and an anti-Semitic polemic, 'Judaism in Music'). Tedious, confused and pompous as these works may be, they contain his ideas about the purpose of the arts and their fusion in the *Gesamtkunstwerk*. At the same time Wagner began working on the libretto – it was another innovation of his to write all his libretti himself – of the work that would become the fifteen-hour-long four-opera Ring Cycle, the story of a magic ring that brings doom to all who lust after its power.

With the sounds of revolution still ringing in Wagner's ears, it is no surprise that these writings were suffused with what Marxist critic Georg Lukács termed 'romantic anti-capitalism' – a rejection of the bureaucratic strictures and money motivation of the bourgeois system which however stopped short of advocating class struggle, instead favouring a return to some supposed halcyon era. In Wagner's eyes, the fractures of modern life and art could be healed by putting theatre back at the heart of society, a position it had held (so he asserted) in unified communities of the past – to be specific in ancient Greece. The dramatic *Gesamtkunstwerk* would unify the arts while paradoxically allowing 'each one to attain its full value for the first time': for example, music and painting would give up narrative, since they would be accompanied by a libretto; likewise, poetry could stop trying to paint pictures with words. But perhaps the most important aspect of the *Gesamtkunstwerk* was that it would also unify the audience, both within itself and with the performers onstage, and thereby create a community, a people – a *Volk*. In order to achieve this, Wagner would put an end to social segregation by opening theatre doors to the whole community, not just the lolling rich, as had been the case in ancient Greece, where some amphitheatres seated 14,000 people. Just as with the arts, this unifying process would allow the members of the audience to fulfil themselves as individuals: as Wagner wrote, 'only in communism does egoism find itself completely gratified'.[4] But Wagner's idea of communism was quite unlike the one proposed in Marx and Engels' *Communist Manifesto*, which was published a year before his 'Art and Revolution': it was nationalist not internationalist, being based on the idea of the unity of a *Volk*, and it was as conservative as it was progressive, hoping to create a better future by looking back to an imaginary ancient world.

Wagner's nationalism was very much of its time, but his reverence for classical theatre was nothing new; the Italians had been looking back to antique drama since the fifteenth century. Before then theatre had been largely religious and open air, medieval mystery plays and more profane entertainments taking place in cathedral precincts or market squares. Theatre's classical turn began in the Italian city of Ferrara in 1486, with a production of Roman playwright Plautus' *Menaichmi* – on which Shakespeare's *Comedy of Errors* is based – in a courtyard of the ducal palace. This courtyard had been a market square until the duke annexed it thirteen years earlier, absorbing a formerly public space into his private realm, a process discussed in Chapter 4. This permitted performances beyond the authority of the Church, which generally disapproved of secular theatre, and at the same time the audience was privatised: whereas anyone could watch in the market square, the public was now only allowed entry at the discretion of the duke, while the duchess and other aristocratic ladies retreated to a loggia overlooking the action – an embryonic royal box.

Palladio's Teatro Olimpico in Vicenza has a radically democratic auditorium.
Seven 'streets' open on to the stage.

A hundred years later the great Venetian architects Andrea
Palladio and Vincenzo Scamozzi designed one of the first purpose-
built theatres since antiquity, but for a very different client. The
Teatro Olimpico was the project of the Olympic Academy of
Vicenza, a group of scholars, merchants and artists, including
Palladio himself, devoted to the study and promotion of classical
culture. Because there was no royal patron, the auditorium of their
theatre is not a hierarchical space: there are no boxes and no privileged viewpoints, just a raked bank of benches like an ancient
auditorium. Taking classicism even further, the stage has a permanent set depicting a city, an allusion to the *skene* building which
formed the backdrop and backstage areas for Greek amphitheatres. Palladio gives this structure a very Renaissance flavour,
covering it in pilasters and statue-crammed niches. These statues
don't represent emperors, as they would have in princely theatres,

but show instead classical writers and local dignitaries. Also set into the *skene* are apertures disclosing seven *trompe l'oeil* 'streets', actually shallow passages that use perspectival recession to create an illusion of greater depth. These open on to the stage at different angles, taking the democratisation of the auditorium even further: there is no ideal position with a privileged view of the action.

Although several theatres at the time put the city on the stage, the democratic arrangement at Vicenza was unusual. Most theatres belonged to dukes or princes and had a very clearly delineated visual hierarchy: the ducal loggia was raised above and behind the rest of the audience, and the stage was oriented to his vision. This mimicked the relationship of the duke to the city, as viewed from a loggia of his palace, and so formed a microcosm of the state. In contrast to the ideally placed duke, the spectators below had a distorted view of the city, making them visually aware of their subordination, a very Renaissance trick. This arrangement became the norm for theatres all over Europe for the next two hundred years. A typical example is the opera house built by the Margrave of Bayreuth in 1748. It's a kind of baroque jewel case with the margrave's box – lousy with putti and topped with a huge gilded crown – as its sparkling centrepiece.

Wagner wasn't the first to try and shake drama from its feudal slumbers. In 1784, five years before the French Revolution, the utopian architect Claude-Nicolas Ledoux had designed a ground-breaking theatre for the town of Besançon. This starkly neoclassical structure is not part of a palace, as most earlier theatres had been, although it was not the first to make a break for free-standing monumentality; that honour goes to Frederick the Great's Berlin Opera, built on a specially cleared square off Unter den Linden in 1745 and much praised by Voltaire, who thought France's theatres woefully medieval in comparison. Inspired by the writings of theatrical reformers like Voltaire and Diderot, Ledoux returned to the semicircular amphitheatres of antiquity. He wrote of wanting to 'establish a new religion' with the building, which would reject the riotous decoration of previous theatres in order to focus attention on the moral lessons being illustrated onstage. He would also clear out the private boxes of the aristocracy, those 'vast aviaries where the powers of the earth cling to their high luxurious perches',[5] partly in order to create a totally visible microcosm of society, but also to prevent monkey business behind the swags. To complete his social microcosm, Ledoux also proposed providing seats for the poorer members of the audience, who had until now stood in the flat pit in front of the stage, coming and going at will throughout the performance and making a lot of noise – and a terrible smell, he sniffily remarked.

If this had all been carried out as planned, the traditional social order of the theatre would have been reversed: everyone would have been seated in one sweeping amphitheatre, with the most expensive seats closest to the stage, and the cheapest up in the rafters. In Paris the aristocracy had vigorously resisted calls for this kind of change for years. They used their theatre boxes as markers of status, as places to conduct their social lives and extramarital affairs, and didn't much like the thought of the applecart being overturned: in an amphitheatre-style auditorium they would have become both not visible enough (unable to display their presence) and too visible (they wouldn't have been able to carry on behind curtains). In the end Ledoux's levelling ambitions had to be modified: boxes were provided for the nobility and the commoners remained in the pit, although they were now seated.

Ledoux's irreducibly Enlightenment ideal of visual discipline – as he put it, 'one sees well everywhere, one is well seen, which contributes to the pleasure of the spectacle and maintains decency' – corresponds to the contemporary concept of the panopticon, a structure which coerces by its transparency.[6] Invented by British philosopher Jeremy Bentham, the panopticon is a circular building with cells arranged around its perimeter, the inhabitants of which can be observed from a central watchtower. They can't see into the watchtower and so they never know if they are actually being watched, but because of the constant *possibility* of surveillance, they constantly modify their behaviour. Eventually discipline becomes internalised – inside each of the prisoners grows an eye watching their every move. Bentham proposed the panopticon as a humane model for prisons, a way of getting rid of chains and dungeons, and also thought the idea might be profitably applied to factories. It was Ledoux's innovation to apply this kind of visual discipline not just to prisons or factories but to entertainment and the theatre – in other words, to the whole of society, not just its lower reaches.

This contrasts with the 'visual regime' (to slip into barbarous academic language) of earlier theatres. In the open-air amphitheatres of the ancient world the eyes of the crowd were directed at the actors, at the *skene* building behind them, which represented the city or domestic space, depending on the backdrop used, and then at the view beyond the *skene*. Since amphitheatres were carved into the nearest available slope – usually the acropolis that stood at the centre of most Greek cities – the view would be of the city below and beyond it the natural world, whether valley, ocean or forest. It would be crass to suggest that this demonstrates that the ancients had a more holistic view of the world, or that each age has its own homogeneous approach to theatre (of course Greek spectators also peered at each other), but the contrast to theatre in the Middle Ages is instructive. Instead of looking down and beyond to nature, the medieval crowd looked up to temporary stages erected in the market square or in front of the cathedral, giving the actors a mercantile or ecclesiastical backdrop, depending on the performance. Later, for Renaissance princes, the enclosure and privatisation of theatres and the use of perspective provided means to create a strictly controlled visual regime in which the performance was unmistakably for the eyes of the ruler.

This continued up to the nineteenth century, but alongside the idea of the monocular theatre there developed a culture of mutual exhibitionism in which aristocrats used their boxes to measure their social standing and to preen and carry on their semi-public private lives. Ledoux was still working within this tradition but gave it an Enlightenment twist: instead of mutual display under the watchful and ordering eye of the monarch, total visibility – or panopticism, to give it its Benthamite name – is an abstract and omnipresent (because internalised) means of social control for the coming post-absolutist age.

While he was designing his theatre Ledoux made a mysterious and highly suggestive engraving that emblematises his ideas about vision, enlightenment, society and theatre. The image shows an enormous eye with a reflection in its iris of the auditorium at Besançon. Perhaps it is the eye of an actor looking out at the audience, which is reflected by him, suggesting that he is their stand-in on stage, and the play is the image of society. From high above the auditorium comes a sunbeam, literally enlightening the spectators but also regulating their behaviour because no one can hide their misdeeds in a twilit box. Does this enlightening ray come from God or from within the cranium of an actor? Does it represent the more general idea that vision, or surveillance, is itself enlightening? Or could it be the architect looking with satisfaction upon his creation, bringing enlightenment and order, via the carefully graded social stratification of the auditorium, to the people?

Ledoux's hopes for a levelled audience were finally achieved ninety years later by Richard Wagner, although he gave the idea a spin of his own. When we left Wagner, he was on the run from the German authorities after the failed revolution of 1849. Though he was finally allowed to return from exile in 1862 it was not a happy homecoming. He was beset by illness, marital decay, adulterous scandal and financial incontinence – and the inevitable angry creditors, who included by this point most of his

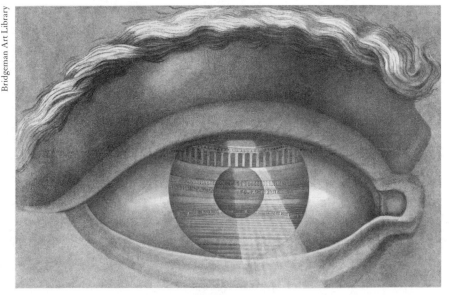

Ledoux's allegory of the theatre as a realm of enlightenment

friends. He was in desperate need of paying work, and his life was a series of brief stays in dreary towns before moving on to escape the debt collectors. The year 1864 found him in Stuttgart and on the brink of disaster, when a miracle occurred. Earlier that year his biggest fan had been crowned King Ludwig II of Bavaria, and one of the eighteen-year-old monarch's first acts was to summon the composer for an audience. This was not as straight-forward as the king had hoped. The composer was in hiding, and when Ludwig's agent finally tracked Wagner down, he had diffi-culty convincing him that he was not a bailiff. Wagner must have been flabbergasted when he heard Ludwig's proposal: he would be spirited away to Munich, have all his debts settled and be provided with limitless backing for the completion of the Ring Cycle.

To begin with the relationship went well. Ludwig had idolised the composer since encountering his work at the age of thirteen, and Wagner loved nothing more than being idolised. To be fair, he was also genuinely touched by the devotion and artistic sympathy of the young king. If his acceptance of royal patronage seems surprising, bearing in mind that we last encountered the composer manning the barricades in Dresden, exile had poured icy water on his revolutionary fervour, which had never been republican to begin with. Meanwhile, his concept of the *Volk* had grown ever more chauvinistic, and his outlook had taken a mystical turn, partly inspired by the lugubrious philosophy of Arthur Schopenhauer, who counselled Buddhist resignation to a world of illusion. In the king he found someone who shared his revulsion at the quotidian and his most deeply held beliefs about the centrality of art to life and drama to society. These beliefs were to find their ultimate expression in a grand theatre intended to be a monument to Wagner and to Ludwig, and which ended up being disastrous to them both.

Shortly after Wagner arrived in Munich, he advised the king that his old comrade Gottfried Semper would be the best candidate to design a theatre for the Ring Cycle. However, the architect and the composer had always had a rather fractious relationship, and they disagreed on the form the building should take. Like the king, Semper thought a grand permanent structure would be more suitable, whereas Wagner still harboured reformist zeal and sometimes expressed the extreme notion that his works should be performed for free in a temporary wooden structure that could be dismantled or even burned after the festival, along with the scenery, props and score. An apparently despairing Semper, strung along for three years by the indecisive king, scheming courtiers and evasive composer, eventually wrote to Wagner: 'your works . . . are too great and rich for illegitimate stages and wooden sheds'.[7]

In the end Wagner was won over to the idea of a permanent stage, but this wasn't going to be like any other opera house: first, the auditorium was to have a single sweep of terraced seats, removing social distinctions as in an ancient amphitheatre and putting an end to the theatre as a space of social display. This would allow people to focus on the drama. Second, the orchestra was to be submerged in a gap between the stage and the auditorium. This was not an unprecedented innovation – Ledoux had proposed the same thing for his theatre at Besançon. However, Wagner had special reasons for a subterranean orchestra, which would allow the creation of a flawless *Gesamtkunstwerk* in which the action on stage was accompanied by music that apparently came from nowhere. Third, the stage was to be framed by a double proscenium, creating what Wagner called a *Mystischer Abgrund*, a 'mystical abyss' separating the spectators from the play, making clear that this was a sacred other realm and simultaneously – another one of those Wagnerian paradoxes – pulling the viewers irresistibly in by focusing their attention on this framed and floating moving picture.

But although the people of Munich applauded the operas that Wagner staged in their city, the planned festival theatre – so extravagant, and for a *foreigner* – was felt to be a step too far. It was seized on by factions in the court and press antagonistic to the composer and king, and by Munich's musical world, which was envious of the outsider's success. Wagner's state-funded profligacy, his arrogance and his scandalous affair with his conductor's wife, Cosima von Bülow, didn't do much for his reputation either, and by 1866 the king was compelled to ask him to leave Munich – temporarily, he assured him, although the composer never returned to live there.

Wagner's enthusiasm for a Munich theatre had in any case been cooling for some time: he wanted to find a place where his art would be worshipped, not subjected to political interference and journalistic vituperation. The king was not so sanguine and fired off volleys of impassioned telegrams. 'If it is the Dear One's wish and will,' ran one of these missives, 'I will joyfully resign the throne and its empty splendour, and come to him, never to part from him again . . . to be united with him, above and beyond this earthly existence, is the only thing that can save me from despair and death'.[8] Wagner sensibly demurred; the same year Bavaria joined Austria in a disastrous war against Prussia, and even he could see that the king had other things on his plate, although this didn't stop him from emotionally blackmailing Ludwig into publishing a ludicrous letter denying his affair with Cosima; nor did it stop the king from running away from his government just as war broke out.

In 1870 Prussia went to war again – this time against France – and won, again. In the wake of victory the Prussian chancellor Otto von Bismarck felt emboldened to complete his project of unifying the German states. With Bavaria incorporated into the Reich, Ludwig became a Prussian puppet. He resented submitting to his hated uncle Kaiser Wilhelm, so he retreated from his public duties to a world of the imagination. He frequently had plays and operas staged in his private apartments, complaining, 'I can no longer get any illusion in the theatre with people staring at me all the time and following every movement of my face with their opera glasses. I want to see the spectacle, not be a spectacle myself for the multitude'.[9] For this marooned monarch the theatre's role as a spectacular feudal microcosm was defunct. Instead, drama was a means of escaping from harsh political realities into an immersive illusion that flooded out from beyond the proscenium to engulf his entire life. In this sense Ludwig was not a feudal relic but a precursor of the twentieth century.

Wagner's works had long confirmed Ludwig's ideals of the unity of art and life, and now, in the keenly felt absence of the composer, they inspired a series of kitsch architectural projects – an alternative universe designed along Wagnerian lines. Ludwig commissioned scenery painter Christian Jank, who had worked on backdrops for Wagner, to sketch out his fantastic castle Neuschwanstein (New Swan Stone). This spindly turreted building, perched on an Alpine summit and decorated with murals depicting scenes from the myths that had inspired Wagner, was intended to emulate the abode of the Grail knights in *Lohengrin*. Ludwig also built two other palaces, Linderhof and Herrenchiemsee, neither of which he occupied for long. Unlike the medievalising Neuschwanstein, these replicated elements of Versailles in homage to Louis XIV – Ludwig called himself the moon king, a nocturnal counterpart of his absolutist hero. In the grounds of Linderhof were follies inspired by Wagner's operas. The Grotto of Venus re-created the scenery from act one of *Tannhäuser* using the most up-to-date technology: its concrete stalactites were lit by electric lights, their colours shifting automatically between red, blue and green, and an artificial waterfall ran down the wall, emptying into an artificial lake. Ludwig was sometimes rowed across this on a little shell-shaped boat dressed – it is alleged – as Lohengrin, the swan knight.

Ludwig's transformation of life into theatre didn't come cheap. By 1885 he had personal debts of fourteen million marks, and whenever members of his government advised him to rein in his spending, he sacked them. So in 1886 his cabinet conspired to have him diagnosed insane by a panel of four doctors, none of whom had ever examined the king. It is hard to say if he actually was mad; at the beginning of his reign he was nothing worse than peculiar, and he was by no means an incompetent ruler. However, frustration and loneliness made him turn inwards, and by the 1880s his behaviour had become extraordinary: he lived nocturnally, refusing to attend to matters of state; he broke off his engagement to a duchess and had scandalous affairs with young equerries and actors; and he held conversations with invisible interlocutors such as Marie Antoinette. The day after he was deposed Ludwig drowned in mysterious circumstances in Lake

Ludwig II as the swan knight Lohengrin, on his boat in the Grotto
of Venus at Linderhof

Starnberg, along with one of the doctors who had signed his declaration of insanity.

Sixteen years earlier, as Prussia was mobilising for its war against France, Wagner had been tied up with a campaign of his own, the never-ending struggle to establish a festival theatre. That year he and Cosima identified the margravial opera house in Bayreuth – which had the largest stage in Germany at the time – as a possible setting for the performance of the Ring Cycle. However, on visiting the town he realised that its opera was far too small and inflexible for his purposes. Nevertheless Bayreuth would, he thought, make the perfect spot for a purpose-built theatre: though it was sufficiently far from his enemies in Munich, it was still in Bavaria, the realm of his friend and sponsor. It was also in the very centre of Germany, and thus well positioned to realise Wagner's dream of a state theatre for a new nation, although this came at the expense of Ludwig's dream of a Bavarian-led national resurgence – the king was devastated when he realised that Wagner had finally abandoned Munich.

With the location decided upon, Wagner began looking for funding. 'Wagner associations' were set up all over Germany, and subscriptions solicited by a gang of enthusiastic disciples, but although the composer was now famous, obtaining sponsorship was a painful process. He was just able to scrabble enough money together to take on two architects, Karl Brandt and Otto Brückwald, who designed a building bearing a striking resemblance to Semper's earlier plans for Munich. Ludwig had given Semper's drawings to Wagner, along with a substantial donation, and the composer eventually and rather sheepishly admitted to the architect, 'although clumsy and artless, the theatre is executed according to your designs'.[10] The foundation stone was laid in 1872, and the building was finally, after many crises, completed in time for the first festival performance of the entire four-opera Ring Cycle in 1876. (The score had been completed in 1874, twenty-six years after Wagner began work on it.)

Pilgrims to the first Wagner Festival, including Kaiser Wilhelm, the Emperor of Mexico, Grieg, Bruckner, Saint-Saëns, Tchaikovsky, Liszt and Ludwig II (who attended incognito), arrived at the town's train station and made their way up the processional avenue to the theatre perched on its hill. There they found a building quite unlike any existing grand opera. For a start it was in the middle of nowhere – many visitors ruefully complained about the lack of comfortable facilities in the town. It had none of the sparkle of the Paris Opera or of the margravial opera house down the hill.

Neither did it share the sober grandeur of Semper's opera in Dresden, although it did borrow Semper's triumphal arch-as-entrance motif. The building had been constructed cheaply from timber and brick, and the inside was if anything more of a shock. The auditorium fully realised Wagner's reforms: it was bare and simple (no velvet swags or golden cupids here), with only a series of columns jutting further and further into the auditorium, leading the viewer's gaze to the stage, which was framed by a double proscenium. Below the stage was a submerged orchestra pit, and the audience itself was seated on rows of undifferentiated seats – 1,650 in total – as in a Greek amphitheatre. The chairs were not upholstered and must have been excruciating places to endure a five-hour opera.

The behaviour of audiences was equally odd. Mark Twain, who attended in 1891, observed that in Bayreuth 'you seem to sit with the dead in the gloom of a tomb'.

> Here the Wagner audience dress as they please, and sit in the dark and worship in silence. At the Metropolitan in New York they sit in a glare, and wear their showiest harness; they hum airs, they squeak fans, they titter, and they gabble all the time. In some of the boxes the conversation and laughter are so loud as to divide the attention of the house with the stage.[11]

In Bayreuth this kind of carry-on was strictly forbidden, and an atmosphere of hushed devotion prevailed; nevertheless not everyone was satisfied. After the first festival Wagner's own mood was one of catatonic depression. Though the crowd was rapturous, the enterprise was a financial disaster, leaving him with a deficit of 150,000 thalers. Five months later he was still sulking, and Cosima, now his wife, noted in her diary, 'R. says how sad it is that he has now reached the stage of wishing to hear nothing more about the Ring of the Nibelungen and wishing the theatre would go up in flames.'[12] There was only one more performance at Bayreuth in Wagner's lifetime.

Spartan amphitheatricality in Wagner's Festival Theatre

Wagner was not the only person to be disappointed by the premier: his close friend Friedrich Nietzsche was devastated. At first Nietzsche had shared Wagner's dream of a community united by art and wrote passionate defences of the composer's work. But Nietzsche, who had been suffering from worsening health for years, was driven away from Bayreuth a nervous wreck before the festival was over. 'My error was this,' he reminisced. 'I travelled to Bayreuth with an ideal in mind, and so I was doomed to disappointment. The preponderance of ugliness, deformity and over-ripeness utterly repelled me.'[13] After his own experiences during the Franco-Prussian War, he found Wagner's nationalism and anti-Semitism increasingly disgusting, an ironic consummation of the new Germany's banality and chauvinism. The prosaically bourgeois national audience could never live up to Nietzsche's dreams of a community united by a transcendent aesthetic experience. After Bayreuth Nietzsche retreated into a self-imposed exile of off-season spa towns and deserted ski resorts, transferring his affections to Bizet and writing ever-more vicious denunciations of his former friend. In a book published shortly before he went insane Nietzsche asked, 'Is Wagner a man at all? Is he not rather a disease? Everything he touches he contaminates. He has made music sick.'[14]

Nietzsche's reaction was characteristically prescient: after the rise of Nazism, and in light of Hitler's support of the Bayreuth Festival, many saw Wagner's music as a poisonous, dangerously seductive concoction. One of his most trenchant critics was the German philosopher Theodor Adorno. Adorno, who was Jewish and a Marxist, spent the Second World War in Californian exile, his neighbours in Los Angeles including Bertolt Brecht, Arnold Schoenberg and Thomas Mann. In this bizarre milieu, alienated by both his capitalist hosts and the fascists he had escaped, he wrote plangent critiques of the high art of his own country, especially the totalitarian impulses he detected in Wagner's music, and of the mass-produced art of the American 'culture industry'.

Adorno identified the Wagnerian *Gesamtkunstwerk* as a precursor of Hollywood, which he thought had much in common with the spectacles that had manufactured consent to the Nazi regime. Wagner's novel insistence on darkening the theatre so that all attention would be focused on the immersive illusion onstage, his megalomaniacal directorial personality, his submersion of the orchestra in a hidden pit so that no one could be distracted by the musicians at work, and his attempt to force all the arts together in order to create a sensory assault that prevented the observer from maintaining a critical distance: Adorno found all these techniques echoed and amplified in the movies. 'The occultation of production by means of the outward appearance of the product – that is the formal law governing the works of Richard Wagner,' said Adorno. Or to put it more plainly, 'The product presents itself as self-producing.'[15] For Adorno, this way of looking at theatre and cinema is problematic because it coincides with a certain way of looking at the world. In a capitalist society the work that goes into making things – from operas to cars to films – is hidden, and so it is easy to forget they are not natural, but are actually made by people who have rights and needs (and agendas) of their own. Like the joins between music and poetry in Wagner's operas, the cracks in capitalist society are smoothed over by an overpowering illusion of wholeness. But Adorno does identify a positive element in Wagner: the fragments can never be brought together. The pieces do not fit. And there is a possibility that an awareness of this failure of the *Gesamtkunstwerk* can bring our attention to the failure of capitalist society: 'The disintegration into fragments sheds light on the fragmentariness of the whole'[16] – or, as Leonard Cohen sang, 'there is a crack in everything: that's how the light gets in'.

Although Adorno, with his haut-bourgeois German background, was highly resistant to the charms of popular culture, he did have a surprising weakness for the films of the Marx Brothers: his book on the pernicious effects of capitalist reason, *The Dialectic of Enlightenment*, cites only one Marx – Groucho. Despite his snobbish scepticism about the new medium, and despite his own classical training, Adorno enjoyed the orgiastic destruction of the set of Verdi's *Il Trovatore* at the climax of the Marx Brothers' 1935 film, *A Night at the Opera*. The subversion of high culture begins when Groucho impersonates the tyrannical director of the opera house and Harpo substitutes the sheet music for *Take Me Out to the Ball Game* for the opera score, respectively revealing the dictatorial tendencies inherent in opera and the interchangeability of high and popular culture in the modern age. When these tricks are discovered all hell breaks loose, and in order to evade capture,

Groucho jumps from the director's box, and Harpo and Chico take to the stage dressed in Gypsy costumes so that they can sabotage the performance. As the tenor performs his aria, the police close in, and Harpo climbs the ropes backstage, switching the backdrop from bucolic scenery to tram stop to costermonger's handcart to a battleship with its guns pointing directly at the audience. Finally, Harpo scampers up and down the scenery, tearing the paintings to shreds, and eventually extinguishes the lights, bringing the production to a halt.

From an Adornian standpoint this gradual dismemberment of the medium seems an act of embodied criticism of the false wholeness of opera. Although the movies themselves carry on the tradition of illusionism – take it indeed to new levels – there are elements in cinema, such as Harpo Marx, with the potential to shatter this illusion. Many of these elements came from the traditions of popular entertainment from which film originally descended and which it attempts to subsume beneath its false totality, but some are too anarchic to be successfully integrated into a conventional narrative structure. The studio insisted on giving *A Night at the Opera* a dopey romantic plot in which true love conquers all and the bad guys get their comeuppance – the Marx Brothers were no longer allowed to distribute their insults even-handedly, as they had done hitherto – but this motley patchwork splits at the seams, and in retrospect all the smeared-on schmaltz fades from the memory, leaving only the image of Harpo, running up a backdrop, for ever.

Film had a ragamuffin, homeless childhood. Far from the marmoreal solidity of nineteenth-century opera, it belonged to the nomadic world of popular entertainment. Movies were shown in sideshow blackout tents – 'black tops' – at circuses, and in adapted shopfronts. Eventually, as the economic potential of film became clear, permanent cinemas were built along the lines of vaudeville theatres – the kind of buildings where the Marx Brothers began their trade. Vaudeville theatre architecture adopted the historical mishmash employed by bourgeois entertainment venues like Opera Garnier, using the new technologies of electric light and industrial terracotta to produce spectacular facades and marquees that jutted into the street. This tradition continues in London and New York, where certain areas are dominated by the architecture of entertainment – Tottenham Court Road, for example, has long been menaced by the Dominion Theatre's grotesque colossus of Freddie Mercury.

Cinemas in turn clothed themselves in a riotous patchwork of historical forms. The American 'picture palaces' of the 1920s represent the pinnacle of this tendency. One of the most outrageous is Grauman's Chinese Theatre on Hollywood Boulevard. With its handprint-studded forecourt and lurid oriental decor, it's an opium den of the masses. Cinema's theatrical drag act was popular in Germany too, albeit not with everyone. Siegfried Kracauer, a well known journalist who had trained as an architect (and was a childhood friend of Adorno's), frequently wrote on the topic of popular entertainment, which he thought distracted the new urban classes from Germany's febrile political situation, lulling them into a false sense of security. In a 1926 article entitled 'Cult of Distraction' Kracauer criticised the pretensions of cinemas to the fake unity of theatres – to the status of the Wagnerian *Gesamtkunstwerk*. Instead, he wanted cinemas to expose the cracks. 'In the streets of Berlin,' he wrote ominously, 'one is not seldom struck by the momentary insight that one day all this will suddenly burst apart. The entertainment to which the general public throngs ought to produce the same effect.'[17]

Kracauer was not the only critic of grandiose theatrical cinemas; architects such as Erich Mendelsohn were also trying to find an idiom more suitable for the new medium. Mendelsohn started off as an expressionist with a fondness for flowing organic curves instead of the sober angularity associated with high modernism. A bizarre 1917 observatory, the Einstein Tower in Potsdam, is his fullest statement of this early tendency, a bulbous erection pulsating with the life force of the universe. Mendelsohn was not sniffy about designing commercial architecture – he also did office blocks and department stores – and his clients appreciated his talent for creating striking effects on a relatively low budget. His sweeping glass facades were powerful advertisements when illuminated at night, displaying their irresistible contents to passers-by and making the street an extension of the shop floor.

In a similar vein his cinemas, such as the Universum in Berlin, designed in 1926, chucked out the chintz of earlier movie palaces, using curves and light to produce an advertising architecture outside – following Semper's earlier opera houses, the curves expressed the sweep of the auditorium – with a restrained interior that did not try to compete with the images on screen. After all, the cinema was, like Wagner's theatre at Bayreuth, plunged in darkness during screenings, so why waste money on gilded caryatids? In Mendelsohn's words there would be 'no Rococo palace for Buster Keaton, no wedding cake in plaster for *Potemkin*'; instead he helped introduce the streamlined look that would become known as art deco.[18] The bastard progeny of his Universum Kino soon populated the world: in many provincial towns an art deco cinema was the most prominent – if not the only – representative of architectural modernism. Mendelsohn himself designed one of the very first modernist buildings in Britain, the De La Warr Pavilion at Bexhill-on-Sea – another venue for mass leisure.

One of the grandest art deco cinemas is the Radio City Music Hall in New York's Rockefeller Center. Like the final scene of *A Night at the Opera*, this building marks the moment when opera and vaudeville were simultaneously overcome and subsumed by cinema. John D. Rockefeller Junior was first inspired to start work on his gargantuan city-within-a-city when he heard of the Metropolitan Opera's plan for a downtown opera house. The Met wanted an old-school free-standing edifice at the confluence of broad avenues but didn't have the cash for such an ambitious undertaking. Enter Rockefeller, who spotted the potential of a commercial development with a beacon of high culture at its heart. However, after the crash of 1929 the Met was forced to bow out, so instead the site went to a more cash-rich entertainment consortium led by vaudevillian Samuel 'Roxy' Rothafel. The music hall's gigantic auditorium, which can seat up to 6,000 spectators, was fitted out in sleek art deco style by Donald Deskey, with an enormous radiant sunburst surrounding the stage.

When it opened in 1932 Radio City was intended as a venue for high-class revues, but it was not a success – the hall and stage were so big that the performers were lost in space, their expressions invisible and their voices inaudible to the audience – and so films came to dominate the programming. In contrast to the enlightening ray of discipline envisioned in Ledoux's engraving of a theatre, the rays around this stage represent the beam of a projector, bounced off a silver screen into the eyes of the masses.

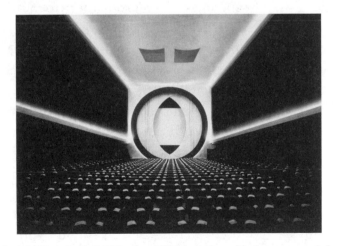

Frederick Kiesler's Guild Theatre, NYC (1929), melds the screen and the eye

We are unmistakably under a new visual regime, but what does this mean for the audience? Is cinema really a weapon of mass distraction, as Kracauer would have it, or does it also have the power to open our eyes? In order to answer that question, I'll turn to the work of another one-time German expressionist, Hans Poelzig. Like Mendelsohn, Poelzig found early success designing theatres and cinemas. In 1919 he fitted out a former circus as a 3,500-seater playhouse for famous theatrical impresario, and later Hollywood director, Max Reinhardt, whose spectacular productions continued Wagner's project of uniting the arts, using all the technological devices at hand to form an overwhelming *Gesamtkunstwerk*. Reinhardt and Poelzig's Grosses Schauspielhaus in Berlin was an incredible artificial grotto dripping with stylised stalactites and glowing with multicoloured lights – like Ludwig's Venus Grotto in Bavaria but for the entertainment and escapism of the urban masses. In contrast, Poelzig's later cinemas went, like Mendelsohn's, for a simpler look: his Kino Babylon strips decoration away in a confirmation of the Wagnerian strategy of focusing attention on the screen. But just because the audience is immersed in the flickering shadow play at the back of this platonic cave, that doesn't mean that the shadows haven't something to say about the objects that cast them. In his earlier expressionist phase Poelzig had also designed the film sets for a 1920 horror film, *The Golem*, whose director and star, Hans Wegener, was a former member of Reinhardt's troupe. In this retelling of an ancient Jewish legend, a rabbi in medieval Prague creates a monstrous slave from clay, which inevitably gets dangerously out of control. One of the central scenes features a curious architectural-cinematic allegory, which serves to demonstrate that not all films, not even all popular films, are brainless affirmations of the status quo. In the scene in question the rabbi is summoned to the palace to entertain the emperor, so he conjures a vision on a magical screen – a film within a film – showing the history of the Jews. When the philistine courtiers jeer at the pathetic sight of the wandering Jew, the palace begins to collapse, and the emperor is only saved by the timely intervention of the Golem. In gratitude, the emperor, who was about to exile the Jews from the city, grants them leave to remain. For all its questionable exoticism, we can perhaps read this as a warning to the audience.

Although architecture figures prominently on stage and screen it is for the eyes only, but there is a parallel tradition of three-dimensional navigable entertainments. These were at first exclusively aristocratic, such as Marie Antoinette's fake village at Versailles, or Ludwig II's grottoes, but at the dawn of the twentieth century the people were admitted into their own fantasy worlds – the theme parks. There were popular precedents in the form of pleasure gardens such as those at Vauxhall in London and the world's fairs of the second half of the nineteenth century, but in the age of mass leisure and electrification these grew bigger, more popular and more immersive. Some of the first and most famous theme parks were on Coney Island – a 'foetal Manhattan' in Rem Koolhaas' phrase, a place where 'the strategies and mechanisms that later shape Manhattan are tested'.[19]

Coney's development really took off with the construction of the Brooklyn Bridge in 1883, allowing the urban masses to flee there from the city. The island's first self-contained entertainment complex was an artificial steeplechase complete with mechanical horses and an elaborately landscaped track. It was enormously successful, giving proletarian riders a taste of the sporting life without the need for wealth or equestrian training. Two other developments completed the ensemble. Luna Park, which opened in 1903, had a pasteboard skyline designed by an architecture school dropout. Punctuated by over a thousand spires and domes, this city of the imagination was brilliantly illuminated at night – electrification allowed the beach to be lit too, thus permitting leisure by shifts and stoking the island's reputation for debauchery. Finally there was Dreamworld, the project of a Republican senator who went on to develop the Chrysler Building, which included such delights as a half-scale town permanently occupied by midgets (complete with midget parliament), a city block full of hysterical inhabitants that burned down on the hour, every hour, and a mock Vesuvius whose eruptions regularly flattened the toy-town on its slopes. The infinite rehearsals of these mechanical cataclysms were finally brought to an end when Dreamworld and Luna Park themselves burned down before the Great War, and in 1938 New York's merciless planner Robert Moses swept away many of the remaining profane entertainments in favour of a more tasteful – and far less interesting – landscaped park.

Coney Island offered a getaway from Manhattan for people who couldn't afford foreign travel but, as Rem Koolhaas noted, this fantastic excrescence, with its fake plazas, theme restaurants, malls and radiant spires, was gradually reabsorbed into the city itself. When the resort returned to the city it was in some cases accommodated under one roof, as in the case of the extraordinary Haus Vaterland in Berlin. This former cafe on Potsdamer Platz was remodelled in 1928 by architect Carl Stahl-Urach, designer of the expressionist sets for Fritz Lang's Mabuse films, to incorporate a cinema, a ballroom and a variety of themed restaurants. There was a Wild West bar, complete with a 'negro and cowboy jazz band', and a Viennese wine tavern where you could eat Sachertorte (the original recipe had been exclusively licensed to the Vaterland's proprietors) and admire a panorama showing the spire of St Stephen's against a starry sky, below which a model tram crossed the Danube. There was also a Bavarian *Bierkeller* with a backdrop showing the Zugspitze glowing in an artificial sunset, a Japanese tea house, a Hungarian tavern with Gypsy violinists and in the Vaterland's most Wagnerian room a 'Rhine Terrace' with a diorama giving the impression that one was overlooking the Lorelei rock. Twenty Rhine maidens danced between the diners, and every hour an artificial thunderstorm darkened the scene. In Siegfried Kracauer's words, the 'Vaterland encompasses the globe,' albeit a 'world every last corner of which is cleansed, as though with a vacuum cleaner, of the dust of everyday existence.'[20] It was a 'pleasure barracks', a 'shelter for the homeless', helping lowly office workers forget the monotony of their work, conning them momentarily into believing they were bourgeois.

The comparison with later fun parks such as Disneyland, opened in 1955, is obvious, although it was Walt Disney's intention to create a cleaned-up de-sexed substitute for 'dirty, phony' funfairs of the Coney Island type.[21] Ostensibly for children, Disneyland infantilised its adult visitors, sugarcoating the scary Cold War world for a nation that would never leave home. It's no accident that the central architectural feature of Disneyland, and the logo of the Disney Company, is based on Ludwig's castle Neuschwanstein, another hideaway from reality, its gates now open to the masses.

With the advent of computer games such as Duke Nukem 3D this fantasy kingdom has merged with domestic space and been privatised in the process. But unlike the enfoldment of theatre in the Duke of Ferrara's palace, this privatisation does not permit consumer control of content, which is ceded instead to the entertainment industry. Furthermore, such privatisation strips away entertainment's social element, that frisson of sexual possibility that belonged to Coney. Now the invention of autism machines like Google Glass threatens to take this desocialised zone into the public space of the street, degrading and monetising our interactions – and perhaps our sense of reality.

Highland Park Car Factory, Detroit
(1909–10)
Architecture and Work

And I saw big squat buildings with great endless windows behind which men were trapped like flies, moving but barely moving, as if they were struggling against I don't know what impossibility. Was that Ford? And then all around and above as high as the sky, a heavy, muffled, multiple noise of torrents of machinery, hard, stubborn machinery turning, rolling, groaning, always close to breaking but never breaking.

Louis-Ferdinand Céline, *Journey to the End of the Night*[1]

A day's output of chassis at the Ford factory, Highland Park, August 1913

Detroit, once centre of industrial modernity – home of the production line; of Motown and techno, the music its rhythms inspired; and of that most dreamily American product, the car – lies ruined, a wasteland of abandoned buildings and vacant lots. Whole downtown blocks have been vapourised – as if the Cold War Soviets had actually hit an American target – and in their place urban farms have sprouted, offering a disturbing glimpse of the future of the West. Will we return to the land as post-industrial peasants, strip-farming among the strip malls? At its peak in the 1950s Detroit was the fourth-largest city in the States, with a population of two million, the highest national median income and the highest proportion of homeowners. Then capital abandoned the city for more easily exploited labour markets, and now only 700,000 live here, a vertiginous drop that has left vast swathes of its 140 square miles deserted, its middle classes fled or plunged into penury, and their homes foreclosed.

Many of its factories, which once churned out four of every five cars in the world for General Motors, Chrysler and Ford, have fallen silent, among them a forlorn building in the northern suburb of Highland Park. A long, plain, four-storey block, its relentless rows of dusty windows now look blankly on to the street. But it was here, just before the First World War, that two Americans – one an anti-Semitic industrialist called Henry Ford, the other an architect and rabbi's son named Albert Kahn – came together in an unlikely partnership that changed the world. Their gargantuan factories produced one of the first mass-market cars, the Model T, but they also, as Ford himself was fond of pointing out, produced *men*. Ford's aim was to change society by changing the way it worked. I'll trace the strange journey of Ford's ideas – from the car plant where they were born to the houses we all live in – because work doesn't just happen in factories or offices, but also in living rooms and kitchens.

Henry Ford towered over the twentieth century that he helped to create, an indefatigable self-publicist who was hated by many but loved by a great many more. (Teddy Roosevelt, an incorrigible limelight-hogger himself, once peevishly complained that Ford's fame eclipsed that of the presidency.) Ford's ideas changed America and then the world, but although he became a revolutionary, he was at heart a deeply conservative man, just one of the many contradictions that characterised his strange personality.

Born on a farm during the American Civil War, he had a lasting suspicion of the metropolis, but created factories the size of cities. He loved the countryside and yet altered it for ever – automobiles meant suburbanisation. His cars helped free Americans, but his factories enslaved them. He venerated the past and yet helped dig its grave. He straddled the worlds of rural idiocy and industrial slavery, a crackpot colossus with a quenchless thirst for snake oil and an unerring instinct for the lowest common denominator (Upton Sinclair said his pronouncements were 'shrewdly addressed to the mind of the average American, which he knew perfectly because he had had one for forty years'[2]). He insisted on sexual propriety in his workers but had a long affair with a much younger woman. A sentimental lover of children, he persecuted his own son even when the latter was on his deathbed. Dementedly anti-Semitic, he banned the use of brass in his factories because it was a 'Jew metal'[3] – where it was used, it was coloured black to escape his notice – and his ghostwritten ravings had a marked influence on Nazism – he was decorated by Hitler in 1938 – and yet his factories employed more black Americans than any other business, helping to create a large black middle class. Finally, he adored traditional American buildings, which he bought and shipped wholesale to his historical theme park, but his factories pitilessly dispensed with the architectural past.

Unlike the fantastic factories I described in Chapter 4 – the tobacco mosque, for example, or AEG's turbine-factory-cum-temple, which were encrusted with status symbols borrowed from religious buildings – Albert Kahn's contemporary plant for Ford at Highland Park was pared down to the bare minimum. This huge shed, apparently more glass than structure, was part of a new wave of workplaces known as 'daylight factories', which super-seded the dark satanic mills of the eighteenth and nineteenth centuries. Daylight factories employed the new invention of steel-reinforced concrete (Albert Kahn and his brother patented their own highly successful system) to open up huge apertures for glaz-ing, whereas earlier brick structures had only been able to support a limited number of smaller windows without collapsing. Because light could now penetrate further into the interior, and because reinforced concrete could cover huge spans, factories could be made deeper and deeper, permitting production on a previously unthought-of scale.

The concrete frames that made this possible can be clearly read in the grids of Kahn's facades, undisguised by render, paint or ornament. It wasn't that Kahn couldn't do historical pomposity – his domestic and public buildings are a twiddly hotchpotch of dead styles, and it must be said that the Highland Park plant's street facade is lightly embellished – Kahn evidently thought that architectural nudity wasn't fit for public consumption. Neither was he unconcerned about the public image of his client; indeed, the vast impersonality of his plants became a symbol of Ford's mystique, the tabula rasa upon which he engraved his personality cult. Kahn's austere approach was simply the last word in architec-tural rationalisation, with all extraneous bobbins scraped off for *Fordist* reasons.

Fordism (called *Fordismus* in Germany and *Fordizatsia* in Russia, a truly global phenomenon that appealed to fascists, communists and capitalists alike) is a way of thinking that has become second nature to us today but was truly revolutionary in its time. It was born of Henry Ford's determination to reduce costs and raise wages in order to create a true mass market and a product with which to saturate it. By balancing ultra-efficient production with voracious mass consumption, Ford thought he had found a solution to one of the perpetual problems of modern capitalism – although he would never have put it so abstractly – that of over-production. Because manufacturers constantly struggle to raise output and push down costs, including wages, there is a tendency to run out of people to sell things to (with rock-bottom wages, who can afford consumer goods?).

Ford's solution, the popular car, was something new and controversial. His financial backers wanted him to build expensive luxury models, and thought that there would never be a mass market for automobiles. The money men abandoned him several times, and it was only on his third attempt to start a business that he found success. Consumerism was disturbing to Ford's contemporaries, who proudly languished beneath the yoke of Victorian propriety. While patriarchs and preachers still belaboured the ears of the young with the virtue of thrift, Ford remarked to the papers, 'No successful boy ever saved any money. They spent it as fast as they could in order to improve themselves.'[4] This attitude caused uproar, but it also made Ford the richest man in the world.

In order to achieve his aim of cheap cars for all, between 1908 and 1927 Ford offered only one ultra-standardised product, the Model T, which, he famously remarked, was available in 'any colour, as long as it's black'. Upton Sinclair, author of a tendentious novella about Ford called *The Flivver King* (flivver was one of the Model T's many nicknames), shared the popular disdain for the car's looks:

It was an ugly enough little creation he had decided upon; with its top raised it looked like a little black box on wheels. But it had a seat to sit on, and a cover to shelter you from the rain, and an engine which would run and run, and wheels which would turn and turn. Henry proceeded upon the theory that the mass of the American people were like himself, caring very little about beauty and a great deal about use.[5]

In the end Ford turned out to be wrong (more about that later); nevertheless, his Model T, one of the first really affordable cars, sold fifteen million units before it was discontinued under pressure from more alluring competitors. Its plain appearance was – just like the factories that made it – the direct result of the rationalisation of the production process. The body was largely built from flat panels made in Ford's own plants – until now car manufacturers had relied largely on parts made elsewhere – which were easy to produce and quick to assemble, so while the result was boxy, it was very cheap.

Ford, or rather his engineers, whose ideas he always claimed as his own, was forever tinkering with production, to speed it up, cut costs and maximise output. At first the factory at Highland Park was arranged in levels, with smaller parts being assembled on the upper storeys. Once complete, these passed down through holes, lifts and chutes to the first floor, where gangs of workers assembled the body at fixed stations. Eventually each finished body was lowered to the ground floor to be fitted to the chassis. Because the product and its parts were always (largely) the same, Ford could have highly specialised machines built to replace general-purpose lathes, saws and drills; these new machines also replaced skilled craftsmen, so he could employ cheaper unskilled labour. The machines and the gravitational workflow sped production up enormously, but the greatest leap forward was yet to come.

In 1913 Ford and his engineers hit on the idea of the mobile assembly line. In his own reminiscences Ford claimed to have been inspired by the swinging carcasses of Chicago's stock-yards, which moved on hooks from butcher to butcher, but his breakthrough was less the result of a momentary flash of inspiration than of an organic flow of small innovations, each leading to greater and greater speed. Turning the logic of the gravitational workflow on its side, an engine component called the flywheel magneto was moved on a conveyor belt past workers. Because the men didn't move but the work did, all pauses in the production process were eliminated, and the time it took to make the magneto was cut from twenty minutes to five. This innovation was quickly extended to the entire production process, and by 1914 the chassis itself was being pulled along by a chain conveyor.

Previously it had taken 12 hours 38 minutes to complete an entire vehicle, but the assembly line slashed this to just 1 hour 33 minutes. The result was a breakthrough five-hundred-dollar car and a radical transformation of the way people worked. To make such cheap cars profitably, the 15,000 men at Highland Park had to produce 1,400 cars a day, eventually accounting for 50 per cent of the cars made in the world. Each man on the line was given smaller and smaller parts of the car to complete, until he reached the pinnacle (or nadir) of specialisation, reduced to a cog in a giant machine, condemned to endlessly repeat the same limited actions. This clearly dehumanising process was defended by Ford, who airily opined, 'The average worker, I am sorry to say, wants a job in which he does not have to put forth much physical exertion – above all, he wants a job in which he does not have to think.' But this was a case of do as I say, not do as I do. Ford admitted on another occasion, 'Repetitive labour – the doing of one thing over and over and always in the same way – is a terrifying prospect to a certain kind of mind. It is terrifying to me.'[6]

Complex actions were photographically dissected in Frank and Lillian Gilbreth's
'motion studies': in long exposures small lights were attached to subjects' hands in order
to record actions, with the subjects themselves reduced to faceless blurs

These 'terrifying' innovations were part of a new approach to work that developed around the turn of the twentieth century, pioneered by Ford, Frederick Winslow Taylor, whose systematic analysis and reorganisation of labour processes became known as Taylorism, and husband and wife team Frank and Lillian Gilbreth, inventors of the motion study. Ford claimed never to have read the work of Taylor (credibly enough – he wasn't keen on books), but although there were differences in their approaches they shared the view that production could be optimised by dissecting the work process. The division of labour had been a

central feature of the Industrial Revolution since the eighteenth
century, but scientific management – as it became known – took
this to its ultimate limit. By reducing the motion of the body to
its smallest constituent parts, all 'useless' or 'unproductive'
actions could be eliminated, thus speeding up production and
maximising profit. Unlike earlier phases of manufacturing,
which split the production process between workers, scientific
management divided the *workers themselves*: each individual was
no longer a whole, but a complex of motions that could be taken
apart and put back together like components of a machine. The
new architecture of the factory line was a Frankenstein's lab in
which humans were destroyed and reassembled to twitch like
galvanic frogs in time with the speeding belt. French novelist
Louis Ferdinand Céline, who visited Detroit in the 1920s,
described the sensory assault of the factory, which remade men,
but not in the paternalistic sense Ford had in mind:

> Everything shook in the immense building, and you, too, from
> the soles of your feet right up to your ears, gripped by the vibra-
> tion that came from the window panes and the floor and the
> machinery, the jolting, vibrated from top to bottom. It turned
> you into a machine yourself, overwhelmed, every ounce of flesh
> quivering in the furious howl which filled and surrounded your
> head, and then, lower down, churned your insides and mounted
> back up to your eyes in little jolts, abrupt, numberless, relentless.
> [. . .] When at six o'clock everything stops, the noise stays with
> you, and it stayed with me throughout the night – the noise, and
> the smell of oil, just as if I'd been given a new nose and a new
> brain forever. It was as if by yielding, little by little, I became
> someone else – a new Ferdinand.[7]

Apart from fragmenting labour and labourers, the invention of
the moving production line also laid the way for the dreaded

'speed-up'. It soon dawned on Ford and his managers that in order to increase profits, the conveyor needed only to whizz by a little faster. This generated its own mean logic: those men who could not keep up were fired, and supervisors, always on hand with their stopwatches to measure the minimum time in which an action could be completed, whether screwing on a nut, welding a panel or completing an entire car, were forever revising down their timings so that every man had to work as fast as the fastest man on his best day. The factory as reconceived by Kahn and Ford had become a machine for squeezing the maximum profit from the workers inside.

Ford's plants facilitated his rationalising mania. The buildings had to be as cheap as possible – even historian Reyner Banham, an enthusiastic fan of industrial architecture, speaks of 'an air of grudging meanness' about Kahn's early plants – while providing the optimum conditions for Fordist production. This meant wide-open spaces, uninterrupted by pillars or walls, to accommodate bulky machinery and a huge workforce (and to allow every action of the workers to be minutely supervised), plenty of daylight streaming through wide windows and, perhaps most importantly of all, the potential for almost infinite reconfiguration. Like Trotsky and Mao, Henry Ford believed in permanent revolution. His engineers were always coming up with new and improved layouts for the production line, and this meant that the architecture had to be open to change too.

Kahn's building at Highland Park, with its expansive open-plan interiors, allowed this to a certain extent, but within four years of its completion it was obsolete. The birth of the moving assembly line had necessitated a new factory form. Instead of multiple storeys and the gravitational flow of ever-larger components to the finished car on the ground floor, the new building needed to be long and low in order to accommodate the lateral progress of the conveyor, and infinitely extendable in any direction, which made the increasingly built-up suburban setting of Highland Park inadequate too. The limitations of Highland Park become clear in a photo of 1914: a sloping wooden platform has been stuck to the exterior wall so that car bodies can slide down onto the chassis emerging from the building on the ground floor. The ever-expanding process has begun to send out tentacles beyond the building, an expansion that would culminate in a world empire of production and distribution, from a rubber plantation called Fordlandia in the Amazon to dealerships in England. Perhaps more than anything else, it was the contingency of Ford's buildings – his and Kahn's reconception of architecture as a process rather than something fixed and eternal – that marks them out as new. No longer borrowing the artifice of eternity from ancient temples and mosques, these workplaces are channels for a shifting system of flows.

In order to accommodate this conception of production, Ford and Kahn began work on a new site in the countryside west of Detroit, next to the River Rouge. The Rouge, as the plant was known, began as a shipbuilding factory during the First World War – which Ford, a lifelong pacifist, opposed bitterly, until he decided to profit from it instead. Converted to tractor and then car production after the war, the plant expanded as vast new buildings were added to the complex. Because these were single-storey with huge areas of glass – including glazed roofs, which meant that daylight could penetrate buildings however broad – reinforced concrete was abandoned in favour of lightweight steel frames, even cheaper and quicker to erect.

The Foundry Building was added in 1921, the Glass Plant in 1922 (Ford was the only carmaker to produce its own glass), the Cement Plant in 1923, the Power House and Open Hearth Building in 1925, the Tire Plant in 1931 (which used rubber from Ford's Amazonian plantation), and in 1939 the Press Shop, an enormous L-shaped building – one leg of which was 505 metres long, the other 285 metres – where body panels were cut and moulded. At its peak in the 1930s the Rouge complex was the size of a city: it covered two square miles, employed 100,000 workers and produced 4,000 cars a day. Raw materials were shipped in from Ford's mines via a specially dug canal, and within 28 hours had been transmuted into a car dispatched via a dedicated railway: 'From ore to auto', so the slogan went. This was the first vertically integrated operation in the world and perhaps the most complete example of vertical integration ever. Meanwhile, Ford's reach, which had spread to encompass a world empire of suppliers and distributors, also began to infiltrate the domestic sphere of his workers.

Ford's home invasion was a response to the discovery that the assembly line, though fast, wasn't quite as fast as he had hoped. The rationalised production process turned out to have one crucial flaw: workers, made of flesh and wayward thoughts, were not as dependable or obedient as machines. Ford had degraded labour, stripping it of all self-direction and creativity, but his factories brought together these degraded workers in their thousands, facilitating organisation against his methods. Resistance was inevitable. 'Soldiering' – the intentional slowing down of work – was rife, and absenteeism chronic (10 per cent in 1913). The working conditions meant he couldn't keep staff either: turnover reached an incredible rate of 370 per cent per year, which meant that in 1913 he had to hire 52,000 people to sustain a staff of 14,000. Beyond these individual forms of protest, there was also a growing clamour for unionisation, which Ford bitterly opposed.

So in 1914 Ford took a decision that set the industrial world reeling and sent his popularity through the roof: he doubled his workers' pay to the famous five-dollar day. The newspapers reacted hysterically, with headlines like 'World's Economic History has Nothing to Equal Ford Plan', 'New Industrial Era is Marked by Ford's Shares to Labourers', and 'Crazy Ford, They Called Him, Now He's to Give Away Millions'. Within a week the company had received 40,000 job applications, and twenty-four hours after his announcement a crowd of 10,000 desperate job seekers had gathered outside the Highland Park plant – in the end they were dispersed by riot police.

What was not immediately apparent was that the five-dollar day was not the simple profit-sharing scheme Ford portrayed it as. Not all workers would get it: they first had to prove themselves worthy. In order to sort the wheat from the chaff, Ford set up the Orwellian-sounding Sociological Department, which at its peak employed fifty investigators. These clipboard-wielding spies visited employees in their homes to make sure that they complied with Ford's commandments: thou shalt not live in sin; thou shalt not live in squalor; thou shalt not take in boarders (who might indulge in inappropriate relations); thou shalt not drink (Ford was a vociferous teetotaller) – and to dictate improvements, both moral and architectural. The aim was to produce a diligent, healthy, upstanding workforce with an insatiable appetite for consumer goods, and the money, unfrittered on booze and gambling, to buy them with.

Ford's paternalism was not entirely unprecedented: earlier workers' settlements established by British industrialists of a 'phil-anthropic' bent, such as the Cadbury workers' village Bourneville, were often publess and chapel-filled, reflecting the dour religiosity of their founders. What *was* new was the degree of organisation and intrusiveness that Ford brought to bear on his experiment in social engineering, and the degree of hypocrisy, for Ford, though insisting on sexual propriety in his workers, was involved in a decades-long extramarital affair with a woman thirty years his junior. The extension of surveillance into the home continued the expansionary logic of the Fordist system. From workplace to bedroom – from ore to whore, one might say – the system demanded control over every aspect of the production process, now expanded to incorporate consumption; his workers had to be able to buy his cars, or the project would fall flat. The home had become part of the factory and was – just as much as a glass or tyre plant, a steel press or an iron foundry – a site of production, reconceived as a total process, and thus also subject to the improvements of scientific management.

But Ford's imperial troops eventually retreated from the battlefield of the home. In 1921 he gave up on social engineering and shut down the Sociological Department. Continuing demands for unionisation had embittered Ford. He would not countenance bargaining with his employees and felt that his five-dollar munificence was going unappreciated. That year he instituted a speed-up that squeezed the same output from 40 per cent fewer workers, which allowed him to sack 20,000 men, including 75 per cent of his middle managers. As a result, his profits for 1921–2 jumped to $200 million. At the same time his attitude towards discipline hardened, and he turned from carrot to stick.

The man wielding that stick was Harry Bennett, an ex-prizefighter with underworld connections. Ford tasked Bennett – already head of human resources – with setting up the Sociological Department's successor body, the Service Department. Composed of thugs, ex-cons and former athletes, this was a private army of spies and enforcers, constantly on the lookout for signs of unionisation and underperformance, given free rein to bully, harass and fire employees. After the crash of 1929, when there was increased pressure from above to cut wages and staff numbers and an endless number of desperate men willing to work for any money in whatever conditions, the Service Department instigated a reign of terror. Ford employees were arbitrarily beaten while queuing to receive their pay, talking was forbidden, visits to the toilet were only permitted when cover was available, and breaks were reduced to a fifteen-minute lunch. Bennett's men tolerated absolutely no perceived transgressions: one worker was fired for wiping grease off his arms, another for buying a chocolate bar while on an errand,

and another for smiling on duty. Ford himself behaved increasingly erratically, setting his managers against one another, undermining the authority of his own son – a president at the company – and taking his approach to organisation to Maoist extremes. In his quest for total control whole departments would be wiped out overnight, and formerly powerful executives could turn up to work to find that the boss had smashed up their desks with an axe.

It was around this time that Ford also developed a passion for folk dancing.

But in 1937 Ford's attempt to crush the unions backfired horribly. Workers on their way to distribute a pamphlet titled 'Unionism, not Fordism' at the Rouge were stopped by Harry Bennett's thugs and violently assaulted. Unfortunately for Ford, several journalists and photographers were also present at the scene, and despite the Service Department's best efforts to beat them into submission and destroy their cameras, some photographs of what was dubbed the Battle of the Overpass made it into the papers. The result was a national scandal, with many placing the blame for the violence squarely on Henry Ford himself. Public support for the United Automobile Workers union surged, and in the end a broken and enfeebled Ford was compelled to accept unionisation at his plants. In later years he subsided into cantankerous senility, his triumphs obscured by a thickening fog of bad decisions and declining success. But although Ford, in closing the Sociological Department, had withdrawn from the domestic realm, his ideas and those of the other scientific managers had a powerful afterlife in America and Europe, bringing rationalisation into private lives and blurring the line between work and rest.

The most visible – and most unexpected – results of Ford's project developed across the Atlantic. Kahn's spare and clean sheds had an enormous influence on European modernists, who saw America as a 'concrete Atlantis', in Reyner Banham's

pregnant phrase: an actually existing land of mythical grandeur, where geometric forms as solid and pure as the pyramids
pointed to an heroic new way of life. American industrial buildings were latched on to by young European architects because
they heralded a future of white-hot technology, but in their
hands factories became homes. The publication of the Deutscher
Werkbund annual of 1913 was a seminal moment. In this book
Walter Gropius, future head of the Bauhaus school of art and
design, published fourteen mysterious and somewhat doctored
photographs that would have an enormous impact on avant-
gardists across Europe. One image showed the towering
cylinders of grain elevators in Buffalo, another a tall unfinished
warehouse in Cincinnati; Kahn's glazed shed at Highland Park
was included too.

These postcards from the future were reprinted in many other
works, including Le Corbusier's famous *Towards an Architecture* of
1923 (Le Corbusier doctored the prints yet more to make the buildings look even 'purer'), and they became touchstones of
Americanismus – the 1920s fascination with all things transatlantic.
But Europe had a long way to go before it caught up with American
technology and the prosperity it promised. When he published the
pictures Gropius himself was building a factory in Germany which
had adopted this American look but not the techniques behind it.
For decades historians assumed that Gropius's famous Faguswerk,
a factory in the Ruhr, was steel-framed. It certainly looks it: the
extensive glazing bends audaciously around corners to reveal the
absence of load-bearing piers. However, more recent research has
revealed that this is only a trick: the brick 'infill', carefully recessed
between the windows, is what actually holds the building up.
Trick or not, this structure helped usher in a craze for the industrial aesthetic. So too did Le Corbusier's faux-industrial villas
– also made of brick. Le Corbusier chose to carefully render his
walls, painting them white to achieve the appearance of concrete.

He said he wanted houses to be made 'on the same principles as the Ford car', and proposed a mass-produced system of reinforced concrete construction. War-ravaged Europe was suffering an unprecedented housing crisis, and industrial prefabrication offered hope of homes for all. This hope turned out to be unjustified, but if houses couldn't yet be made that way, they could at least be made to *look* that way.

Real and illusory high-tech Americanismus: a Mercedes advertisement shot outside Le Corbusier's brick and stucco house for the Werkbund exhibition, Stuttgart (1927)

Albert Kahn, however, did not share the modernists' enthusiasm for the industrial look:

I can see a very close analogy between the modern industrial building and the modern box-like, flat-roofed house, so many of which are erected today. At that, while I admire many of the modern factories, I can't say as much for many of these houses. Indeed, much already done and being done under so-called Modernism, is to me extremely ugly and monotonous.[8]

Kahn, despite running one of the biggest architectural practices in the world – in 1929 he was producing one million dollars' worth of new buildings a week – was self-effacing to the point of anonymity. In his public pronouncements he constantly attributed the genesis of his own buildings to 'Mr Ford's ideas' and proclaimed architecture to be '90 per cent business, 10 per cent art'. He had rearranged his own practice as a production line years before he began working for Ford, turning the traditional craft-based atelier of the genius architect into a collaborative and highly rationalised plan factory. Vertical integration, via the combination in one office of 400 designers, draughtsmen, clerical staff and mechanical and structural engineers (Kahn's was one of the first firms of architects to directly employ engineers), and the organisation of these specialists into project teams, allowed the streamlined production of an enormous quantity of industrial buildings – among them over 1,000 structures for Ford, 127 for General Motors, 521 factories in the USSR and numerous domestic and public buildings. So it is unsurprising that Kahn – who criticised 'temperamental prima donnas' – disliked Le Corbusier's 'notoriety-seeking' and 'inexplicable' buildings. For Kahn (and Ford) architectural simplicity was suitable for the workplace, where economy was king, but in the domestic realm, suffused with traditional values, older styles were more appropriate – and necessary to disguise the economic realities of the home in a Fordist age. This horses-for-courses approach was true functionalism in Kahn's estimation.

However, apart from the adoption of the 'purity' of Kahn's

industrial architecture for the external appearance of modernist houses, there was a deeper Fordist transformation of domestic life itself: the revolution that Ford had unleashed could not be escaped by a retreat into historical fantasy. In fact American theorists had been applying the ideas of scientific management to the home for years before Ford. The pioneering writer Catharine Beecher had first advocated a rational reorganisation of the kitchen in 1842, so one could argue, turning the conventional narrative on its head, that scientific management actually began in the home rather than the workplace. Chicken-and-egg questions aside, these attempts to reform the home and the factory demonstrate that traditional boundaries between labour and rest, home and workplace were blurring. Working-class homes, which had traditionally been sites of production (where goods were handcrafted), were now privatised as their residents went to work in factories – although as ever they remained places of work for women, who now had the double burden of factory labour and housework. Wealthier homes on the other hand had always been separated into domestic space for the owner and workspace for the staff, but as servants became unaffordable and middle-class women turned into domestic labourers, the working areas of the home attracted the attention of taste makers and reformers: enter Beecher, with her ergonomically designed kitchen.

Despite America's early lead in sorting out the home for the middle-class housewife, it was in Europe that these rationalising ideas really took off, albeit with a distinctly different political slant. Christine Frederick's enormously influential treatise *The New Housekeeping*, published in the States in 1913 and translated into German in 1921, had asked, 'If the principles of efficiency can be successfully carried out in every kind of shop, factory, and business, why couldn't they be carried out equally well in the home?' This question was eagerly taken up by a number of European architects, including Austrian Margarete Schütte-Lihotzky. Lihotzky was a political radical who later joined the Austrian Resistance and was imprisoned for five years by the Nazis as a result. One of the first female architects in Vienna, in her early career she was involved in the creation of leftist settlements on the outskirts of that city, and later in the building of workers' flats. This attracted the attention of German architect Ernst May, who hired her in 1926 to help reconstruct Frankfurt – which was desperately short of housing – along socialist principles. Within five years he and his team had built a 'New Frankfurt' of 15,000 flats, the majority of them for workers.

Lihotzky created her revolutionary Frankfurt Kitchen for these new homes. A good Marxist, Lihotzky saw the home as a site of production and women's confinement there as an impediment to their education, employment and political engagement. She was also a devotee of scientific management, and by conducting time-and-motion studies of women at work, she reorganised the kitchen to cut out wasted movement and optimise food production workflow, thus giving women time (she hoped) to take part in more politically and economically significant activities. Taking her inspiration from the kitchens of trains, the floor space of the Frankfurt Kitchen was long and narrow, the worktops were flush, the cupboards carefully placed, and the sink, bin, drying rack and oven all arranged to create an easy-to-clean assembly line for housework.

But Lihotzky also translated another, more problematic element of Taylorism into her Frankfurt Kitchen. One of the major aims of housing reformers at the time was to separate working-class kitchens from living spaces, up to now united as *Wohnküche* –'living kitchens'. They had the best of intentions in doing so: they wanted to make the home more hygienic and safe, and to dignify the labour of women by giving them a proper workplace of their own – a factory for food. However, many female New Frankfurters disliked the isolation of their new kitchens. They were separated from the life of the family and trapped in a tiny space – small for efficiency's sake, but too small for company or supervising children. The very fittedness of these first fitted kitchens also deprived their users of the opportunity to personalise their surroundings, and many women complained that they missed their old-fashioned living kitchens.

Like Ford's factories, the Frankfurt Kitchen was an attempt to remake the workplace rationally, and to remake people as fitter, happier and more productive. But, just like Ford, Lihotzky ignored the texture of everyday life, thus whittling away at the things that made work bearable or interesting. Lihotzky also left fundamental questions about gender roles unasked, reinforcing the idea that housework is just for women. However, these were not the first attempts to solve the problem of the relation of the two worlds of rest and work, home and factory in the industrial era. Some had taken a more holistic approach towards this question, taking into account the fine grain of human experience, our individual quirks, our need for variety – and our need for pleasure.

Born in 1772 in France, Charles Fourier worked for a long time but without a great deal of success as a travelling salesman. First-hand experience of the scams, waste and unfairness of the early industrial world and of the violence of the French Revolution (in which he lost his inheritance) led him to vilify what he contemptuously referred to as 'civilisation'. Inspired by his commercial background and the example of Newton, he compiled a minute and slightly deranged (or is it deviously satirical?) catalogue of civilisation's many failures and hypocrisies, including thirty-six varieties of bankruptcy and seventy-six kinds of cuckoldry. His solution was to propose the voluntary formation of communities – 'phalanxes'– which would allow their members to share and thus reduce the burden of 'civilised labour, which, far from offering any allurement either to the senses or the soul, is only a double torment'.[9] A pioneering feminist, he included the problem of domestic labour in his calculations. He saw housework as an insurmountable obstacle to happiness, since it trapped women in a routine of idiotic and unrewarding drudgery. Arguing that, 'Social progress . . . [is] brought about by virtue of the progress of women toward liberty,'[10] he suggested that domestic labour be centralised and shared. In order to allow the burden of work to be spread equally and fairly, Fourier proclaimed that the ideal phalanx would comprise 1,620 members, a number corresponding exactly to the full range of human types according to his baroquely complex schema, so allowing for the perfect combination of varying characters and talents.

The buildings in which this new way of living would flourish were called phalansteries. In his bizarre writings (he asserted that the sea would one day turn into lemonade, and that people would reach heights of seven feet and live for 144 years) Fourier described these structures in great detail: 'Instead of the chaos of little houses which rival each other in filth and ugliness in our towns, a Phalanx constructs for itself a building as perfect as the terrain permits.'[11] At the centre of this grand structure there would be meeting rooms, libraries, educational facilities and concert halls, all supplied with water pipes, central heating, ventilation and gaslight. These spaces were to be united to the workshops and residential quarters, which would be apportioned according to income – Fourier was not opposed to class divisions – by long iron-and-glass covered walkways not dissimilar to Kahn's later industrial buildings. It was a high-tech machine-age utopia, and like Ford's plants the layout of the phalanstery was determined by the flow of production, but what was being made here went far beyond mere money: it was pleasure itself.

In addition to all the specialised spaces enumerated above, the phalanstery was to contain rooms dedicated to the pursuit of the 'passions'. This points to the most original aspect of Fourier's utopian vision, his focus on psychology. For Fourier, the perfect society does not just minister to the material wants of its individual members, but also to their sensual needs, which he enumerated, following Newton's example, as if they were natural laws. This led him to an emphasis and a startling degree of candour on matters of sexuality. He condemned traditional marriage for being a form of sexual slavery especially onerous for women. Instead, Fourier said that everyone required what he called the 'amorous minimum' – the satisfaction of their sexual desires no matter how unconventional. He thus argued for the toleration of homosexuality (he was a big fan of lesbianism); for the institution of administered orgies at appointed hours in a dedicated room in the phalanstery called the Court of Love and for 'amorous philanthropy', in which lithe young things would minister to the needs of the elderly and disabled. Toleration is the wrong word for Fourier's approach: he did not encourage a wishy-washy liberal response to human diversity; he revelled in difference, which he argued promises the greatest and most interminable pleasure for all. Satiation – the one great danger in his utopia – can only be kept at bay by endless variety. Fourier extended this reasoning to labour, arguing, 'In work, as in pleasure, variety is evidently the desire of nature.'[12] Since any task gets tiresome after one or two hours he proposed a constant swapping of professional roles; Fourier, despite his organisational mania, would have hated Ford's factories.

Fourier's followers, including his American translators, cut out his references to sexuality in order not to terrify their prudish audiences, a bowdlerisation that incensed the old man. However, thus shorn of its more hair-raising aspects, Fourierism spread like wildfire. In France one of Fourier's most successful disciples was an iron stove manufacturer named Jean-Baptiste-André Godin, who built an enormous commune – he called it a Familistère – for his workers in Guise, near Paris. The large glazed shared spaces of these buildings and the centralised cleaning and cooking facilities closely followed Fourier's phalanstery, and the experiment was highly

Apartments, cooperative shops, a garden, nurseries, schools, a swimming pool and a theatre made up the Familistère built by Godin for his workers in the 1850s

successful. Founded in 1846 and later given over to cooperative ownership and management by the workers, the Familistère was only closed in 1968, when the company was taken over by Germans.

Fourier's ideas had a much greater if more evanescent impact on the other side of the Atlantic, where in the 1840s there was a national craze for collective working and living, and numerous communities sprang up with startling names like Utopia, Ohio. The most famous of these was Brook Farm, set up in the countryside outside Boston by a Unitarian minister named George Ripley in 1841. To house the commune Ripley began work on a large phalanstery

> one hundred and seventy-five feet long, three stories high, with attics divided into pleasant and convenient rooms for single persons. The second and third storeys were divided into fourteen houses, independent of each other, with a parlour and three

sleeping rooms in each, connected by piazzas which ran the whole length of the building . . . The basement contained a large and commodious kitchen, a dining-hall capable of seating from three to four hundred persons, two public saloons, and a spacious hall or lecture room.[13]

Nathaniel Hawthorne, who was briefly a member of this phalanx, immortalised his experience in a roman-à-clef entitled *The Blithedale Romance*. Unconvinced by the project, he gently mocked the aspirations of the settlers: 'We meant to lessen the laboring man's great burden of toil, by performing our due share of it at the cost of our own thews and sinews. We sought our profit by mutual aid, instead of wresting it by the strong hand from an enemy, or filching it craftily from those less shrewd than ourselves (if, indeed, there were any such in New England).'[14] But economic problems quickly led to the collapse of the commune – quite literally, when the yet incomplete and uninsured phalanstery building burned to the ground in 1847. However, Hawthorne identified other sources of potentially calamitous discord: in *The Blithedale Romance* communal life disintegrates when a tangled network of desire develops between the narrator, his puritanical friend Hollingsworth and two young ladies. Hawthorne was familiar with Fourier's work, and in one scene in *The Blithedale Romance* his narrator mischievously brings the suppressed erotic element to the surface.

I further proceeded to explain, as well as I modestly could, several points of Fourier's system, illustrating them with here and there a page or two, and asking Hollingsworth's opinion as to the expediency of introducing these beautiful peculiarities into our own practice. 'Let me hear no more of it!' cried he, in utter disgust . . . 'Nevertheless,' remarked I, 'in consideration of the promised delights of his system, – so very proper, as they certainly are, to be appreciated by Fourier's countrymen, – I cannot but wonder that universal France did not adopt his theory at a moment's warning . . .' 'Take the book out of my sight,' said Hollingsworth with great virulence of expression, 'or, I tell you fairly, I shall fling it in the fire!'[15]

Hawthorne implies that the suppression of Eros by reformers like the mini-Robespierre Hollingsworth can lead only to social discord, and one might speculate that if Eros had not been suppressed in the American phalansteries, these communities might have had a bit more to offer their increasingly disillusioned inhabitants than hard work and bad food. There was a lesson for Ford too in *Blithedale* and in Fourier as a whole: by refusing to satisfy the sensual needs of consumers and workers, Ford's enterprise was doomed to failure.

Ford's attempt to create a harmonious and optimally profitable industrial universe turned sour because he tried to chase pleasure out of the spheres of production and consumption. Ford's Sociological Department took a prescriptive and antiquated view of sexual morality, and in trying to impose his own hypocritical Victorian values on his workers at home, he alienated their emotional lives from work at the very same time as attempting to reconcile the two. Then, sensing his failure, he turned from administrative compulsion (via the sociological survey and the five-dollar day) to the brute force of his Service Department, and was doomed. Meanwhile, Ford's rival Alfred Sloan at General Motors had spotted a chink in the armour of the world's greatest manufacturer. There was no way GM could out-rationalise Ford, so instead they decided to offer consumers a wider range of more attractively designed products, putting sensual pleasure back into the sphere of consumption although not addressing the parallel problem of the denial of pleasure in labour. Nonetheless by the mid-1920s GM was outselling Ford for the first time, and after resisting the entreaties of his executives for years, in 1927 Ford was finally convinced to discontinue the Model T in favour of the more seductively styled Model A – now available in several colours besides black. But Ford had lost his advantage, and he would never regain his position as the world's greatest manufacturer.

Michael Ochs Archives / Getty Images

Sex in the Rouge: Martha and the Vandellas perform their 1965 hit 'Nowhere to Run'.

Despite Ford's own failure, Fordism itself survived – and indeed flourished – after the Second World War by mutating into something that would have deeply disturbed its founder. This change was fuelled by credit – of which Henry Ford, ever watchful for 'Jewish' finance, disapproved – and sex. The new Fordism erupts into seductive life in a performance of Martha Reeves and the Vandellas' hit 'Nowhere to Run', which was filmed on the assembly line of the Rouge in 1965. (Motown's boss, Berry Gordy, had worked at the factory before starting his record label.) Three

young and impossibly glamorous singers dance among the workers building Ford Mustangs, with the implicit equation of the
women, as consumable sex objects, with the interchangeable mass-
produced parts around them. The song's producers actually used
car parts – shaken snow chains – to create an insistent percussive
effect running throughout the track, a precursor of the starker
industrial sound that was to emerge from Detroit with techno in
the late 1980s. The rattling chains refer to the tortured and inescapable relationship described in the song, but they are also the
sound of the all-pervasive force of industrial capital, which has
invaded the realm of Eros via pop culture: 'nowhere to run,
nowhere to hide'. Rest has become 'leisure' and pleasure has
become work – a pretext for consumption.

An archly self-aware celebration of the same process appears
in satanist and avant-garde artist Kenneth Anger's short film
Kustom Kar Kommandos. Filmed the same year as the Vandellas'
video, this three-minute slice of pastel-hued homoerotica shows
a young man lovingly buffing the paintwork of his car to the
soundtrack of the Phil Spector-produced hit, 'Dream Lover';
incredibly, the film was funded by a $10,000 grant from the Ford
Foundation.

Ford would not have approved. Nevertheless, in later life –
seeming to realise that he had gone wrong somewhere but still
unable to acknowledge the importance of sensuality – Ford had
begun to grope backwards towards American utopianism, arguing that rural life should be industrialised, and industrial life
agriculturalised, as he put it. By this he meant that he wanted to
decentralise industry, so that the huge factory complexes that he
had created were broken up into smaller establishments spread
out in bucolic settings. His aim was for workers to reunify work
and life in some kind of prelapsarian industrial Eden. However,
his Arcadian impulse could never have competed with the more
potent attempts of late Fordism to harness the power of the

domestic sphere that had developed after the war: the use of advertising and pop culture to eroticise labour and consumption in the home. The crucible in which this alchemical process took place was the kitchen, where, in a perverted fulfilment of Ford's hopes, domesticity was industrialised and industry domesticated.

The middle-class American dream of the rationalised kitchen, which had begun in the 1840s with Catherine Beecher, was now marketed to a much broader section of the populace, the new middle class, with its disposable income provided by Fordist labour. Capitalists wanted to reabsorb some of this 'surplus' wealth back into their profits, and by portraying the work of the housewife as an effortless joy, advertising – its imagery rife with sexual innuendo – powered up the home, and labour and consumption within it, with an electrifying erotic charge, making the kitchen and its gadgets irresistible symbols of very traditional femininity. Thus domesticity was brought completely into the industrial universe, as a site of mingled consumption and labour but on a purely individualistic footing. Despite the emphasis on pleasure, there is nothing of Fourier's phalanstery here. There is no shared reduction in the burden of domestic chores – the promise of 'workless washdays' turned out to be an empty one as manufacturers ramped up hygiene standards in order to keep people buying more and more specialised appliances. There are no futuristic glazed streets, stately pleasure domes or provisions for the 'amorous minimum', just lonely greed dressed up as happiness. Nor is there anything of Margarete Schütte-Lihotzky's political vision for the modern kitchen. The kitchen is painted as a place of consumption, not work, although of course work still goes on there, and its users are not freed by convenience but enslaved by it.

These two approaches towards work and the home – Fourierist and Fordist – met in their death struggle on another continent far from the steamy kitchens of American suburbia. The Soviet Union might seem an unlikely place to find Fordism, or Fourierism for that matter, as party orthodoxy saw Fourier as a faintly bonkers precursor of 'scientific socialism', but Ford was lionised during the Russian Revolution. His portrait was hung beside Lenin's in factories, and the party invited Albert Kahn to build hundreds of plants between 1928 and 1932 as part of the first five-year plan. (Initially most of these produced tractors, but they were later converted to build the tanks that crushed the Nazis.) The popularity of Fordist ideas in the USSR demonstrates a peculiar similarity between capitalist and communist economies, both of which tend to disregard the importance of satisfaction in work in favour of the imperatives of hyperproduction, whether in the cause of profit or some future utopia. However, during the heady early years of the USSR – before Stalinist orthodoxy closed like a vice – there was room for more imaginative rethinkings of the way that life and work might be organised in a communist utopia. Lenin himself was deeply inspired by a Fourierist novel, *What Is to Be Done?* by Russian writer Nikolai Chernyshevsky, which proposed the construction of gigantic glass communes dispersed throughout the countryside.

Feminism also flourished, and revolutionaries such as Alexandra Kollontai, later Soviet ambassador to Norway, the first female ambassador in the world, argued that under communism traditional families and gender roles would wither away, childcare would be collectivised and free love would reign. Such ideas blossomed in architecture, and a group of young visionaries called the constructivists designed (but did not build – there was very little money or opportunity for building during the post-revolutionary period) structures that would usher in new communal ways of living and working. The most famous of these was Vladimir Tatlin's 1919 Monument to the Third International, a gigantic canted tower of high-tech iron and glass, designed to hold rotating assembly rooms. The unbuilt tower points eternally to a glorious future, unlike the static, status-quo-affirming Eiffel Tower to which it is a riposte.

In later years the constructivists managed to get a surprising amount of work built, even during Stalin's first five-year plan. Mosei Ginzburg's famous 1930 Narkomfin building in Moscow is a touchstone of late constructivist design, a huge communal house designed to be a 'social condenser' – a means of reshaping society by bringing people together in new combinations. It was meant to be a prototype for all future Soviet housing, but in reality very few domestic buildings were put up during this period. Industrialisation was a much higher priority for the party, and most urban citizens continued to live in dirty overcrowded tsarist apartment blocks. The contrasting abstraction of Ginzburg's clean white structure was inspired by European modernists like Le Corbusier – and by the machine aesthetic, which was also in vogue in Russia during the 1920s and early 1930s – but Ginzburg wanted these formal innovations to adorn a socialist utopia, not just the villas of rich industrialists. Accordingly, the Narkomfin building was to contain a public kitchen and dining room, a gym, a reading room, child-care facilities and shared clothes-washing facilities – so far, so Fourierist. The idea was that in the communist future sleeping would take place in private individual cells, and all other activities, both leisure and labour, would be shared. Even sex would be unchained by the revolution.

But the constructivists – tempering their aspirations to fit in with party orthodoxy, which had retreated from the enthusiastic idealism of the 1920s – recognised that people could not suddenly be forced into this new way of life. To ease the transition, the Narkomfin building included a variety of living spaces, gradated from traditional flats to dormitories. The 200 prospective residents were meant to come in one end as bourgeois nuclear families, and pop out the other as shiny new communists: this was the home reconceived as a production line for people, not just 'a machine to live in', which was Le Corbusier's fundamentally different indus-trial metaphor. Social change is built into the structure – not indeterminate change, as in Ford and Kahn's River Rouge plant, but change towards a preconceived form, communism. Despite its Fourierist touches, the Narkomfin building also shared something of Ford's approach to domesticity: both attempted to eradicate private life, whether by paternalistic supervision in the case of Ford's Sociology Department, or by minimising private spaces in Ginzburg's building, in order to harmonise domesticity and labour, fusing the two in an optimally productive relationship.

This 'utopia' never came. Just as the Narkomfin building was completed Stalin tightened his grip on thought and expression, imposing his own deeply backward views on society. The same year he shut down the Zhenotdel, the women's section of the party, thus ending attempts to revolutionise gender roles. Uncle Joe didn't much like modernist architecture either: he wanted people to live in bombastic classical apartments, not futuristic laboratories for a new way of life. Foreign influences were henceforth considered deeply suspicious, and Ernst May and Margarete Schütte-Lihotzky, who had fled Nazi Frankfurt to help build the new Russia along with numerous other left-leaning Germans, were forced to leave the country. Many native modernists were not so fortunate, and ended up being 're-educated' or worse. The Narkomfin building was one of the first canaries to fall off its perch in this airless coal mine. Shortly after its completion a party bigwig insisted on having a private penthouse constructed on the roof exactly where a communal terrace was meant to be, and its builders felt compelled to denounce their effort as a failed experiment. Future housing projects bowed to Stalin's retrograde ideas, and utopian communalism fell out of fashion for decades.

After many years of hibernation, however, these ideas re-emerged blinking into a brave new Soviet dawn. In the wake of Stalin's death in 1953 Nikita Khrushchev initiated a thaw in Russian intellectual life. For a while concepts that had been unmentionable in the 1930s crawled out of the woodwork, and constructivism was reassessed: it was no longer counter-revolutionary 'formalism' but a homegrown socialist art movement to be (cautiously) proud of. The residents' committee of the Narkomfin building, which had fallen into neglect and its facilities adapted to other uses, petitioned for a reinstatement of the original communal areas and programmes. This was never granted, but for a while Fourierist ideas of shared cooking, cleaning and childcare were in the air. In fact, between 1957 and 1959 a variety of housing types were considered as part of a crash programme of home building, during which millions of citizens were rehoused in clean new apartments. Both communal *and* private kitchens were promised, as adherents of late-Fordist ideas about work and domesticity battled Fourierist-style communalists for supremacy in Soviet architecture. On the one hand it was argued that Russians needed private well-appointed homes as sites for communist consumption, and on the other that dormitories with shared facilities were more in accordance with socialist principles. Combinations of the two were also suggested, with the proposal that consumer goods be publicly owned so that they could be rented out by private householders.

Eventually the Fordists won the argument, to the lasting economic detriment of the USSR, which could not sustain American levels of consumerism. But it seemed for a while that it might: this was the tantalising era of Red Plenty, to borrow Francis Spufford's name for the brief period when the USSR seemed to be overtaking the capitalist West. These days, with the ignominious collapse of the Soviet empire still fresh in our memories, we tend to forget that there was a moment – between the launch of Sputnik in 1957 and the Cuban Missile Crisis of 1962 – when Russia seemed like it might win the Cold War. The Soviets had embraced and even surpassed Western technological achievements; they were winning the space race (Yuri Gagarin went into orbit in 1961); their economy was growing faster than any other bar Japan's; they were producing an incredible number of engineers and scientists;

and they were leading the field in cybernetics in order to create – it was desperately hoped – a microchip-planned economy. Khrushchev knew that he had to offer the Russian people, worn down by decades of war, famine and enforced ideological conformity, a concrete hope of a better future – no longer some misty communist Neverland, but a real, unambiguous fulfilment of current needs and wishes. In an abysmal misjudgement, the year 1980 was chosen as the one in which Soviet society would overtake America. In twenty years the communist cornucopia would overspill, in Spufford's words, with 'Ladas quieter than any Rolls-Royce. Zhigulis so creamily powerful they put Porsche to shame. Volgas whose doors clunked shut with a heavy perfection that made Mercedes engineers munch their moustaches in envy.'[16]

People really believed this stuff, and not without reason. Previously unheard-of material comforts were becoming available to ordinary Soviet citizens. Shops were full, and the streets were packed with people dressed in bright new clothes. But the party – which was all too aware of the inadequacies of the country's creaking corrupt economy – knew that Khrushchev's vision was unattainable. He was deposed in 1964, his promises officially forgotten, but they lived on in the minds of Russians, steadily eroding the legitimacy of the party. So why on earth did Khrushchev make his ludicrous promise of 'communism in twenty years'? The blood-soaked Stalin era weighed heavily on his conscience, for a start, and it seems he genuinely wanted to make amends by delivering the happiness that communism had always held out to its adherents. But this was as much a response to international as domestic politics.

In 1959 the world's two superpowers had locked horns on one of the most bizarre battlegrounds in history, a show kitchen at the American National Exhibition in Moscow. The famous 'kitchen debate' that took place there between Khrushchev and Vice-President Nixon was a pivotal moment in the Cold War, when the Fordist American dream of mass consumerism went head to head with the Soviet ideal of Red Plenty. The American show kitchen was consciously intended as propaganda by white goods – or rather pastel pink and canary-yellow goods, for in true late Fordist style the units and appliances supplied by General Electric were available in a wide variety of colours. Consumer choice, then as now, stood in for democratic representation: this was pure kitchen-sink politics.

The futuristic machines on display included a robotic floor-washer and a mobile dishwasher. Faced with all this automation, Khrushchev asked Nixon, 'Don't you have a machine that puts food into the mouth and pushes it down?' His remark brims over with contempt for capitalist greed and sloth but does nothing to disguise the fact that he had been wrong-footed by the everyday opulence on display. The terms of the Cold War had been changed: the Americans, who were losing the space race at the time, had withdrawn to the home front, and Khrushchev's insistence on victories won in space and the lab could not compensate for the more tangible defeat in the arena of the kitchen. No matter that the Russian papers pointed out (quite rightly) that few Americans could afford such high technology and that most US homes were bought on crippling mortgages; people queued in their thousands to file past these artefacts from another civilisation, each visitor being implanted with a seed of candy-coloured doubt. There was no longer any Fourierist alternative of communally shared labour on offer. Late Fordism – with its welding together of consumption and production, work and pleasure in the private home – prevailed, and those rattling chains echoed across the Iron Curtain: 'nowhere to run, nowhere to hide'.

Fourier, with his emphasis on communal living and sensory pleasure, might seem to offer an alternative to this late Fordist consensus. But Fourier, as I've hinted a few times during this chapter, was not so far from Ford after all. His mania for categorisation descends from the same Enlightenment motives that lie behind Ford's rationalising approach to work, and with his emphasis on 'passions' he strangely anticipated the condition of late Fordism. 'A general perfection in industry', he argued, 'will be attained by the universal demands and refinement of the consumers, regarding food and clothing, furniture and amusements.'[17] He continued: 'My theory confines itself to utilising the passions now condemned, just as Nature has given them to us and without in any way changing them.'[18]

But, as it turned out, passions *were* altered by being industrialised. Fourier wanted to pin down and dissect protean human sexuality just as minutely as Ford cut up the worker's body, and the scars left by his surgeon's knife can be seen today in the reports of marketeers, whose investigations into the fifty-seven varieties of desire are carried out in the service of consumerism. As a result, pop culture and advertising have supplied us with new objects of desire, suffused with the glow of promised erotic pleasure. By taking on board the areas of human experience suppressed by Henry Ford and incorporating them into the realm of consumption, late Fordism successfully and profitably integrated passions into industrial society. But there is one aspect of Fourierism that has never been realised, Google workers on beanbags notwithstanding. 'Life,' Fourier wrote, 'is a long torment to one who pursues occupations without attraction. Morality teaches us to love work: let it know, then, how to render work lovable, and, first of all, let it introduce luxury into . . . the workshop.'[19] In our post-Fordist era, when manufacturers have stopped paying workers enough to buy their products and shipped their operations to cheaper labour markets instead, the luxurious workshop seems further away than ever. The sea hasn't turned into lemonade yet, either.

E.1027, Cap Martin
(1926–9)
Architecture and Sex

And thou, O wall, O sweet, O lovely wall,
That stand'st between her father's ground and mine!
Thou wall, O wall, O sweet and lovely wall,
Show me thy chink, to blink through with mine eyne!
William Shakespeare, *A Midsummer Night's Dream*

Eileen Gray's villa rests on the rocks of the Riviera like a beached liner.

A dark spot bobs in the waters of the Riviera, a puncture wound in the glittering surface of the sea. Slowly the waves return the object to the shore. There, watched over by a villa that had obsessed him for decades, the body of Le Corbusier, the twentieth century's most famous architect, lies as if sunbathing on the beach. Some have speculated that his death on this glorious August day in 1965 was a suicide. He had become gloomy and withdrawn after the recent loss of his mother and his wife, and he had remarked to a colleague, 'How nice it would be to die swimming toward the sun!'[1] This is not a story about death, however, but of love – and sex. It is the story of Le Corbusier's mad passion for the house on the cliff and the resentment of the designer of that house, Eileen Gray. Motionless stone may seem the anaphrodisiac opposite of living flesh, but in this chapter I'll reveal the secret sex life of buildings, their capacity to enflame and arouse. It's a story about houses made for lovers, structures that thwart love and people who love buildings themselves. Although some of the characters that populate this story – like the woman who married the Berlin Wall – may seem extreme cases, the fact is that our sex lives mostly take place in architectural surroundings. So what do buildings do to our libidos?

Before I try to answer that question, let's go back to the scene I described above: the sun-drenched beach, the celebrity corpse and, most important of all, the cliff-top villa. Though it was Eileen Gray's first architectural work, the house at Cap Martin is a superbly accomplished piece of design. Its streamlined white form rests on the rocks like a beached ocean liner, its terraces and windows overlooking the Mediterranean below. The nautical theme continues in the furniture and fittings, which are inspired by the romanticism of holidays on boats and trains – 'le style camping' as Gray called it. Everything is cunningly adapted to maximise the available space: drawers pivot rather than pulling out, beds fold into walls, and the whole performs a kind of mechanical ballet. This is architecture brought to twisting, sliding life.

The house is more than just a technical marvel, however; it is also a love poem, a present for Gray's partner Jean Badovici. The name E.1027 is an encoded combination of their initials: E for Eileen, 10 for J (J being the tenth letter of the alphabet), 2 for B and 7 for G. Paradoxically, by disguising their relationship as an anonymous formula Gray speaks volumes about her secretive and enigmatic personality. Even her close friends had little idea of her inner life, and in later years she destroyed most of her personal correspondence. But although she kept her emotional life to herself it seems she was an adventurous and unconventional woman.

Gray left her aristocratic home in Ireland at a young age for the excitement of Paris. There she studied art and socialised with the expatriate lesbian milieu around Gertrude Stein and Djuna Barnes, forming a romantic attachment with a famous chanteuse named Damia, an extravagant character who was notorious for walking her pet panther on a leash. One of Gray's most enduring relationships was with Badovici, editor of an architectural review and fourteen years her junior. In 1924 he asked her to build him a house, and after its completion in 1929 the couple spent most of their summers there. The structure is very much determined by its purpose as a lovers' retreat. The central living room can also be used as a bedroom, a 'bedroom-boudoir' as Gray called an earlier dual-purpose room she designed. Its focal point is a large divan that unfolds to become a bed.

On the wall above this piece of furniture Gray pasted a marine chart inscribed with the words *L'invitation au voyage*, the title of a poem by Baudelaire. The poem's subject could hardly be more appropriate:

> My child, my sister,
> Think of the rapture
> Of living together there!
> Of loving at will,
> Of loving till death,
> In the land that is like you!
> [. . .]
> There all is order and beauty,
> Luxury, peace, and pleasure.

Baudelaire could almost be describing this secluded spot overlooking the sea at Cap Martin. The poem continues:

> Gleaming furniture,
> Polished by the years,
> Will ornament our bedroom[2]

But unlike Baudelaire's patinated antiques the furniture in E.1027's bedroom-boudoir shone with the machine finish of chrome and glass.

Gray had not always been such a technophile; she made her name as a furniture designer creating art nouveau lacquerwork, such as a chair with arms like writhing snakes, a piece later owned by Yves Saint Laurent. She learned the technique of lacquerwork, a painstakingly slow process requiring the application of numerous slow-drying layers, from a Japanese craftsman in Paris. But as the century progressed she moved away from such handcrafted 'theatricality', as she later disparagingly called it, turning instead to cuboid forms influenced by the work of the De Stijl movement. In E.1027 her modernist furniture reaches its apogee and starts to evolve into something else – to disappear. At one end of the spectrum her pieces in the 'camping style' fold away to become portable and almost invisible, while at the other extreme pieces are built into the walls or seem to become the walls themselves. The furniture playfully re-enacts the transition between her two careers, from interior designer to architect: one grows organically out of the other.

The bedroom-boudoir of E.1027

Her borderline furniture/architecture is embodied nowhere more perfectly than in the screens she designed. Gray made many of these throughout her career, and always used them in her own houses. They were often translucent: some were made of cellulose (an early plastic) and others of wire mesh. One famous example from the early 1920s was made of black-lacquered panels that pivot on steel rods. This piece of furniture developed from a hall she had designed for a house on the rue de Lota in Paris. This room was lined with similarly shaped panels, which seemed, at the end of the hall, to curve inwards and disintegrate. Moving through the space, one had the impression that the building itself fragmented as one moved from the public realm of the street towards its private, inner recesses.

The 'brick screen' that Gray developed from this interior was a further step towards mobile architecture: the solidity of a wall disintegrates into manipulable units, allowing the viewer to see through the barrier. In Gray's work architecture, usually static and opaque, dissolves to become mobile and transparent. Her screens divide – and unite – architecture and furniture, seen and unseen, private and public. The implications of this for sexuality are enormous. Throughout history, architecture has been used to keep sex out of sight, and our sex lives are conventionally hidden between the four walls of our bedrooms. The story of Gray's house illustrates what happens when these walls begin to break down.

Gray continued her use of screening devices in E.1027, most notably at the front door. The living room is shielded from the building's entrance by a curved cupboard that prolongs the experience of entering the building. Gray described the journey into a house in sensual, almost erotic terms, as 'a transition that still keeps the mystery of the object one is going to see, which keeps the pleasure in suspense'. In an even more visceral statement, one that would give Freudians a field day, she said, 'Entering a house is like the sensation of entering a mouth which will close behind you.'[3] Besides prolonging the feeling of penetration, the screen also protects the occupants from the eyes of visitors, acting as a marker for the ambiguity of the central space, which is public and private, both a place for making love and for receiving guests. Three stencilled phrases in the hall seem intended to slow visitors further. By the entrance to the living room is *entrez lentement* (enter slowly); by the entrance to the service area, *sens interdit* (a phrase literally meaning 'forbidden direction', which also sounds like 'forbidden feeling' and perhaps 'without prohibitions' – *sans interdit*); and beneath the coat hooks, *défense de rire* (no laughing). Gray's jokey admonitions warn incautious visitors to avoid potentially embarrassing interruptions, but they also seem to hint at the paradisiacal freedoms of her lovers' retreat, where nothing is forbidden.

One regular visitor at E.1027 was Le Corbusier, a close friend of Badovici. Le Corbusier, as he called himself – he was born Charles-Édouard Jeanneret – became the most prominent figure in twentieth-century architecture not least because he was a skilled self-publicist and a tireless promoter of the 'new architecture'. He was also politically ruthless and willing to work with any regime – including the Vichy government – if he thought it would get things built. His structures span the world, from a museum in Tokyo to an entire state capital in India. Yet despite his global success he developed a lifelong obsession with Gray's little house by the sea. He wrote a rapturous postcard to her after a stay there in 1938: 'I am so happy to tell you how much these few days spent in your house have made me appreciate the rare spirit that dictates all the organisation inside and out. A rare spirit that has given the modern furniture and installations such a dignified, charming, and witty shape.'⁴ This was partly his gratified ego responding to the many Corbusian touches in Gray's villa. The slender steel columns, or *pilotis* as Le Corbusier called them, which lift the structure above the ground and which Gray had added at Badovici's suggestion; the accessible roof; the horizontal windows and open-plan interiors: all these conform closely to Le Corbusier's 'Five Points of Architecture'. But leaving aside these formal similarities, Gray's house strayed quite far from Le Corbusier's programme. This divergence stemmed from a fundamentally different idea of what architecture should be.

She explicitly argued against Le Corbusier's most famous maxim. 'A house,' she said, 'is *not a machine to live in* [my emphasis]. It is the shell of man, his extension, his release, his spiritual emanation.'[5] In accordance with this principle, she humanised the machine-made sterility of modern design with playful and personal touches such as the chair based on the Michelin Man, the life ring on the terrace and the stencilled puns on the walls.

In a further divergence from Le Corbusier's canon, Gray did not provide the uninterrupted spaces the master had insisted on. His houses, with their pioneering ribbon windows and open-plan interiors, had a tendency to transparency, and he once wrote that a building should be 'like an architectural promenade. One enters and the architectural vista shows itself immediately to view.'[6] Gray's buildings are more opaque. Although it has generous ocean views, E.1027 is full of screens and obstructions, making the experience of moving around it labyrinthine and suprising. Gray's ideal of living was more secretive than Le Corbusier's. 'The civilized man,' she wrote, 'knows the modesty of certain acts; he needs to isolate himself.'[7] The many visual obstacles in E.1027 contrive to provide this modesty while preserving the airiness of the open plan.

By the early 1930s Gray's relationship with Badovici had become strained. She found his infidelity unendurable and objected to his raucous drinking sessions. Gray was an independent person who refused to be tied down by people or possessions, no matter how close they had once been to her, and so she left the villa she had created at Cap Martin. After she had gone Badovici occupied E.1027 alone, with Le Corbusier his frequent guest. In 1938 – perhaps during the same visit that inspired his congratulatory note to Gray – Le Corbusier asked Badovici if he could add a series of murals to E.1027's walls. The resulting paintings are garish and jarring, disrupting the calm and balanced spaces of Gray's original design. The images, which bear more than a passing resemblance to Picasso's work, depict naked women in erotic poses. Some, inspired by a formative journey that Le Corbusier made to Algeria in his youth, seem to show harem or brothel scenes. A large mural in the living room represents two nude women with a child floating between them. One of these figures has a swastika on her chest – Le Corbusier never satisfactorily denied the charge of Nazi sympathies. What is going on in this strange and provocative painting – is it an imagined birth scene? A reference to Gray's sexuality?

Whatever their significance to Le Corbusier, Gray – who regarded them as a violation of her creation – was appalled by the paintings. But she was not stung to action until Le Corbusier wrote a journal article on them in 1948. In one passage he damned the house with faint praise: 'This house that I animated with my paintings was very pretty, and could well have existed without my talents,' he condescends, adding, 'The walls chosen to receive nine large paintings were the most colourless and insignificant walls.'[8] The insult was compounded by the omission of any reference to Gray. It was not the first time that her name had been erased from the historical record, an instance of the institutional sexism that still plagues architecture, and in succeeding decades E.1027 was often attributed to Badovici alone or even to Le Corbusier himself.

Badovici then wrote to Le Corbusier – at Gray's request, her biographer Peter Adam surmises: 'What a narrow prison you have built for me over a number of years, and particularly this year through your vanity . . . [E.1027] served as a testing ground, embodying the most profound meaning of an attitude that formally banished paintings. It was purely functional, that was its strength for such a long time.' Le Corbusier's sarcastic reply seems directed at Gray:

You want a statement from me based on my worldwide authority to show – if I understand your innermost thoughts – to demonstrate 'the quality of pure and functional architecture' which is manifested by you in the house at Cap Martin, and has been destroyed by my pictorial interventions. OK, you send me some photographic documents of this manipulation of pure functionalism . . . then I will spread this debate in front of the whole world.'[9]

As nasty as it is disingenuous, his reply contradicts his earlier effusive praise of the villa. It also contradicts an unequivocal statement he had made on the topic of wall paintings. 'I admit the mural is not to enhance the wall,' he wrote, 'but on the contrary, a means to violently destroy the wall, to remove from it all sense of stability, weight, etc.'[10]

In the same year that this embittered debate was taking place Le Corbusier wrote to Badovici criticising numerous aspects of the building. Tellingly, he particularly objected to the screen in the entrance hall. He called it 'pseudo' and suggested that Badovici should have it removed. The screen of course keeps the living room private from the prying eyes of visitors. It seems his murals in E.1027, like his attempt to remove the entrance screen, were intended to render the villa transparent. He painted one mural – 'a means to violently destroy the wall' – directly onto the screen itself, incorporating Gray's stencilled words *défense de rire* and *entrez lentement*. By his symbolic removal of the walls, it seems that he intended to look into the house, and with the erotic scenes he painted, he supplied the imagined objects of his voyeuristic fantasy.

There is an extraordinary photograph of Le Corbusier at work on the murals. Apart from his pipe he is completely naked, the only known photograph to show him so. His decision to paint these images while nude speaks to the fact that he must have understood the act as a primitive violation of the architectural space. We can turn to another modernist pioneer here, an Austrian architect named Adolf Loos, for an insight into the contested

Le Corbusier at work on his murals at E.1027 (the scar on his thigh was caused by a propeller in a boating accident)

– and surprisingly sexualised – place of wall painting within modern architecture. Loos is a pivotal figure because he was one of the earliest and most vocal critics of architectural decoration, his views heralding the stripped-down, minimalist appearance of twentieth-century design. He was a great inspiration to both Le Corbusier and Gray – Gray's first architectural design is based on one of his drawings. In his 1908 essay 'Ornament and Crime' Loos argues, with his own distinctive logic, that 'the evolution of modern culture is synonymous with the removal of ornamentation from objects of everyday use . . . The urge to decorate one's face and anything else within reach is the origin of the fine arts. It is the childish babble of painting. But all art is erotic. A person of our times who gives way to the urge to daub the walls with erotic symbols is a criminal or a degenerate.'[11]

In his writings Loos placed great importance on the separation of public facades from private interiors. His buildings have plain white exteriors, which in his day were considered scandalously minimal, even naked. His interiors on the other hand employ complex spatial effects and rich materials such as marble and fur to create a feeling of sensual intimacy. Gray's interiors pick up on this cocooning effect, while Le Corbusier in contrast extends the blankness of Loos's facades into his interiors, and merges the public and private with his long windows and hybrid spaces, which are neither entirely inside nor outside. In her fascinating book *Privacy and Publicity* Beatriz Colomina points out that Le Corbusier was very conscious of the difference between his approach to building and that of Loos. He reminisced: 'Loos told me one day: "A cultivated man does not look out of the window; his window is a ground glass; it is there only to let the light in, not to let the gaze pass through."'[12] In contrast to Corbusian transparency, Loos's windows are usually obscured by built-in furniture, curtains or screens, devices that Gray would later use to complicate her own interiors. In E.1027 Le Corbusier was willing to tear down such barriers with his own hands.

Le Corbusier was not the only twentieth-century architect with voyeuristic tendencies. Transparency is an ubiquitous feature of modern buildings: from Bruno Taut's 1914 Glass Pavilion to Norman Foster's 'gherkin', over the course of the last hundred years the traditional opacity of the masonry wall has been gradually abandoned in favour of a diaphanous insubstantiality. There are technological reasons behind this development: innovations in structural engineering such as reinforced concrete frames and cantilevered floors have allowed architects to eliminate load-bearing walls and increase the use of glass and open plan spaces. However, transparency wasn't simply a side effect of scientific progress. If society hadn't changed too the glazed public structures of the nineteenth century, such as the Crystal Palace and Paddington Station, would never have become the private homes of today.

Everything that had formerly seemed stable went into crisis after the Industrial Revolution – our relationships, our social rules and our architecture. As Marx wrote of the modern experience, 'All that is solid melts into air.' From the outset avant-garde architects understood architectural transparency as a rejection of bourgeois individualism, which had been protected for so long by the ornamented facades of the nineteenth century. 'To live in a glass house,' said Walter Benjamin, 'is a revolutionary virtue par excellence.'[13] Pioneers like Bruno Taut and Paul Scheerbart agreed, and wrote impassioned manifestos prophesying the communal utopia that would result from a world of glass houses in which everyone could see what the neighbours were up to, although at the start of the twenty-first century this sounds more like a totalitarian hell. There was a sexual aspect to this slightly cranky vitalism: nudism was a constant preoccupation, with popular credence being given to the idea (still current in Germany, its place of origin) that the body should be exposed to healthy fresh air and sunlight. And where there's sex, there's sexism. Paul Scheerbart's bizarre fantasy novel of 1914 entitled *The Grey Cloth with 10 Percent White* describes the marriage of a visionary architect to a woman whose modest grey dresses don't clash with his pavonine glass structures. The condition of their marriage is that she will be contractually bound to dress drably for the rest of their lives, playing second fiddle to the real star of the show, her husband's transparent buildings.

After the First World War the ecstatic rhetoric of these pioneers was superseded by a sober objectivity, but the fact was that privacy – and sexuality – would never be the same again. The carefully segregated public areas of the nineteenth-century house – the hall, parlour and dining room – gradually lost their integrity and fused with formerly private spaces, as in the now-common arrangement of the open-plan living room-kitchen-diner. These spatial mutations corresponded to a changing society: large sections of the middle classes could no longer afford servants and so the kitchen was transformed into a site of conspicuous consumption, a communal area in which friends and relatives could congregate to celebrate the rite of cookery, these days elevated on an altar of polished granite worktops according to the word of Jamie Oliver.

New spatial arrangements also corresponded to changing morality: as Victorian prudery gave way, sex ceased to be an unspeakable or invisible act. In the absence of domestic staff, the phrase 'not in front of the servants' faded from bourgeois lips, and open-plan living melted the glacial frigidity of middle-class propriety. The process hasn't stopped. Just as walls have turned to glass, bodies and acts formerly considered private have become unashamedly public, to the point where the previously invisible is now inescapable. Celebrity sex tapes, reality TV shows and Internet porn have irreversibly blurred traditional definitions of obscenity; our every act is observed by the state via CCTV, every online thought monitored by the National Security Agency. Voyeurism has become part of modern consciousness, with an appeal that extends well beyond perverts and bohemian artists. The first architectural expressions of this change were built in the early years of the twentieth century, when architects like Le Corbusier broke down the walls of the modern house, but the story of architecture and sex goes back a lot further than this.

Architecture has always had a place in the stories we tell about love, whether as a setting for the action or taking a more active role. One of the earliest examples of architectural erotica is the Roman myth of Pyramus and Thisbe, the story of a pair of young neighbours who fall in love despite their parents' enmity. It has been retold countless times – *Romeo and Juliet* is the most familiar example – its permutations recording radical alterations in the relationship between sexuality and architecture over the centuries. The first known example of the tale is from AD 9, when the Roman poet Ovid wrote of the young lovers,

> Now, it so happened, a partition built
> between their houses, many years ago,
> was made defective with a little chink;
> a small defect observed by none, although
> for ages there; but what is hid from love?
> [. . .]
> There, many a time, they stood on either side,
> Thisbe on one and Pyramus the other,
> and when their warm breath touched from lip to lip,
> their sighs were such as this: 'Thou envious wall
> why art thou standing in the way of those
> who die for love? What harm could happen thee
> shouldst thou permit us to enjoy our love?
> But if we ask too much, let us persuade
> that thou wilt open while we kiss but once:
> for, we are not ungrateful; unto thee
> we own our debt; here thou hast left a way
> that breathed words may enter loving ears,'
> so vainly whispered they.[14]

The wall, stone-deaf and stony-hearted, ignores the lovers' plea, so instead they arrange an illicit nocturnal meeting by a deserted tomb. Thisbe arrives on the scene first but as she is waiting a prowling lioness scares her away. In her haste she loses her veil, which the lioness – her mouth bloodied from a recent kill and doubtless annoyed by Thisbe's escape – mauls. Pyramus now shows up and while fruitlessly searching for his lover stumbles across the bloody veil. Assuming that Thisbe has been eaten he falls on his sword. At this point Thisbe reappears and, understandably upset by what has transpired in her absence, stabs herself too.

Besides being a cautionary tale about the virtue of punctuality, the myth centres on the use of architecture as a barrier to sex and warns us about what happens to people who try to overcome it. We can consider the story a sort of origin myth of sex and buildings: it reminds us that one of the roots of architecture lies in the prevention of inappropriate couplings. In many cultures walls have been, and in some cases still are, the proper impediment to improper love, a primordial means of enforcing the marital ownership of women, preventing infidelity, miscegenation and other taboo loves. Although the Roman teller of this tale sets the action in ancient Babylon, with a distinct whiff of classical disapprobation of oriental cruelty, such practices were also true of ancient Athens, the imagined birthplace of Western civilisation. Athenian women could not vote or own property and were hidden away in the furthest recesses of their husband's homes. There, segregated in a room known as the gynaeceum, they spent their days weaving and child rearing, their monogamy architecturally guaranteed. Meanwhile men hosted their friends in the *andron*, a public room used for dinners and parties, for carousing with prostitutes and doing business.

The exceptionally high level of political activity among Athenian males was only possible because they didn't have to work. Democracy was purchased with the architecturally enforced domination of wives, whose labour, along with that of slaves, funded male leisure. The place of women in Greek architecture is perfectly emblematised by the caryatids holding up the porch of the Erechtheion on the Athenian acropolis. These colossal female figures are trapped by their architectural burden, for ever enslaved in order to support the social edifice that constrains them. The fact that caryatids recur throughout Western classicising architecture speaks volumes about the persistence of female subjugation, and when Le Corbusier drew concubines all over the walls of Gray's house, it was an atavistic act: he was trying to return a woman's room to a harem, a prison built from male sexuality, a prison that had to be transparent because it was guarded by the male gaze. But he was closing the stable door long after the horse had bolted.

There are a few centuries to get through before women escape their architectural prisons, however – dull centuries when the Church built barriers to sexuality that were stronger than any physical wall. But 1,340 years after Ovid, Boccaccio's collection of raunchy stories *The Decameron* bursts like a breath of fresh air into the pious asphyxia of the Middle Ages. In Boccaccio's reworking of the tale of Pyramus and Thisbe the initiator of the forbidden communication is a bored housewife imprisoned by her jealous husband. Despite the husband's meticulous precautions, the woman finds a hole in the wall of the marital home, and it just so happens that the adjoining property belongs to an attractive young man. After she gains his attention by dropping stones through the wall, the two begin a whispered relationship. So far, so Greek, but what happens next is decidedly novel. Frustrated by merely conversational intercourse, the woman contrives a plan to get her husband out of the way. Playing on his jealousy, she convinces him that an intruder is somehow getting into the house while he sleeps. Enraged, he resolves to catch this phantom lover by spending every night guarding the front door. While he is there the neighbour crawls through the gap in the wall – assiduously widened by the pair meanwhile – and into bed with the woman.

Boccaccio's tale shows that the sexual imprisonment of women by men is weakening: the protagonist's intelligence destroys her architectural bonds and she is free to enjoy her own sex life with impunity. The bawdy tone of the *Decameron* results from a changed set of sexual rules the keynote of which is an acceptance of the social fact of sexual impropriety that no longer ends in tragedy but in human satisfaction. Society has changed so that individual resourcefulness and wit are more highly valued than medieval piety, and unworkable social mores are revealed as self-defeating foolishness. But though Boccaccio's wall is more porous than the unforgiving masonry in Ovid's tale, it is still a wall and the woman is still a captive in her husband's house.

By the Renaissance things have changed once more: in *A Midsummer Night's Dream* the story of Pyramus and Thisbe is acted out by a group of 'rude mechanicals', much to the amusement − and censure − of their aristocratic audience. These labourers, whether their snotty audience realises it or not, are harbingers of mass society and its democratised art, and their approach to sexuality tells us much about the unstable nature of sex in early modernity. Significantly, the wall in *A Midsummer Night's Dream* is animated, becoming an active participant in the forbidden affair. It is a talking part played by a tinker named Tom Snout: 'This loam, this rough-cast and this stone doth show / That I am that same wall; the truth is so.'

This transformation is an early example of the quintessentially modern process of reification. Reification (in German *Verdinglichung*, literally 'thing-ification') stems from a failure to perceive the forces of capitalism that mould society. Instead of realising that value is created by the work of everyday people, through reification things (commodities) seem to become inherently valuable and to be social actors almost on a par with humans − think of the way markets are described as having personalities, as being bullish, strong or worried. While reification makes man-made objects appear to have a natural life of their own, living people are commodified, objectified, become thing-like, because the only thing they have to sell is themselves – their time, their labour. The result of these apparently contradictory forces is that walls, though built by humans and thus destructible, appear to be God-given barriers that can interact with people on their own terms. So Tom Snout the tinker becomes a wall, his social position literally petrified.

Not only does Shakespeare identify the process of reification right at the dawn of capitalist society, he is also prescient enough to foresee its counterpart in human sexuality: fetishism. Just as walls separated from their place in the network of social production come to life and speak, individual objects or body parts, be it shoes or feet, are separated from the body and stand in for the complete love object. In *A Midsummer Night's Dream* the wall is no longer a mere impediment; it is an accessory, responding when the lovers enjoin it to open its chink. And in a further development of Ovid's theme, the love Pyramus feels for Thisbe is projected onto the wall itself: 'Thou wall, O wall, O sweet and lovely wall', he says as he presses his lips against the stone. Thus the wall becomes a fetish. We have regressed in a sense from Bocaccio's story, in which intelligence overcomes walls. Now the wall has become integrated into human sexuality. This is how voyeurism begins, because for the voyeur the wall is necessary, physically and mentally. He doesn't want unimpeded vision; he (it is usually he) has to see but remain unseen, divided from the object of his love. So although real walls are being broken down, and they have been since Boccaccio, the architecture of sexual repression has entered into human consciousness.

Shakespeare takes a more psychological approach to the story than Ovid or Boccaccio, his inward turn another symptom of modernity. This inwardness comes to a climax with a different kind of storytelling: the pseudo-scientific narratives produced by

Freudian depth psychology. But more revealing than Freud's discredited ideas about repression and voyeurism themselves is a story he tells in his famous 1919 essay 'The Uncanny' (in German the word is *unheimlich* –'unhomely' – a telling architectural metaphor). In this work Freud describes an uncanny experience of his own.

> Strolling one hot summer afternoon through the streets of a small Italian town, I found myself in a district about whose character I could not long remain in doubt. Only heavily made-up women were to be seen at the windows of the little houses, and I hastily left the narrow street at the next turning. However, after wandering about for some time without asking the way I found myself back in the same street, where my presence had begun to attract attention. Once more I hurried away, only to return there again by a different route. I was now seized by a feeling that I can only describe as uncanny, and I was glad to find my way back to the piazza I had recently left and refrain from any further voyages of discovery.[15]

Freud tells it as if the 'unhomely' architecture is willing him to sexual impropriety: the city itself, architectural embodiment of the febrile southern atmosphere, entraps him in narrow streets from which he can only extricate himself with difficulty. But who is really the prisoner in this story? Freud is the captive of his own fear of the female gaze, but he is free to escape back to the piazza, scene of respectable public life. The prostitutes, on the other hand, are imprisoned in their brothels, and could probably not walk through the respectable parts of town without being arrested. The transparency of the windows – as in Amsterdam's red-light district today – does not ameliorate the fact that these women are just as architecturally enslaved as the caryatids in ancient Greece. This is another demonstration of the fact that architectural transparency is not a neutral strategy but a fundamentally gendered one: men can look *in*, but women shouldn't look *out*. The flip side of male voyeurism is a kind of architectural paranoia, in which the windows of the houses stand in for fear of the female gaze. The returned gaze becomes a more and more regular occurrence in modernity (Manet's imperious *Olympia* is a striking case, the outraged reaction to the painting an instance of mass male hysteria) as women cease to be exclusively observed but also observers, and Freud's 'unhomely' feeling is really an expression of male surprise and fear as gender roles shift from their accustomed poles.

This change in gender roles accelerated throughout the late nineteenth and twentieth centuries, as women fought for and won unprecedented control over their own architectural settings. The battle finds literary expression in Virginia Woolf's famous essay 'A Room of One's Own'. Woolf asks why there have been so few female artists, and comes to the conclusion that this is a question of economics and space, asserting that 'a woman must have money and a room of her own if she is to write fiction'.[16] The essay concludes with an explosive outburst as Woolf imagines the final escape from the gynaeceum in acts of multifarious creativity: 'Women have sat indoors all these millions of years, so that by this time the very walls are permeated by their creative force, which has, indeed, so overcharged the capacity of bricks and mortar that it must needs harness itself to pens and brushes and business and politics.'[17]

Tellingly, Woolf's essay was published in the same year that Gray finished work on E.1027. The first modern building to be completed by a female architect, Gray's villa may seem to be a 'room of one's own' on a grand scale, and it is certainly a volcanic expression of those long-repressed female creative forces that Woolf describes. But there is a slight complication: as the coded name reveals, E.1027 is not a room of Gray's own but a house for her and her lover, Jean Badovici. In the end Gray, who felt trapped

Caryatids from a Venetian edition of Vitruvius, 1511

Brothel in Amsterdam

by the relationship, had to flee this self-built prison, which had the constraints of the relationship built into its plan. In fact she went on to build a house in the Alpine village of Castellar that was finally hers alone, but she eventually left this house too, forced out by the onset of the Second World War. It is probable that she would have left in any case: she once said, 'I like doing the things, but I hate possessions.'[18] The burden of bricks and mortar weighed heavily on her mind and compromised the thing most precious to her, freedom. A room of one's own turns out not to be the ultimate in self-determination but another trap, where bourgeois interiority (think of Woolf's streams of consciousness) is substituted for freedom. A room of one's own is after all a possession, a commodity, a set of walls that separates us from others.

The fetishisation of architecture appears in these stories as a kind of metaphor for the modern condition of reification, but there are cases in which this metaphor is brought to startling life. In 1979 a woman called Eija-Riitta Eklöf Berliner-Mauer married the Berlin Wall, hence her bizarre surname – 'Berlin Wall' in German. Mrs Berliner-Mauer is not alone in her tastes, but a vocal member of a group of self-defined 'Objectum Sexuals', established by a woman named Erika Eiffel, who is married to . . . well, you can probably guess. The Objectum Sexuals are united by their shared attraction to inorganic objects, especially large architectural structures, although Mrs Berliner-Mauer explains, 'I also find [that] other manufactured things look good, [such] as bridges, fences, railroad tracks, gates . . . All these things have two things in common. They are rectangular, they have parallel lines, and all of them divide something. This is what physically attracts me.' Crucially, it is the division that appeals.

This behaviour, the reductio ad absurdum of fetishism, may seem the province of damaged libidos, but it is merely an extreme consequence of the more general tendency identified by Shakespeare in *A Midsummer Night's Dream*. When Pyramus and

Thisbe transfer their love to the wall that stands between them, a wall that is for them animated and responsive, they are entering into the Faustian bargain of reification, which animates the world but stills the soul. Mrs Berliner-Mauer is an extreme case, but the Berlin Wall – despite the fact that it cruelly separated many real lovers – had a broader aphrodisiac appeal, as noted by David Bowie in his song '"Heroes"'. At first listen it may seem that Bowie is singing about two heroic lovers divided by the Iron Curtain. But listen more closely (and note the quotation marks around the title): he actually describes a pair standing together on one side of the wall, kissing as they imagine the barrier as an eternal, immutable structure, and the possibility of beating the 'shame' on the other side, 'for ever and ever'.

In fact Bowie is mocking the sham heroism of a couple (based on Bowie's producer Tony Visconti and his West German girlfriend) conducting a love affair on the Western side of the wall. When they kiss they imagine that their love is an act of defiance, but in reality the wall is for them merely an aphrodisiac. Ironically Bowie's poorly understood song contributed enormously to the romantic image of the Berlin Wall in Western minds, and no doubt hundreds of trysts were conducted to his soundtrack. For Bowie listeners and subscribers to the romantic myth of Cold War Berlin, the Wall merely had to act as a symbolic division. A more physical instance of the aphrodisiac quality of walls occurs in gay cottaging, in which glory holes are used to further anonymise participants in anonymous sex acts.

One can speculate that the use of glory holes – apertures cut through the partitions separating lavatory cubicles – originated in more repressive times when anonymity was necessary to safeguard the reputation of closeted homosexuals, but their continued use reveals that the idea of partition and anonymity has an enduring sexual appeal. Glory holes fetishistically separate the cock from the body, reducing the partner to a pure sexual organ devoid of any human qualities besides tumescence. As with Mrs

Berliner-Mauer, the idea of division is crucial here: division between people and division of the body itself. This is a sad indication of the extent to which reification has altered the human soul but at the same time a heartening demonstration of the power of human sexuality to overcome any barrier, even at the cost of that barrier being partially internalised in the process. The irony is that this process of internalisation has corresponded to a tendency of real walls to turn transparent or to melt away from open-plan spaces. The material barriers of our early civilisations have disappeared only to become – after a brief moment of respite before the dawn of modern capitalism corresponding to the period in which Boccaccio was writing – barriers of the mind.

My last example of architectural erotica is a story about what happens when we attempt to demolish these walls rather than live with them. Rainer Werner Fassbinder's film *The Marriage of Maria Braun* describes a woman's struggle to survive and prosper in the hypocritical and materialistic world of post-war Germany. Although the film can be read as a metaphor for the fate of the Western half of the divided country, the Berlin Wall does not appear itself – instead, other divisive structures stand in for it.

The story begins with Maria's marriage on the eve of the Allied assault on Berlin. The opening shot shows a framed photograph of Hitler which is blown apart by an explosion to reveal, through the resulting hole, Maria and her partner being married in a registry office. After the war Maria, who presumes her husband to have been killed, must make her own way in the world, and she ruthlessly employs her erotic capital to this purpose, sleeping with anyone necessary to ensure her survival. In the process she rises from the position of a *Trümmerfrau* – a rubble woman, as the women who scavenged in the ruins of post-war Germany were called – to a secretary and later an executive in a successful West German corporation. Eventually she is wealthy enough to purchase that ultimate symbol of financial independence and bourgeois success, her own home. It is exactly now that she realises that her home is a prison, her apparent rise a hellish descent. In an ambiguous final scene she accidentally blows up her house, herself and her husband by lighting a cigarette after leaving the gas on.

The film ends as it begins, with an explosion and a pile of rubble, Maria once more a *Trümmerfrau*. But is her death really an accident? Perhaps Maria Braun's self-immolation is an attempt to finally escape the trap of architecture, which we think we own but in fact possesses us, and which confines our sexuality to the four square walls of bourgeois domesticity. It is an act of what Walter Benjamin called the 'destructive character': 'where others encounter walls or mountains, there, too, he sees a way . . . What exists he reduces to rubble – not for the sake of the rubble, but for that of the way through it.'[19] In Fassbinder's pessimistic analysis, however, this escape can only come with death.

The final act of my story begins with another explosion. When the retreating Germans bombed St-Tropez in 1944 the flat that Gray had rented in the town, along with most of her drawings and notebooks, was destroyed. The Germans also looted her house in Castellar and used the walls of E.1027 for target practice – Le Corbusier's image with the swastika was riddled with bullets as if executions had been carried out in front of it. Despairing at the destruction of her life's work, Gray moved back to Paris. She did eventually build another house in the countryside near St-Tropez, overseeing the work herself at the age of seventy-five, but she never returned to E.1027.

Le Corbusier's passion for the house was, however, undiminished by the years. He purchased a plot of land overlooking Gray's villa and in 1952 built a tiny lean-to there, a wooden *cabanon*, as shepherd's shacks are called in the south of France.

This one-room holiday home was a present for his wife Yvonne, and like E.1027 it is a masterpiece of minimalism. Although everything has been reduced to the bare necessities, the fourteen square metres of floor space do not feel cramped. There is storage space above the false ceiling, the furniture is mostly built in or folds away, and the lavatory, which Le Corbusier maintained was perfectly adequately ventilated, is hidden behind a curtain. There is no need for a kitchen because there is a connecting door to Le Corbusier's favourite local restaurant, where he and his wife ate every day.

Their shared minimalism aside (and this is a much more spartan version than Gray's), the enormous difference to Gray's villa becomes apparent when one considers the windows of Le Corbusier's *cabanon*. Unlike the expanses of glass he dictated for most of his projects, the *cabanon* has two small square windows overlooking the sea. These have folding shutters that are painted with sexually explicit murals of a couple, and on the wall opposite there is a large painting of a bull-man with a giant phallus. It's a classic case of voyeurism: the windows he insisted on for other people's houses are for looking into, but his own windows, in the only house he ever built for himself, are one-way apertures for him to look out of. He once wrote, 'I exist in life only on the condition that I see.' The *cabanon* is like a birdwatcher's hide perched on a cliff, and the images painted on the insides of the shutters, like the murals he painted in E.1027, provide the spectacle he hoped to see, as if they were some kind of sympathetic magic charm.

Le Corbusier's continued interest in E.1027 did not stop with the construction of his *cabanon*. After Jean Badovici's death E.1027 passed into the possession of his sister, a Romanian nun, and eventually the property was sold at auction. Perhaps concerned that any offer he made would attract unwanted attention, Le Corbusier persuaded a Swiss friend, Marie-Louise Schelbert, to buy the building on his behalf. Le Corbusier exerted his influence behind the scenes to ensure that, despite a higher bid from a certain Mr Onassis, she secured the property. Over the following years he insisted that the villa was well maintained by Schelbert, preventing her, for example, from removing the furniture, and he regularly visited the house when staying in his *cabanon* up the road, until one summer he died on the beach overlooked by the house.

With his death we have come full circle, but the strange tale of E.1027 does not stop at this point. The story does not end, but the tone radically changes: we are no longer listening to a tale of sexual obsession, but turning the pages of a cheap airport thriller. Some time in 1980 a Dr Heinz Peter Kägi removed most of the furniture from E.1027, driving it back to his home in Zürich in the dead of night. Three days later Marie-Louise Schelbert – his patient – was found dead in her flat, and E.1027 passed into Kägi's possession. Madame Schelbert's children, suspecting foul play, mounted a legal challenge to the will, but this came to nothing.

According to local rumour, Kägi now began to hold orgies in the villa, seducing local boys with drugs and alcohol, until one night in 1996 he was murdered by two young men in the bedroom-boudoir. The men, who claimed that Kägi had given them gardening work for which he refused to pay, were soon picked up trying to cross the Swiss border and imprisoned. E.1027, long neglected, now fell into ruin. Squatters moved in and the remaining furniture was either stolen or smashed. Numerous attempts to preserve the building failed, until eventually a restoration of Le Corbusier's murals was effected and the house placed under legal protection. It is a sad irony that it is Le Corbusier's unwelcome embellishment of the house that led to the final resurrection of E.1027 as an historical monument and today attracts the most attention. After many years of under-funded and widely criticised restoration, however, the villa has still not been reopened.

But what in the end is E.1027 a monument to? It is certainly a fitting monument to the moment when women finally won the power to build, a struggle that, despite the high-profile success of architects such as Zaha Hadid, is still continuing – architecture remains one of the most male-dominated professions. But it also memorialises something more elusive than this, something harder to pin down: a moment of resistance. The internalisation of walls via the twin processes of reification and fetishism may be ineluctable, even though Gray attempted to escape them with her constant peregrinations and fresh starts. Her restlessness complies with that irreducibly modernist imperative, Brecht's 'Cover your tracks.'

> Go into any house when it rains and sit on any chair that's in it
> But don't sit long. And don't forget your hat.
> I tell you:
> Cover your tracks.
> Whatever you say, don't say it twice
> If you find your ideas in anyone else, disown them.
> The man who hasn't signed anything, who has left no picture
> Who was not there, who said nothing:
> How can they catch him?
> Cover your tracks.[20]

But however many times we leave our belongings behind or escape from unsatisfactory relationships – whether we live in buildings like E.1027, with its transportable camping furniture so suited to the modern condition of homelessness, or out of a refugee's suitcase like Walter Benjamin – we cannot escape the furniture of the soul, our attachment to things that tie us down. If, however, Gray's house fails to escape the bourgeois rootedness of the traditional home, it remains a successful resistance to another process of modernity: the radical erasure of walls, of which Le Corbusier was a prime exponent. Corbusian transparency may seem to be a utopian approach to human sexuality, a refusal to accept bourgeois repression. But Le Corbusier's voyeurism goes beyond this into a quasi-totalitarian transparency that is the opposite of sex – one only has to watch *Big Brother* or visit a nudist camp to realise how utterly unerotic complete visibility can be. And indeed, after the co-option of architectural transparency by corporations as a symbol for an organisational transparency that does not really exist, the original utopianism of the concept is revealed to be more fragile than the glass from which their buildings are made. Gray's house – in this sense a halfway home – with its ribbon windows, screens and obstructions, adopts the transparent tendency while simultaneously attempting a heroic yet compromised resistance to its negative aspects. Whether, in our age of webcams, glass towers, CCTV, universally available porn and reality TV, there is any escape from total transparency, is another question.

Finsbury Health Centre, London
(1938)
Architecture and Health

When I was still a child, no other character in sacred history seemed to me to have such a wretched fate as Noah, because of the flood that kept him trapped in the ark for forty days. Later on, I was often ill, and for days on end I too was forced to stay in the 'ark'. Then I realised that Noah was never able to see the world so clearly as from the ark, despite its being closed and the fact that it was night on earth.

Marcel Proust, Pleasures and Days[1]

Abram Games' banned 1942 propaganda poster featuring the Finsbury Health Centre

In blacked-out London's grimy nights invisible figures armed with nothing more than tin hats and buckets full of sand watched from towers and rooftops – intently or with chilled boredom – for German incendiaries falling from the skies. One of these watchers in the dark was an Indian immigrant named Dr Chuni Lai Katial.

Handsome, socialistically inclined and very well connected (a 1931 photograph shows him with Charlie Chaplin and Mahatma Gandhi), Dr Katial was shortly to become Britain's first Asian mayor. Before the war he was chairman of the public health committee of Finsbury, a deprived inner-city borough of London, and his firewatching was given a special piquancy by the possibility that his own baby might be burned or blasted by the bombs, the child in question being the Finsbury Health Centre. Dr Katial had fought long and hard to open the centre in 1938, and now it stood half-buried in sandbags, a necessary precaution since its facade was largely made of those unmistakable signifiers of architectural modernity, glass bricks (the glass cracked under the weight, but otherwise the building survived the war unscathed). In this context transparency also had another connotation: health. For it is one of the enduring ideas of modernity that sunlight has invigorating properties, and just as the glass facade admitted these healing rays, the light emanating from the centre at night was meant to be a beacon – now extinguished to hide the building from the Luftwaffe – shining out in the filth and darkness of the slums.

I haven't begun my story about architecture and health in medias res for merely dramatic effect. War may not be father of all, but it was one of the parents of modern healthcare: the rise of the nation state and of imperialism, with the concomitant need for a professional standing army, led to an entirely new official interest in the size and health of the population. Military and naval hospitals in eighteenth-century Britain inspired architects across Europe, and the dire treatment of wounded and sick soldiers during the Crimean War (1853–6) spurred Florence Nightingale's long campaign to reform hospitals back home. Later, the poor health of volunteers for the Boer Wars (1880–1902) caused a national scandal in Britain: only two fifths were fit to fight, and fear of martial incompetence, and the resulting disintegration of empire, provided an impetus to improve the living conditions of the working class.

Dr Katial (rear left) hosted a meeting of Charlie Chaplin and Mahatma Gandhi at his home in London's East End in 1931

But although changes were made, the nation's health remained in a parlous state well into the 1930s. The biggest killer was tuberculosis, responsible for 30,000–40,000 deaths a year, and the connection with overcrowding and unsanitary conditions was clear. Finsbury, for example, with its tightly packed impoverished population, was a breeding ground for the disease. The housing stock was appalling: 2,500 cellars were used for sleeping and living, and 30 per cent of the population lived more than two people to a room. As a result, the average male life expectancy was fifty-nine and the death rate was 18 per cent higher than in Hampstead, which was much less densely populated. Apart from warfare and imperial insecurity, in places like Finsbury there developed another impetus for improved healthcare: municipal socialism.

A Labour council was elected for the first time in 1934, both in the borough and London-wide, and a result of this sea change was the Finsbury Plan, which aimed to clear slums and build schools, housing and healthcare facilities. The health centre was one of the first fruits of this plan. By incorporating a full range of services under one roof and making them available free to all at the point of use, the building was also a harbinger of that later, singularly great British institution, the National Health Service. The political significance of the building was clear enough to contemporaries, and deeply divisive: in a wartime propaganda poster designed in 1942 by Abram Games, a rickety boy in a filthy basement is hidden behind a facade depicting the centre. The picture is emblazoned with the ambiguous slogan 'Your Britain: fight for it now.' The war cabinet hated the image, and Winston Churchill ordered all copies of it destroyed. 'Churchill may have been a great wartime leader,' Games later recalled, 'but he'd never visited a slum. I saw the war as a catalyst for achieving the things that Britain needed, but I think he saw those who supported the welfare state as communists.'[2]

Wealth has always been intimately tied up with health and architecture. Before the twentieth century hospitals were only for the poor; the rich could afford to be visited by doctors in the comfort of their own homes. This led to very different experiences of illness, and although medicine was often worse than useless it also led to different outcomes, since poor patients rarely left the filthy hospitals alive.

One rich and celebrated invalid, Marcel Proust, whose father was a famous doctor (his book *The Hygiene of the Neurasthenic* reads like a checklist of his son's symptoms) suffered from a variety of ailments throughout his life. Proust spent three of his final years cooped up in an hermetically sealed cork-lined room as a precaution against the sounds, scents and sunlight that irritated his illness and distracted him from his work. The room has been re-created in the Musée Carnavalet in Paris, albeit with fresh cork – the original panels were black with soot from the anti-asthma powders Proust burned there, which, along with the galaxy of uppers and downers he was addicted to, can have done his health no good whatsoever. Isolated from the rest of society, and frequently high as a kite, Proust recalled figures from his past, delineating the vagaries of time and its distension by the experience of illness.

Illness also affects our understanding of space: whether it's the pulsating walls conjured by a fever, the invalid's shrunken universe reduced to the poles of bedroom and bathroom and the hurried journeys between, or the almost insurmountable obstacle course that the world presents to the infirm, architecture's relationship to health is not just a problem of catastrophic illness, of hospitals and clinics, but also one of everyday life.

Ten years before the Finsbury Health Centre was built, an attempt to make everyday life healthier had begun south of the river in London. The Peckham Experiment, as it was known, was initiated by doctors Innes Pearse and George Scott Williamson, who wanted to study a working-class community's health and habits in order to find ways of improving these. Like many reform-ers of the time, their aims were eugenic – 'to see that only the fit marry and beget' – and so the experiment began as a small club where local families of reproductive age could use a nursery, lawyer, laundry and social club for a subscription of sixpence a week.[3] In exchange, the doctors were able to conduct periodic examinations of the members. They found that the health of the locals was in a terrible state – by their reckoning, only 9 per cent were free from 'disease, disorder or disability' – so they decided to establish a more elaborate facility in Peckham.

Funded by wealthy philanthropists who shared their concerns about the reproductive health of the nation, Pearse and Williamson hired architect Owen Williams to build a sparkling glass-walled building which elicited the praise of no less a figure than Bauhaus director Walter Gropius, who called it 'an oasis of glass in a desert of brick'. Opened in 1935, the Pioneer Health Centre was a three-storey structure with a central court, at the bottom of which was a swimming pool. The pool could be viewed from the cafe and the workrooms on the upper levels, the idea being that the sight of people exercising would encourage others to join in. This encapsu-lated the whole philosophy of the Peckham Experiment: the doctors would not tell families to improve their lives, but provide them with concrete examples of better living, from which they could learn and benefit – and pass their experiences on. Hence the transparent facade, which was meant to advertise healthy living to the community at large. Although this might seem admirably unpatronising, the reason for the hands-off approach was eugenic: only those whose genes deserved to survive – those who took responsibility for themselves – would benefit. The transparency of the building was also necessary so that the doctors could observe their experimental subjects, 'looking through the glass walls of the Centre, as the cytologist may under his microscope watch living cells grow'.[4]

The Finsbury Health Centre was designed with very different aims in mind. Peckham was not a slum, and its residents were mostly tradesmen and skilled labourers, but Finsbury was a much poorer area. The health problems of its residents were correspondingly more acute, as would have been only too apparent to Dr Katial. So when he was planning his centre, he had in mind a place where diseases could be treated, not some kind of human Petri dish. He found his model at a conference of the British Medical Association in 1932, where a radical architectural practice named Tecton presented drawings for a TB sanatorium it was proposing for the East End. At the time the sanatorium was an archetype of modern design, and so it was an ideal test case for a group of young architects wanting to make their mark in the world.

That modernism should be entwined in a *danse macabre* with tuberculosis is hardly surprising. As dispersed rural populations were concentrated in squalid industrial cities, infections had risen, until by the turn of the twentieth century TB was the greatest killer of adults in Europe and the USA. Before its bacterial cause was discovered it had been thought that a combination of bad air, dirt and heredity was responsible for the disease. After Robert Koch spotted the bacillus wriggling down his microscope in 1882 the possibility of contagious transmission was confirmed, but until an antibiotic cure was discovered in 1946 a strange regime of magical and symbolic treatments became medical orthodoxy. Sunlight, fresh air and rest were believed to stave off the disease, so droves of rich sufferers made the pilgrimage to the Alps for extended 'cures', a phenomenon captured in Thomas Mann's *Magic Mountain*. In this 1924 novel dim-witted everyman Hans Castorp visits his consumptive cousin, who is recuperating in the mountains, and discovers that he is temperamentally suited to this otherworld of the sick. Arriving from the 'flatlands', as the sufferers derisively refer to the rest of the world,

Castorp spots a long building 'arrayed with so many balconies that, from a distance as the first lights of evening were being lit, it looked as pockmarked and porous as a sponge'.[5] Balconies were the essential element of sanatoria: it was on them that patients would lie for their daily two-hour *Freiluftkur* – 'fresh air cure' – on chairs that also became staples of modern design. Aalvar Aalto's Paimio Chair, designed for his sanatorium in Finland, is a particularly famous example.

Hans Castorp's love affair with the sanatorium was shared by designers across Europe, who applied the 'hygiene of the optical' (to borrow Bauhaus master László Moholy-Nagy's phrase) to all sorts of buildings, institutional and domestic. Big windows, flat roofs – for sunbathing, however miserable the climate – chrome furniture and white walls completed the clinical look, and lent architects the aura of scientific expertise that now accrued to the medical profession. The promiscuity of the metaphor was such that it became the subject of parody: 'Modern man,' Robert Musil wrote in *A Man Without Qualities*, 'is born in a hospital and dies in a hospital – hence he should also live in a place like a hospital.'[6] Hygiene was a powerful modernist trope, a versatile metaphor that could stand for all sorts of ideas. Newness and cleanliness were not just aesthetic choices; they could, for example, represent a rejection of the nervous strain caused by the modern city, as in Josef Hoffmann's serene white Purkersdorf Sanatorium for nervous complaints situated outside Vienna, that capital of neurotics – Mahler, Schoenberg, and Schnitzler received treatment there. More sinisterly, hygiene could mean racial hygiene, or eugenics, as we saw in Peckham. On the other hand, it could stand for a rejection of the bourgeois traditions behind middle-class cluttered interiors, and the unequally distributed dirt of industrial society, as was demonstrated by a famous sanatorium at Hilversum in the Netherlands called Zonnestraal – sunbeam.

Built by Jan Duiker and Bernard Bijvoet between 1925 and

1931, Zonnestraal has an almost intangible concrete structure that is a paean to the healing power of light, which in this case also represented enlightenment in a political sense: this sanatorium was not a rich invalids' retreat, but commissioned by the diamond workers' union, the biggest and richest such organisation in the Netherlands. The diamond trade was a lucrative but dangerous business, since the glittering dust thrown off by the production process abraded the lungs. Fittingly, the money collected from the sale of this dust paid in part for the sparkling sanatorium, where workers could spend time breathing in the altogether more whole-some pine-scented air of the surrounding forests.

The Finsbury Health Centre was part of this international movement of socially conscious, hygienic, modern design. The most prominent member of the practice that designed it, Berthold Lubetkin, had an impeccable modernist pedigree. Born to a wealthy Jewish family in Tiflis, Georgia in 1901, Lubetkin moved to Moscow to study art in 1917 and watched the revolution unfold from his bedroom window. This teenage encounter with political radicalism and the heady artistic atmos-phere of revolutionary Russia had a lifelong influence on his architectural ideas – he remembered this time 'when history crashed through the barriers of everyday convention' as one 'of open, delirious joy'. Lubetkin was no fan of later Stalinist ortho-doxy, and he regretfully added that this 'was a short-lived period' of freedom.[7] After travelling around Europe for ten years, including a stint studying in Paris with pioneering concrete expert Auguste Perret, who had also taught Le Corbusier, Lubetkin came to London in 1931.

Unlike many refugees from totalitarian Europe, however, Lubetkin stayed put. Others found the relative openness of America more appealing and moved on, but Lubetkin thought he detected an opportunity for a charismatic and ambitious young architect in stuffy old England. There was a small but vocal modernist scene, and it was with people associated with this scene, including the future architect of the National Theatre, Denys Lasdun, that Lubetkin formed Tecton. Short for *architecton*, the Greek work for architecture, the practice was unique in Britain in having a collective name. This advertised the collective spirit of the group, which rejected the existing feudal structure of the profession, in which teams of anonymous office juniors laboured to create projects which would be signed off by a big-name architect, a situation that persists today. In the straitened circumstances of the Depression there were not many opportunities for such a radical group, but they made their mark in 1934 with the unlikeliest of commissions, a penguin pool at London Zoo. The famous double-helix ramp, made possible by the engineering expertise of Ove Arup – who was to collaborate with Tecton and Lubetkin for many years – was an early iteration of one of Lubetkin's central ideas, the social condenser. Originated by the constructivists, the social condenser was a building that brought people together in new relationships, making new ways of life possible. Bringing penguins together might seem to be somewhat lacking in revolutionary potential, but this was design as propaganda: it was meant to advertise Tecton's skill and the playful utopian potential of modern architecture to the public at large – and to potential patrons.

Tecton was finally able to put its ideas about the social purpose of architecture into practice when Dr Katial, inspired by its proposed TB sanatorium, commissioned a health centre for Finsbury in 1935. The resulting building was the first modernist structure to be erected by a municipal authority in Britain, and its plain white surfaces and glass bricks made a striking statement of difference in the surrounding slums. However, it also has a distinctly classical flavour: it is serenely symmetrical, and its spreading wings open to embrace the visitor rather like the colonnaded forecourt of St Peter's in Rome. Once across the little footbridge that forms the

*Tecton's Penguin Pool at London Zoo advertised the playful side
of modern design to the public*

ceremonial approach to the centre, the visitor entered a bright
reception area scattered with informal seating. This made a big
change from the familiar lines of chairs in dingy waiting rooms,
and was meant to create the impression of a sort of social club
where people could drop in at any time, without being intimidated
by medical professionals. In other words, it was meant to be – like
the penguin pool – a social condenser, but this time for humans.
Murals by Gordon Cullen added to the administrated chirpiness
of the atmosphere, exhorting visitors, 'Live out of doors as much as
you can.' The slightly bossy tone highlights the building's double
purpose: as well as a social club, it was also meant to be a 'mega-
phone of health', educating the local community and helping to
prevent, as well as cure, disease. But it went about this in a very
different way from the Pioneer Health Centre in Peckham: gone

are the creepy eugenic undertones, and instead there is a straight-forward educational and transactional environment. We should probably be grateful that this paternalistic approach was adopted by the NHS after the war, whereas the Peckham Experiment ran out of steam and funds, and its health centre is now – inevitably – luxury flats.

The Finsbury Health Centre's facilities included one of the first women's clinics, a TB clinic, a mortuary, a dentist, a foot clinic, a cleansing and disinfection station, and a flat for people whose homes were being fumigated. The building was divided into a central core housing permanent functions, such as the reception, lecture hall for educational public talks and lavatories, while the two wings were occupied by clinical and office spaces that could be subdivided or opened up as needs dictated. This was a conscious recognition by Tecton of the rapid evolution of modern medicine, and belies the static symmetry of the plan: classical architecture – most architecture, for that matter – is not built for change, whereas this was a structure designed with social change in mind. It was a revolutionary conception by English standards and an attempt to answer one of the enduring problems of designing for health and human life, which are fluid and mutable rather than solid as concrete or marble. The centre's indeterminacy follows the lead of Ford's plant at River Rouge. This synergy is emblematic of the way the welfare state grew up as an adjunct of Fordist capitalism. Ford may have closed his Sociology Department, but the idea survived, albeit detached from the corporation and enfolded in the state. Welfare was a way of observing and disciplining the bodies of workers, not only in the factories, but also at home and at rest, in order to maximise productivity.

But the forward-looking plan should not disguise the fact that the building also cast a glance back: the two wings, designed to permit maximum penetration by daylight and fresh air, were

The Finsbury Health Centre was originally surrounded by Victorian slums

informed by an outdated medical paradigm – miasmatic theory. Since antiquity the observation that some diseases occur in clustered outbreaks has inspired the idea that they are caused by bad air, or miasmas, emanating from decomposing matter. Eventually, 'pavilion'-type hospitals were designed with this theory in mind, with separate buildings for each ward, allowing – it was believed – the healthy penetration of fresh air. That these ancient ideas didn't have an impact on architecture until the eighteenth century can be attributed to the fact that earlier hospitals were not built to heal: in the Middle Ages they were factories for works of charity and the production of grace.

Initially attached to the great religious houses, hospitals were places where pilgrims could rest, and the poor, sick and elderly could be cared for and eventually die in the faith, while those dispensing charity had their souls cleansed by good works. These buildings' plans, like the monasteries from which they grew, were dictated by their religious functions, as in the Hôtel Dieu at Tonnere in France. Here sufferers lay in beds in a massive hall, at one end of which was a light-filled chapel placed so that the inmates could watch or at least hear Mass (consuming the sacrament during communion had died out earlier in the Middle Ages; instead, sight of the eucharist was the key to salvation).

As merchants and princes grew richer and more powerful in the fourteenth and fifteenth centuries, they too began to endow charitable foundations. At the same time a renewed interest in ancient learning inspired a return to classical architecture. One of the most successful attempts to blend the classical and Christian traditions together was proposed by Italian architect Filarete for the city of Milan in 1456. Completed 350 years later, his Ospedale Maggiore was divided into two halves. On the left four men's wards were arranged in a cross around a central altar which could be seen from all the beds, and on the right there was a similar arrangement for women. Around the perimeter were administrative buildings, and the eight courts created by this plan were filled by an ice store, pharmacy, wood yard and kitchen. In the middle of the building's central court was a church. The plan is eminently rational – rational, that is, if you believe that the main function of a hospital is saving souls. In subsequent centuries cruciform designs became popular throughout Europe. One such plan, devised by a German architect named Furttenbach in the mid-seventeenth century, was conceived in the form of the crucified Christ – whom, Furttenbach wrote, 'stretches out his merciful arms over the beds of the suffering . . . shares his merciful heart in the presentation of the Mass and in the place of the upper altar bends his holy head towards Christianity. Thus we may see in this hospital building a lovable figure and be reminded constantly of the suffering and death of our own Saviour.'[8]

But as the Church's power waned and the nation state began its rise, the function of hospitals started to change. Absolutist monarchs used hospitals to exert their control over society. In 1656 Louis XIV established the Hôpital Géneral, which was not a physical building but a regime under which various undesirables were incarcerated, often in chains. Beggars, vagrants, the idle, the infirm, the insane, epileptics, the venereally diseased and young women who had fallen or 'seemed likely to fall' into debauch – fully one per cent of Paris' population – were locked up in the hospitals at Bicêtre and Salpêtrière. Inmates of the latter hospital were finely graded following a policy of what John Thompson and Grace Goldin called 'divide and conquer': each idiot, each maniac and each melancholic had his or her cell, which – because of the building's low-lying site – periodically filled with Seine water and sewer rats. This mass incarceration, which Michel Foucault called 'the Great Confinement', was repeated across Europe: for example, in England there were houses of correction and later workhouses. In the Bethlem Royal Hospital, which under its nickname Bedlam became a byword for insanity, inmates were subjected to the stares and laughter of the paying public: advertising the attractions within, a statue on the gate represented 'raving' madness bound in chains. Foucault attributes this new approach to illness and insanity to the Enlightenment and the growth of the market economy, and to a corresponding exclusion of unreason and the economically inactive. There was no longer any room for the 'idle': their families, who had to work, hadn't the time or money to look after them, and they had to be locked away to prevent their moral poison from spreading.

Alongside this drive to control the civilian populace, the rise of European imperialism meant that governments also required bigger, fitter armies. Since soldiers were now expensively trained professionals rather than just expendable levies, attention turned to facilities for their health and recuperation. British army

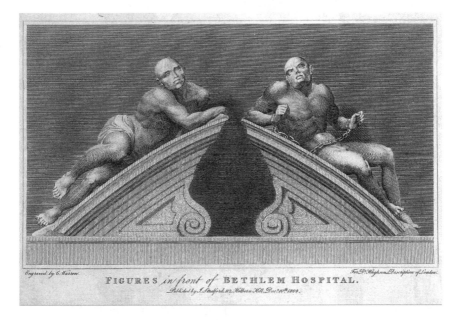

Engraved by C.Warren.   For D.Hughson's Description of London.

FIGURES *in front of* BETHLEM HOSPITAL.
Published by J.Stratford, 112 Holborn Hill, Dec.10th 1808.

Figures of 'melancholy' and 'raving' madness from the gate of the Bethlem Royal Hospital, London by Caius Cibber (c.1676). The chains worn by the manic figure were not merely allegorical

physician John Pringle observed in an influential 1750 tract that convalescents in requisitioned hospitals almost invariably died, whereas those lodged in makeshift, permeable spaces – in haylofts, barns and tents – were more likely to survive. Taking this as confirmation of the theory that disease was caused by bad air, he recommended the dispersal rather than the concentration of the sick and wounded. This idea found early architectural expression in the Royal Naval Hospital at Stonehouse, Plymouth, completed in 1765. The complex housed 1,200 sailors in ten three-storey pavilions arranged in strict military formation and linked by colonnades. It was so popular with patients that soldiers sometimes crept in from a nearby army hospital, and had to be evicted.

In 1787 two members of a commission tasked with rebuilding

the ancient Hôtel Dieu hospital in Paris visited Plymouth, where they were greatly impressed to find that their plans had already been realised. Their own hospital, founded on the Île de la Cité in in the seventh century, had by the end of the eighteenth century sprawled to cover both banks of the Seine and a bridge in between. Wards had also been built out on piers over the river, and a warren of cellars slung beneath, hanging like swallows' nests over the murky water. This high-density approach was all very well when the primary function of a hospital was saving souls, but by the late eighteenth century the rising power and professionalisation of medicine, backed by the state's desire to expand its power over the populace, led to doctors wresting control of hospitals from the religious orders. The profession was now free to throw its weight around and put its miasmatic theories into action. Consequently, the overcrowded Hôtel Dieu – one survey found 2,377 patients there, many of them sleeping eight to a bed – came to be reviled as 'the most dangerous place in the world'. Reforming doctor Jacques Tenon was horrified by its 'narrow, dark passages, where the walls are dirtied with spittle, the floor soiled with filth oozing from the mattresses and from the commodes when they are emptied, with pus and blood from wounds or venesections [bloodletting]'.[9] In 1772 a fire killed nineteen patients and caused a huge outcry. In response over 200 proposals were made for the Hôtel Dieu's reconstruction along healthier lines. The majority of these adopted the pavilion plan.

Over the next hundred years pavilions triumphed. A century of conflict seemed to confirm the healthy properties of the dispersed plan. During the Crimean War, for instance, Florence Nightingale found British soldiers dying at a rate of 42 per cent in a requisitioned Ottoman barracks at Scutari. The overcrowded building's sewers had completely rotted away, allowing a reservoir of excrement to accumulate below; the intermittent water supply, meanwhile, was found to be trickling through the decomposing carcass of a horse. In contrast, a prefabricated military hospital at Renkioi achieved a mortality rate of only three per cent. Designed by Isambard Kingdom Brunel, its dispersed wooden huts, each of which housed about fifty men in two wards, were covered with highly polished tin to reflect the sun's heat. Renkioi was greatly admired by Nightingale, who was a staunch adherent of miasmatic theory, and when she returned to Britain she agitated for reform. Hospitals should, she argued, be at most two storeys tall, and courtyards should be eliminated, since they allowed bad air to collect. 'Cross ventilation' was key if wards were to be healthy, and that meant that they had to be located in isolated architectural units so that a breeze could blow through windows on both sides. The resulting units became known as Nightingale wards, although she merely popularised the design. The pared-down interiors allowed the free flow of air, and the regimented rows of beds could be easily supervised by nurses – thus imposing the military character of these buildings' antecedents on civilian populations. The Nightingale ward's form was dictated as much by a passion for Foucauldian visual discipline as by miasmatic ideas. 'Every unneeded closet, scullery, sink, lobby and staircase,' Nightingale wrote with martinettish vim, 'represents both a place which must be cleaned, which must take hands and time to clean, and a hiding or skulking place for patients or servants disposed to do wrong. And of such no hospital will ever be free.'[10]

Although it was an imperfect representation of the nature of disease, miasmatic theory and its architectural analogues did manage to reduce the number of deaths in hospitals by thinning out patients and improving sanitation; it scored an even bigger hit in the form of Joseph Bazalgette's great London sewer network. But eventually it became clear that reforms based on miasmatism were not the complete answer, and at the same time Pasteur and Koch's discoveries demonstrated the mechanics behind contagion, thus confirming germ theory. The pavilion plan was finished, but certain ideas associated with miasmatic theory refused to die: the importance of sunlight, for instance, and of fresh air, lingered in the imagination well into the twentieth century, as the transparency and quasi-pavilion plan of the Finsbury Health Centre demonstrates. Built after the confirmation of germ theory but before the widespread use of antibiotics, the centre existed in a strange seventy-year interregnum in which magical thinking about the bactericidal effects of sunlight persisted. One of its facilities was a solarium, where slum-dwellers could bask in artificial rays, a common treatment at the time.

Solid, expensive architecture has a tendency to lag behind changes in society and technology, and new health practices have often necessarily been instigated in buildings from another era. When the National Health Service was set up in Britain after the Second World War, the eighteenth- and nineteenth-century hospitals it inherited were often rickety and ill suited to modern medicine. But the nonsimultaneity of the simultaneous, as German philosopher Ernst Bloch called it, can create surprisingly cosy bedfellows: the prevalent Nightingale wards *were* suited to post-war state surveillance and we're-all-in-it-together-ism. Partly a wartime hangover, medical communalism was also a by-product of scientific developments. The increasing complexity and cost of medical technology meant that the rich could no longer be treated at home, or even in private clinics, so hospitals became more complete microcosms of society, albeit divided into public wards and private rooms for the very wealthy. The social experience of the hospital ward is one of the favourite subjects of the Carry On series' vivisections of the post-war British psyche. The second and most successful of these films, 1959's *Carry on, Nurse!*, introduced those staples of hospital comedy, the stern matron with her inescapable gaze and military bearing, and the nubile nurse. These two perform a sort of stick and carrot routine, enticing the (invariably male) body of the patient into the microcosmic welfare state of the hospital so that it can be surveyed and disciplined by the firm smack of government. The comic situations in these films all rest on the attempted evasion of state power by the little man and the awkwardness resulting from different classes being thrown together under conditions in which even the most rudimentary privacy has been stripped away. Ultimately, however, everybody rubs along together under the disciplinary gaze of matron, and social democracy survives.

Decrepit pavilions and Nightingale wards finally began to be swept away in 1962, when funding was made available for an extensive programme of NHS hospital building, signed off by Enoch Powell. Their most popular replacement was an arrangement borrowed from business architecture and nicknamed the matchbox-on-a-muffin, a high-rise tower on a broader podium block. This design was a response to rising ground rents, which made spread-out pavilion designs hugely expensive; to changes in medical knowledge, which meant that cross-ventilation was no longer the objective of hospital design (indeed, it was now understood to spread germs); to developments in building technology, such as lifts and air conditioning, which allowed deep plans to be ventilated without windows; and to advances in nursing and surgical techniques, which meant that protracted bed rest was no longer the primary form of care. Instead, patients were treated and shipped out as quickly as possible, and as a result wards grew smaller to prevent contagion, and subservient to the technical areas – imaging departments, operating theatres and other clinical spaces. In the matchbox-and-muffin hospital these services tended to occupy the podium (muffin), where they could spread out and be reconfigured as necessary, while the more static wards were stacked in the matchbox tower above. These towers also had an ideological function, especially in European cities, where they advertised the modernity, power and presence of the welfare state in monumental form, rivalling the towers of the private sector.

This power could not survive unchallenged, and in the crisis-ridden 1970s deinstitutionalisation began its creeping progress. Framed as a humanitarian reform under the euphemistic term 'care in the community', the closure of mental institutions, facilitated by the invention of antipsychotics like chlorpromazine (which allowed patients to be imprisoned much more cheaply in their own minds), and of care homes for the elderly was primarily an ideologically driven attempt to shrink the state by neoliberal governments. In the absence of investment, hospital expansions were reduced to ground-hugging accretions of prefabricated sheds, a strange return to the pavilion plans of the previous century. Simultaneously, hospital wards began to fill with the refugees of deinstitutionalisation. I once spent a month in a large London hospital. In the absence of adequate care homes, the ward was full of elderly people, but there were also some more piquant characters: a Gibraltarian maniac who was convinced that witches were flying in through the window to take him away and who kept trying to light cigarettes under the covers, a junkie on whom the old ladies kept a strict but maternal eye, and a man who expired one day in a volcano of vomited blood, splashing the newspaper I was reading in the next bed.

Chronically underfunded and overcrowded hospitals present a growing problem to neoliberal governments, whose citizens expect a functioning healthcare system but have been convinced by vested interests in parliament and the press that the higher tax bill this necessitates is not in their interests. So, spotting an apparently ideologically sympathetic way of paying for public services, John Major's Conservative administration embraced a funding model pioneered in Australia: private finance initiatives. Hugely expanded under New Labour, PFIs injected borrowed capital into the sector, permitting the construction of vast new hospitals, such as the 987-bed Norfolk and Norwich Hospital opened in 2001, without raising taxes. The Norfolk and Norwich, like many PFI hospitals, was built on fields, cheaper than an inner-city site and allowing a languid sprawl of low-density pavilions across the landscape, but less accessible to most of the population. Owen Hatherley described such hospitals, which are 'always on the outer reaches', as designed in 'the PFI manner, which is by now familiar from a thousand New Labour non-projects: a bit of stock brick, a plasticky wavy roof, some green glass, plus a few dashes of jolly colour in the carpets'.[11]

Besides aesthetic insipidity – the result of administrators opting for cheap developer-designed plans – the problem with PFI is that, though it allowed governments to escape making tough choices, the savings were illusory. The deals struck under PFI were in fact appallingly expensive and resulted in the British people paying far more for hospitals than they would have done through raised taxes. This was apparent to many critics from the outset, but its consequences have now become obvious: the interest charged on the loans used to build new hospitals is so high that in order to make repayments other publicly owned facilities are being closed, including accident and emergency departments. If you were a cynic, you might ask if this was not part of the neoliberal agenda from the outset, a hollowing-out of the NHS to make the marketisation of healthcare palatable to the electorate. The dishonest obsession with cutting up-front costs, which has spread throughout British bureaucracy, has also had a devastating effect on the architectural profession. Good design is considered an unnecessary expense, so patrons opt instead for 'design-build' contracts, which cut out architects in favour of developers and their in-house design teams. The results are banal, cripplingly expensive buildings and a profession in crisis.

One potential victim of the shrinking NHS is the Finsbury Health Centre. The building, though listed, has been under-funded for years, and the local NHS trust is desperate to get rid of it, in which case it too will probably be turned into luxury flats. This would have come as no surprise to the health centre's creator, Berthold Lubetkin, who was very quickly disillusioned by the reality of the welfare state. During the war he had retreated to a farm in Gloucestershire, where he looked after hippos and chimps evacuated from London Zoo. His subsequent return to architecture should have been a triumphant one: the national government was now Labour, promising opportunities for building on a much grander scale. Locally, Tecton had been commissioned with completing the Finsbury Plan, and the practice designed a series of groundbreaking housing estates across London. One of these – originally to be called Lenin Court but renamed Bevin Court due to political pressure – features one of the finest staircases in the world, a space-age social condenser for London's working classes. However, post-war socialism turned out to be less sympathetic than Lubetkin had hoped. Cash-strapped bureaucrats had little time for the utopian dreams of architects, and when his plans for a new town at Peterloo were rejected after a long consultation process, he retreated into bilious exile. He had once proclaimed that 'nothing is too good for ordinary people', but in the 1970s he bitterly remarked of his work in Finsbury, 'These buildings cry out for a world which has never come into being.'[12]

Earlier in this chapter I observed that the conjunction of health and architecture is not only experienced in buildings for acute crises, such as hospitals and clinics, but in the spaces of everyday life. The healthiness or otherwise of the quotidian environment has been tackled by people as diverse as Joseph Bazalgette, the doctors behind the Peckham Experiment and the countless modernist architects who agitated for clean-lined sun-filled

Tecton's staircase at Bevin Court (1955). Originally to be called Lenin Court, the building is located on the site of the revolutionary's London home

housing. Today, this struggle continues in Western Europe and America, but in a very different form. For one, the tenets of modernism have been discredited – often for political reasons, as in the post-1970s evolution of hospital design. The modernist office blocks that fill our cities are now seen as anything but healthy, as the technologies that were meant to make deep open-plan spaces habitable – modern materials and air conditioning – have been accused of having the opposite effect, emanating noxious particles and recirculating 'bad air'. Although sick building syndrome is now widely seen in clinical circles as having been a form of mass hysteria, a kind of throwback to miasmatic theory and perhaps a dumb protest against post-Fordist labour practices, there is no denying the fatal reality of legionnaires' disease, which spreads via the air-conditioning ducts of hotels and cruise ships. At the same time, technologies like lifts and escalators have compounded the symptoms of Western affluenza: as infectious disease has been all but eliminated from our cities, we have instead begun to die of inertia – today nobody uses Lubetkin's social-condensing staircase at Bevin Court.

In order to combat this, urbanists including New York City's planning department have started using voguish nudge theory – the idea that people can be prodded gently in the direction of doing the right thing for their health – by designing more prominent stairs, for example, or making steps into 'piano keys' that emit notes when trodden on. It's an updated version of the Peckham Health Centre's hands-off approach, no longer motivated by eugenics but by an ideologically related hatred of regulation and welfare – and much less effective than either. In developing countries, on the other hand, the most elemental problems of sanitation continue to kill huge numbers: one third of the world's population has no access to a lavatory, and diseases caused by overcrowding such as TB are still rife. TB is currently the second-biggest killing disease after AIDS, causing 1.4 million deaths in 2011.[13] Gandhi's dictum 'Sanitation is more important than independence' has a fresh urgency, as the economic powerhouses of India, China and Brazil are revealed as smoggy monsters with feet of clay (or something worse). Whether architecture can do anything about this is the subject of my final chapter.

Footbridge, Rio de Janeiro
(2010)
Architecture and the Future

Life is more important than architecture.

Oscar Niemeyer[1]

Oscar Niemeyer's curvaceous footbridge leads to Rocinha, Rio's biggest favela

A gigantic arse-shaped bridge concludes my investigation into the lives of bricks and mortals – it was an opportunity too Rowlandsonian to resist. With it, we have travelled from the imaginary wooden hut at the beginning of my story to the concrete bottom at its end. We have also come full circle, since the bridge takes pedestrians across a busy road to Rocinha, Rio's biggest favela and a huge agglomeration of 'primitive' dwellings, many of which, with their plumbing, electricity and plasma TVs, are not so primitive at all. Rumour has it that Oscar Niemeyer, Brazil's most famous architect and Last of the Great Modernists, designed his footbridge to resemble a woman's bikini-clad bottom. Although this would be a fitting symbol for this voluptuous city, Niemeyer pointed out that his G-string suspension bridge is actually a direct reference to his earlier design for Rio's *sambódromo*, or samba arena, which crowns the processional route used during carnival. But considering the architect's slavering pronunciations, it's not impossible that his mind was on bottoms. 'Right angles don't attract me. Nor straight, hard and inflexible lines created by man,' he wrote in *The Curves of Time*, his autobiography. 'What attracts me are free and sensual curves. The curves we find in mountains, in the waves of the sea, in the body of the woman we love.'[2]

Palaeozoic sexual attitudes aside, the design was given as a gift and as a gesture of solidarity to the inhabitants of the favela which climbs the mountain behind the bridge. Niemeyer – who also designed the public buildings of Brasilia, the nation's capital and the consummation of modernist planning – was a communist to the end of his 104 years. In 2006 he wrote, 'One day the world will be more just and will take life to a superior stage, no longer limited to governments and dominant classes.'[3] One day perhaps, but 20 per cent of Cariocas, as the people of Rio are known, live in favelas, while down in the rich beach communities of Ipanema and Leblon prices are high enough to make this Londoner's eyes water. Rising disparity is not just a Brazilian problem, although it attains vertiginous extremes here: nearly a billion of the world's people now live in slums. These come in many forms, whether peripheral accretions like Rocinha or older enclaves such as Cairo's City of the Dead, a Mameluke cemetery the tombs of which are inhabited by over half a million people.

Slumification is not the only problem facing architecture: in 2010 the proportion of the world's people living in cities passed 50 per cent for the first time. The majority of urbanites live in the megacities of the developing world, such as Shanghai, Mexico City or even prodigious new forms like the endless sprawl of the Rio/Sao Paulo Extended Metropolitan Region, which has a combined population of 45 million. While cities swell and fuse to become regional megalopolises, the countryside is also urbanising. In China, as Mike Davis wrote in his staggering book *Planet of Slums*, 'in many cases, rural people no longer have to migrate to the city: it migrates to them'.[4] He concluded, 'The cities of the future, rather than being made out of glass and steel as envisioned by earlier generations of urbanists, are instead largely constructed out of crude brick, straw, recycled plastic, cement blocks, and scrap wood. Instead of cities of light soaring toward heaven, much of the twenty-first-century urban world squats in squalor, surrounded by pollution, excrement, and decay.'[5]

Under these conditions of explosive urbanisation, where the distinction between *rus* and *urbe* itself is blurring, where housing shortages and real estate bubbles destabilise Western economies and where so many people live in inadequate buildings made without architects, the biggest challenge facing architecture is the provision of housing for ordinary people. Though this responsibility was met with seriousness and occasional brilliance, albeit more frequently with corruption and ineptitude, by architects, planners and governments in the last century, these days it is consistently shirked. Instead the buck is passed to the private sector or to the poor themselves, and architects are either squeezed out of the design process altogether, reduced to 'adding value' to corporate HQs or to building yet more museums of dubious utility.

I don't want to turn Niemeyer's concrete bridge into a straw man. Though it could be painted as a typically useless icon, his heart was in the right place. He donated the design for free to a programme of favela improvements that includes a large sports centre at one end of the bridge and improved housing at the other. These works, part of the federal Programa de Aceleração do Crescimento (Growth Acceleration Programme – known as PAC), coincided with the recent 'pacification' of the favelas, which has eradicated the most blatant gang activities – although the drug industry continues much as usual in the backstreets – and the insertion of police installations at strategic points. PAC and pacification have also coincided, not coincidentally, with the approaching invasion of the World Cup and the Olympics.

Expenditure on the former has already caused some of the biggest riots Brazil has ever seen: over one million people took to the streets in June 2013. Occupying the roof of Niemeyer's congress building in Brasilia, protestors cast long shadows that made his bowl-shaped roof into an animated Grecian urn, a living symbol of democracy that the architect would surely have approved. The Olympics will be held in Rio in 2016; Rocinha is very close to the tourist beach enclaves, and a good impression must be made on the International Olympic Committee at any cost. But though the marked reduction in gang warfare is certainly to be welcomed, pacification (which involved door-to-door searches without warrant and much reported police racism – black people make up a disproportionate number of favela residents) is perhaps better understood as the invasion by the state of a semi-autonomous zone in order to recoup the value created by its residents, who colonised this previously unused land.

The projects paid for by PAC are similarly questionable: they have so far failed to make much of an impact on the generally squalid and dangerous conditions in Rio's favelas. In Rocinha the euphemistically named Valao, or valley, still pours human waste down an open cataract in the middle of a street, in which children splash and parasitic worms lurk. Projects such as schools and markets have remained unbuilt, or their half-built skeletons shelter homeless squatters, whereas the Niemeyer bridge and the rainbow-coloured new houses and sports centre on either side of it are overpriced cosmetic improvements that do little to resolve the more life-threatening problems of the favela. Visible from cars speeding past on the highway, the shapely bridge is actually a mask, both literal and ideological, for the favela. Likewise, the widely publicised cable car sailing over another favela, Complexo de Alemão, is a hugely expensive white elephant built mainly for the benefit of outsiders. Seen from beyond the slum, it's an unmissable signifier that 'something is being done', and as one favela dweller observed, it allows tourists to gawp at the poor without dirtying their feet. (Following pacification, favela tourism has boomed, although one German visitor was seriously wounded in a shooting in Rocinha in 2012.)

To some it comes as little surprise that PAC has stalled, perhaps even failed in its mission to improve the slums. The favelas of Rio – which began in 1897 – have been subjected to an endless variety of clearances, relocations, invasions and improvements over the last hundred years, as a history written by Catherine Osborn explains. As early as the 1910s many favelas were forcefully cleared in order to make way for the Haussmannisation of Rio. At the time slums were seen – in South America as in Europe – as pestilential incubators of disease, moral decay, crime and political unrest, the latter especially unnerving to post-colonial governments since slums were home to many former slaves and indigenous people. In 1937 a favela policy was outlined for the first time with these prejudices in mind: the settlements were an 'aberration' and should be demolished. But demolition didn't eradicate urban poverty or the spectre of political unrest, so in the 1940s the Catholic Church intervened in the favelas to help stamp out communism – the party itself was banned after winning 24 per cent in the municipal elections in 1947.

Neverthless, in the 1950s the people of the favelas began to organise themselves and petitioned the government for improvements and assistance, and in the 1960s a new municipal officer, sociologist José Arthur Rios, responded with programmes of improvements which for the first time involved residents in consultation. However, the city governor, working for real estate interests who wanted to clear the favelas for redevelopment, stopped these programmes and reinitiated slum clearances, moving over 100,000 slum residents to massive new housing projects known as *conjuntos* on the outskirts of the city. These were too expensive, too badly built and maintained, and too peripheral for many ex-favelados, and they were soon riddled by the same gang violence that plagued the slums: one of them, City of God, was made internationally infamous by the 2002 crime film of the same name. But despite their evident inadequacies, the *conjuntos* continued to be built, which is unsurprising since they made a lot of money for construction companies and the politicians they bribed. 1960s Britain was little better: the notorious leader of Newcastle council T Dan Smith was eventually jailed for accepting bribes from architect John Poulson.

Meanwhile, favela residents' associations clamoured for an end to clearances, arguing that improvements should be made to existing settlements instead, and that if demolition was necessary, people should be rehoused near their old homes. But the government ignored their views until the end of the military dictatorship and the return of democracy in 1985, when the people of the favelas at last got the vote. In the 1992 elections favela-born Benedita da Silva was only narrowly pipped to the mayoralty by Cesar Maia, who made certain concessions to his rival's constituency in order to win its support. The resulting *Favela–Bairro* (Favela to Neighbourhood) programmes lasted from 1994 to 2008, and enshrined the principles of public consultation and of 'preserving the local character' of favelas. Public spaces and public facilities were the focus instead of homes, which meant crèches, infrastructure and social services. The results were impressive, but due to poor materials and maintenance, they have rapidly decayed. Furthermore, the vaunted principles of participation and community support were honoured mainly in the breach. Most programmes were imposed from above, and social services were never provided, or once initiated quickly petered out.

The next wave of improvements came with the 2007 PAC programme, which funded prestige projects such as Niemeyer's bridge and the sports centre at Rocinha, and the cable car in Complexo de Alemão. Most recently, in 2010 Rio's current mayor Eduardo Paes – spurred on by the approaching World Cup and Olympics – announced a new municipal programme called *Morar Carioca*. It was to have a multi- billion-dollar budget and would work in partnership with the Brazilian Institute of Architects on major infrastructure upgrades such as roads, drainage, recreational facilities and social centres. Most impressively, it promised 'the participation of organised society . . . in all stages', undertook to rehouse displaced citizens near their original homes, and pledged to institute zoning regulations that would maintain affordable housing and thus prevent displacement caused by gentrification. But as Osborn concludes:

> Despite the incredible promise of *Morar Carioca* in theory . . . in practice, the programme's name has been used so far by local authorities only to undertake authoritarian and unilateral, often arbitrary, interventions in Rio's favelas. In the historic trajectory of 'to remove or to upgrade', the current city government has arrived at a third contradictory path with *Morar Carioca*: a proclamation of upgrading but a

practice that emphasises home removals, both through overt demolition and enabling of gentrification.[6]

Seen from a larger economic perspective, however, this policy is far from contradictory. The story of Rio's slums is a microcosmic history of global attitudes to housing the poor. In the late nineteenth century slum clearance was seen as the solution – a solution, one might add, that merely moved the poor further from their jobs and communities in order to reclaim valuable urban land. In the first half of the twentieth century municipal socialists, modernist architects and military dictators alike agitated for new housing estates to replace the slums, a programme that was enormously accelerated in Europe by the Luftwaffe and the RAF. But by the 1950s criticism was already being voiced of mass public housing. In Britain sociologists Wilmott and Young noted – in their famous study of the relocation of working-class families from inner-city Bethnal Green to suburban Essex – that communities were destroyed by distant resettlement. In response to this, and to the horrors of post-war planning, architect Cedric Price and historians Reyner Banham and Peter Hall advocated the other pole of idiocy, what they called Non-Plan: a libertarian stance that eventually inspired the unsupervised growth of Docklands.

A reaction also occured in developing nations, where observers began to criticise massive state-funded housing projects as expensive and inefficient, and for producing poor-quality dwellings, arguing instead that 'slums could be the answer'. It was not coincidental that this movement began in US and British colonies, especially in Puerto Rico, where the US administration had been pioneering 'aided self-help' since the end of the 1930s. These experiments were then foisted on the rest of Latin America by Anglo-American-led international bodies, and later funded by the Americans as counter-communist measures. Many architects supported these ideas too, for example British anarchist John Turner. He visited Peru in the 1950s, where he observed the reconstruction of the city of Arequipa after a massive earthquake and recommended that, instead of building new homes for displaced residents, the government could facilitate construction on a much greater scale by instigating a programme of aided self-help. Ideally this would mean providing access to infrastructure, plots, training and subsidised tools and materials while allowing residents to construct – or direct the construction of – their own dwellings.

Turner was not the first planner or architect to advocate self-help, but he was the most vocal and perhaps the most influential, and his ideas were endorsed by the World Bank, then headed by Robert McNamara. During his time as US defence secretary McNamara had massively expanded American involvement in the Vietnam War, but this partnership between a neoliberal butcher and anarchist planner seems less strange if you consider that both were fundamentally opposed to big government, albeit for somewhat different reasons. Turner's intentions may have been good: he thought that locals could build dwellings much more cheaply and attractively than governments could; that if people had more input into their homes, they would be happier with them; and that self-help could cut out reliance on international speculative capitalism. The neoliberals, on the other hand, wanted states to deregulate their building industries and let private enterprise take over the provision of housing through the free market.

But Turner had a bad case of what Marx referred to as the 'cretinous rustic idyll' – he romanticised slums, which are not expressions of self-realisation but desperate measures taken in situations of appalling scarcity.[7] Even worse, Turner's advocacy of self-help was used as an ideological fig leaf by the institutions of global capital. By refusing to supply housing to its tax-paying citizens, the state allows capitalists to extract value from workers twice over: once in the workplace, and once in the home by demanding that they labour for free on their own dwellings. It allows low wages to persist by providing the lowest-cost housing possible. As in every industry, deregulation of housing does not lead to lower costs or higher standards – that's just neoliberal doublethink – much of the costs 'saved' by self-help programmes are simply transferred to the builder-occupiers. And, as Rod Burgess put it in his critique of self-help housing:

> As the crisis in capitalism deepens, the costs of living space, rec-reational areas, urban services, infrastructure, energy and raw materials all increase dramatically. In advanced capitalist and Third World countries alike . . . self-help philosophies are put forward as a solution: build your own house, grow your own food, bicycle to work, become an artisan and so on. To those in the Third World who have done all these things and who are still rarely far from starvation, such appeals to be more self-reliant must strike them as being a rather curious form of radicalism.[8]

How much truer this is today than when it was written thirty years ago. In the end, although Turner's anarchist approach might appeal to survivalist cranks and corporate libertarians, the obvious answer to bad public housing is not to build *no* housing, but to build *better* housing. It's not an impossible task: examples of superb, cheap design abound in developing countries. The Hong Kong architec-tural practice of John Lin, for example, has led several projects in mainland China employing the labour and expertise of local people in order to create economical, energy-efficient and site-appropriate buildings. Impressively, projects such as his courtyard house in Shijia village, Shanxi Province, also attain a striking degree of aesthetic distinction with the most unexalted materials. Most new buildings in the Chinese countryside – especially those funded by migrant sons sending money back from the big city – are trans-planted urban types: multi-storey concrete villas clad in bathroom tiles and, money permitting, ornamented with fantastical accretions in tinted glass and polished tubular steel.

While these have a certain visual distinction of their own, Lin attempts to rework the traditional one-storey courtyard type instead as a transitional object, enduringly fit for purpose as the Chinese village morphs from rural backwater to something else. There is something almost brutalist about his modus operandi of employing what comes to hand – in this case traditional mud bricks – and forming it into semi-familiar vernacular typologies with a modernist twist. In Shijia a concrete frame was inserted to ensure earthquake resistance, but this was infilled with insulating mud bricks, and the whole building enclosed with a punctured brick screen, which shades while allowing the circulation of air. Inside, people and pigs share the dwelling, waste from the latter being used to produce gas for cooking. Ironically, in pseudo-socialist China the project was funded by a wealthy philanthropist.

Three stages in the construction of John Lin's prototype house in Shijia village, Shanxi Province, showing the earthquake-proof concrete frame (top), the insulating mud-brick infill (middle) and the pierced brick screen (bottom)

But though such interventions are admirable, and demonstrate the continued relevance of architectural design in a world of increasingly deprofessionalised building, systemic change is necessary in order to ensure that public housing is constructed on a large enough scale and in a way that actually benefits residents. Although there have been gestures towards the involvement of communities in architecture, these are usually just lip service paid to the political demands of the poor – as we saw in Rio. There the perceived contradiction between the municipal government's proclamation of participation and the actuality of forced evictions is no contradiction at all. It's just a new way of capital stealing value created by people: slums are built by the poor without state oversight, during which time gangsterism and lawlessness are allowed to prevail, then once development has reached a certain pitch these settlements are 'pacified' or invaded by the state in preparation for a different kind of gangsterism, the real estate market.

These days government attitudes to slums tend away from aided self-help and towards gentrification – slum clearance by stealth. Those who profit from Rocinha's urbanisation will not be its current inhabitants, most of whom rent and will therefore not benefit from schemes recognising the legal rights of slum property owners, but their landlords, who live in Ipanema and Leblon. Aided self-help is no longer necessary: the poor have in most cities completely developed the peripheries, and it only remains for capitalists to confiscate the value they have created. This is happening in the West too, to the middle classes. The sub-prime mortgage crisis led to vast numbers of illegal foreclosures, which – as one US congressman put it – represented 'the largest seizure of private property ever attempted by banks and government entities'.[9]

Only political change will stop this process: we are not presented with a choice between 'architecture or revolution', as Le Corbusier put it, but an imperative need for architecture *and* revolution.

When the tables are turned and the periphery reclaims the centre, architecture will at last be built for people, and not for the developers, speculators, landlords and corrupt bureaucrats who profit from it.

Protestors on the roof of Niemeyer's congress in Brasilia complete the building, a living riposte to the frozen sculptures of the gods on the pediment of a Greek temple

Notes

Introduction: The First Hut

1   Michel Foucault, *Language, Counter-Memory, Practice*, ed. D. F. Bouchard (Ithaca, NY, 1980), 142.
2   Henry-Louis de La Grange, *Gustav Mahler, Vol. 4: A New Life Cut Short* (Oxford, 2008), 821.
3   Ibid. 460.
4   Ibid. 213.
5   Henry Thoreau, *Walden* (Oxford, 2008), 102–17.
6   Vitruvius, *The Ten Books on Architecture,* trans. Morris Hicky Morgan (Cambridge, MA, 1914) 40. http://www.gutenberg.org/files/20239/20239-h/29239-h.htm#Page_38
7   Paul Schultze-Naumburg, *Kunst und Rasse* (Munich, 1928), 108.
8   Gottfried Semper, *Style in the Technical and Tectonic Arts*, trans. Mallgrave and Robinson (Los Angeles, CA, 2004), 666.
9   Joseph Conrad, *Heart of Darkness* (London, 1994), 75, 82.
10   Ibid. 52.
11   Samuel Beckett, *First Love* (London, 1973), 29–30.
12   Ibid. 31.

Chapter 1: The Tower of Babel, Babylon

1   In the spirit of my denial of singular points of origin in the Introduction, I should add that these were independently invented in several other places, including the Yangtze basin.
2   Devin Fore, *Realism after Modernism: The Rehumanization of Art and Literature* (Cambridge, MA, 2012), 121.
3   Genesis 11:4.
4   Genesis 11:6.
5   Genesis 11:9.
6   Flavius Josephus, *The Antiquities of the Jews*, trans. William Whiston. http://www.gutenberg.org/files/2848/2848-h/2848-h.htm
7   Exodus 1:14.

8   Jeremiah 51:29.

9   Revelation 14:8.

10 Magnus Bernhardsson, *Reclaiming a Plundered Past: Archaeology and Nation Building in Modern Iraq* (Austin, TX, 2005), 26.

11 Robert Miola, *Early Modern Catholicism: An Anthology of Primary Sources* (Oxford, 2007), 59.

12 Peter Arnade, *Beggars, Iconoclasts, and Civic Patriots: The Political Culture of the Dutch Revolt* (Ithaca, NY, 2008), 113.

13 Thomas Carlyle, *The French Revolution*, vol. 1 (London, 1966), 155.

14 Ibid. 154.

15 Hans Jürgen Lusebrink and Rolf Reichardt, *The Bastille: A History of a Symbol of Despotism and Freedom* (London, 1997), 121–2.

16 Gertrude Bell, *Amurath to Amurath* (London, 1924), vii. http://www.presscom.co.uk/amrath/amurath.html

17 Bernhardsson, 21.

18 Ibid. 44–5.

19 Ibid. 241.

20 www.gerty.ncl.ac.uk/diary_details.php?diary_id=1176

21 Letter to H.B. dated 16 January 1918. *The Letters of Gertrude Bell*, vol. 2 (1927). http://gutenberg.net.au/ebooks04/0400461h.html

22 Bernhardsson, 105.

23 Ibid. 108.

24 Jean-Claude Maurice, *Si vous le répétez, je démentirai: Chirac, Sarkozy, Vilepin* (Paris, 2009).

25 Daniel Brook, 'The Architect of 9/11', *Slate*, September 10 2009. http://www.slate.com/articles/news_and_politics/dispatches/features/2009/the_architect_of_911/what_can_we_learn_about_mohamed_atta_from_his_work_as_a_student_of_urban_planning.html

Chapter 2: The Golden House

1   Wolfgang Kayser, *The Grotesque in Art and Literature* (Bloomington, IN, 1963) 20.

2   Suetonius, vol. 2, trans. J.C. Rolfe (Cambridge, MA, 1914). http://penelope.uchicago.edu/Thayer/E/Roman/Texts/Suetonius/12Caesars/Nero*.html

3   Tacitus, *The Annals*, trans. Alfred John Church and William Jackson Brodribb (New York, 1942). http://classics.mit.edu/Tacitus/annals.mb.txt

4   Ibid.#

5   Gustave Flaubert, *La danse des morts* (1838), 171.

6   The existence of these objects is disputed by mainstream historians.

7   Nikolaus Pevsner, *Outline of European Architecture* (London, 1962), 411.

8   Edward Champlin, *Nero* (Cambridge, MA, 2003), 200.

9   Epistle XC. Seneca, vol. 2, trans. Richard M. Gummere (Cambridge, MA, 1917–25). http://www.stoics.com/seneca_epistles_book_2.html

10   Bernard Mandeville, *The Fable of the Bees* (London, 1989), 73–4.

11   World Bank, 2010.

12   Tacitus, op. cit.

13   Vitruvius, *On Architecture*, trans. Richard Schofield (London, 2009), 98.

14   Nicole Dacos, *The Loggia of Raphael: A Vatican Art Treasure* (New York, 2008), 29.

15   Alexandre Dumas, *Celebrated Crimes, Vol. 2* (London, 1896), 259.

16   Geoffrey Harpham, *On the Grotesque: Strategies of Contradiction in Art and Literature* (Princeton, NJ, 1982), 30.

17   Manfredo Tafuri, *Theories and History of Architecture* (London, 1980), 17. Emphasis in original.

18   Ruskin, from *The Stones of Venice*, quoted in Geoffrey Scott, *The Architecture of Humanism: A Study in the History of Taste* (London, 1914), 121.

19   http://www.vit.vic.edu.au/SiteCollectionDocuments/PDF/1137_The-Effect-of-the-Physical-Learning-Environment-on-Teaching-and-Learning.pdf

20   Miles Glendinning and Stefan Muthesius, *Tower Block: Modern Public Housing in England, Scotland, Wales and Northern Ireland* (New Haven, CT, 1993), 322–3.

21   Jonathan Meades, *Museum Without Walls* (London, 2012), 381–5.

22   See Owen Hatherley, *A Guide to the New Ruins of Great Britain* (London, 2010) and *A New Kind of Bleak: Journeys Through Urban Britain* (London, 2012), and Anna Minton, *Ground Control: Fear and Happiness in the Twenty First Century City* (London, 2012).

23   Augustus Welby Pugin, *The True Principles of Christian Architecture* (London, 1969), 38.

24   Adrian Forty, *Words and Buildings* (London, 2000), 299.

25   Adolf Loos, *Ornament and Crime: Selected Essays*, trans. Michael Mitchell (Riverside, CA, 1998), 167.

26   K. Michael Hays, *Modernism and the Posthumanist Subject: The Architecture of Hannes Meyer and Ludwig Hilberseimer* (Cambridge, MA, 1992).

27   Karl Marx, *The Eighteenth Brumaire of Louis Bonaparte*, trans. Saul K. Padover http://www.marxists.org/archive/marx/works/1852/18th-brumaire/

Chapter 3: Djinguereber Mosque, Timbuktu

1   Robert Bevan, *The Destruction of Memory: Architecture at War* (London, 2006), 7.

2   John Hunwick, *Timbuktu and the Songhay Empire* (London, 2003), 9.

3   N. Levtzion and J.F.P. Hopkins (eds), *Corpus of Early Arabic Sources for West African History* (Cambridge, 1981), 271.

4   Suzan B. Aradeon, 'Al-Sahili: the historian's myth of architectural technology transfer from North Africa', *Journal des Africanistes*, vol. 59, 99–131, 107. http://www.persee.fr/web/revues/home/prescript/article/jafr_0399-0346_1989_num_59_1_2279?luceneQuery=%2B%28authorId%3Apersee_79744+authorId%3A%22auteur+jafr_787%22%29&words=persee_79744&words=auteur%20jafr_787

5   Walter Benjamin, trans. Harry Zohn, in *Selected Writings Vol. 4: 1938–1940*, eds Howard Eiland and Michael Jennings (Cambridge, MA, 2003), 391–2.

6   Georges Bataille, 'Architecture', trans. Dominic Faccini, *October* vol. 60, spring 1992, 25–6, 25.

7   Lewis Mumford, *The Culture of Cities* (London, 1938), 435.

8   Bevan, 91.

9   http://wais.stanford.edu/Spain/spain_1thevalledeloscaidos73103.html

10   James Young, 'The Counter-Monument: Memory against Itself in Germany Today', *Critical Inquiry*, 18, 2, winter 1992, 267–96, 279

11   Friedrich Nietzsche, *Untimely Meditations*, trans. R.J. Hollingdale (Cambridge, 1983) 62.

12   Irina Bokova, 'Culture in the Cross Hairs', *New York Times*, 2 December 2012.

13   Emily O'Dell, 'Slaying Saints and Torching Texts', on jadaliyya.com, 1 February 2013. http://www.jadaliyya.com/pages/index/9915/slaying-saints-and-torching-texts

14   Sona Stephan Hoisington, '"Ever Higher": The Evolution of the Project for the Palace of Soviets', *Slavic Review*, vol. 62, no. 1, spring 2003, 41–68, 62.

15   John Ruskin, *The Seven Lamps of Architecture* (New York, 1981), 184.

16   Neil MacFarquhar, 'Mali City Rankled by Rules for Life in Spotlight', *New York Times*, 8 January 2011.

17   Felix Dubois, *Notre beau Niger* (Paris, 1911), 189.

18   Mumford, 439–40.

19   K. Michael Hays, *Modernism and the Posthumanist Subject: The Architecture of Hannes Meyer and Ludwig Hilberseimer* (Cambridge, MA, 1992), 65.

20   Ibid. 69.

Chapter 4: Palazzo Rucellai, Florence

1   Ayn Rand, *The Fountainhead* (London, 1994), 14.

2   Richard Hall (ed.), *Built Identity: Swiss Re's Corporate Architecture* (Basel, 2007), 14.

3   Anthony Grafton, *Leon Battista Alberti: Master Builder of the Italian Renaissance* (Cambridge, MA, 2000), 18–19.

4   Ian Borden, Barbara Penner and Jane Rendell (eds), *Gender Space Architecture: An Interdisciplinary Introduction* (London, 2000), 363.

5   Robert Tavernor, *On Alberti and the Art of Building* (New Haven, 1998), 83.

6   He is discussing Loos's columnar entry for the *Chicago Tribune* competition. Manfredo Tafuri, 'The Disenchanted Mountain: The Skyscraper and the City', in *The American City: From the Civil War to the New Deal* (Cambridge, MA, 1979), 402.

7   Leon Battista Alberti, *On the Art of Building*, trans. J. Rykwert, N. Leach and R. Tavernor (Cambridge, MA, 1988), 263.

8   Mark Philips, *Memoir of Marco Parenti: A Life in Medici Florence* (Princeton, NJ, 1987), 190.

9   Ibid. 208.

10   David Ward and Oliver Lunz (eds), *The Landscape of Modernity: New York City 1990–1994* (New York, 1992), 140.

11   Philip Ursprung, 'Corporate Architecture and Risk', in Hall (ed.), *Built Identity*, 165.

12   Rand, 300.

13 Cited in Tafuri, 519.
14 William H. Whyte, *The Social Life of Small Urban Spaces* (Washington, 1980) 64–5.
15 www.mori.co.jp/en/company/urban_design/safety.html
16 Marshall Berman, *All That is Solid Melts Into Air* (New York, 1987), 99.

Chapter 5: *The Garden of Perfect Brightness, Beijing*

1   Ezra Pound, *Selected Poems* (London, 1977), 71–2.
2   Jean-Denis Attiret, *A Letter from F. Attiret*, trans. Harry Beaumont (London, 1752). http://inside.bard.edu/~louis/gardens/attiretaccount.html
3   Craig Clunas, *Fruitful Sites: Garden Culture in Ming Dynasty China* (London, 1996), 102.
4   Xiao Chi, *The Chinese Garden as Lyric Enclave* (Ann Arbor, MI, 2001), 134.
5   Ibid. 51.
6   A. E. Grantham, quoted in Geremie Barmé, 'The Garden of Perfect Brightness: A Life in Ruins', in *East Asian History* no. 11, June 1996, 129.
7   Maggie Keswick, *The Chinese Garden* (London, 1976), 164.
8   Cao Xueqin, *A Dream of Red Mansions Vol. 1*, trans. Yang Xianyi and Gladys Yang (Beijing, 1994), 341.
9   Ibid. 310.
10 Attiret, op. cit.
11 Jonathan Spence, *The Search for Modern China* (New York, 1990), 123.
12 G. J. Wolseley, *Narrative of the War With China in 1860* (London, 1862), 280. http://www.archive.org/stream/narrativeofwar1oowols/narrativeofwar1oowols_djvu.txt
13 John Newsinger, 'Elgin in China', in *New Left Review* 15, May–June 2002, 119–140, 137. http://www.math.jussieu.fr/~harris/elgin.pdf
14 Newsinger, 134.
15 William Travis Hanes and Frank Sanello, *The Opium Wars: The Addiction of One Empire and the Corruption of Another* (Illinois, 2002), 11–12.
16 Newsinger, 137.
17 Ibid. 140.

Chapter 6: *Festival Theatre, Bayreuth, Germany*

1   Walter Benjamin, *One-Way Street and Other Writings* (London, 1979), 120.
2   Thomas Mann, 'The Sorrows and Grandeur of Richard Wagner' in *Pro and Contra Wagner* (London, 1985), 128.
3   Mark Twain, 'Chapters from my Autobiography', *North American Review* (1906–7), 247. http://www.gutenberg.org/files/19987/19987-h/19987-h.htm
4   Juliet Koss, *Modernism After Wagner* (Minneapolis, MN, 2010), 18.
5   Anthony Vidler, *Claude-Nicolas Ledoux: Architecture and Social Reform at the End of the Ancien Régime* (Cambridge, MA, 1990), 168.

6   Ibid. 232.

7   Koss, 39.

8   Ernest Newman, *The Life of Richard Wagner: Volume III, 1859–1866* (New York, 1941), 538.

9   Ibid. 215.

10 Koss, 50.

11 Ibid. 57.

12 Ibid. 65.

13 Nietzsche, fragment dated 1878 (author's translation). http://www.nietzschesource. org/#eKGWB/NF-1878,30[1]

14 Nietzsche, *The Case of Wagner*, trans. Anthony Ludovici, (Edinburgh and London, 1911), 11.

15 Theodor Adorno, *In Search of Wagner* (London, 1991), 85.

16 Ibid.106.

17 Siegfried Kracauer, 'Cult of Distraction: On Berlin's Picture Palaces', trans. Thomas Levin, *New German Critique* no. 40, winter 1987, 91–6, 95.

18 Kathleen James, *Erich Mendelsohn and the Architecture of German Modernism* (Cambridge, 1997), 163.

19 Rem Koolhaas, *Delirious New York* (New York, 1994), 30.

20 Siegfried Kracuaer, *The Salaried Masses*, trans. Quintin Hoare (London, 1998), 93.

21 Karal Ann Marling (ed.), *Designing Disney's Theme Parks: The Architecture of Reassurance* (New York, 1997), 180.

Chapter 7: Highland Park Car Factory, Detroit

1   Louis-Ferdinand Céline, *Voyage au bout de la nuit*, (Paris, 1962), 223. Author's translation.

2   Upton Sinclair, *The Flivver King* (Chicago, 2010), 16.

3   Steven Watts, *The People's Tycoon: Henry Ford and the American Century* (New York, 2005), 384.

4   Ibid. 118.

5   Sinclair, *The Flivver King*, 22.

6   Watts, 156–7.

7   Céline, 225–6. Author's translation.

8   Federico Bucci, *Albert Kahn: Architect of Ford* (Princeton, 1993), 175.

9   Charles Fourier, *Selections from the Works of Charles Fourier*, trans. Julia Franklin (London, 1901),59. http://www.archive.org/stream/selectionsfromwoofourgoog#page/ n2/mode/2up

10 Charles Fourier, *The Theory of the Four Movements* (Cambridge, 1996), 132.

11 Charles Fourier, *The Utopian Vision of Charles Fourier*, trans. Jonathan Beecher and Richard Bienvenu (London, 1972), 240.

12 Fourier, *Selections*, 166.

13 Carl Guarneri, *The Utopian Alternative: Fourierism in Nineteenth-Century America* (Cornell, 1991), 185.

14 Nathaniel Hawthorne, *The Blithedale Romance* (Oxford, 2009), 53–4.

15 Ibid., 18.

16 Francis Spufford, 'Red Plenty: Lessons from the Soviet Dream', *Guardian*, 7 August 2010.

17 Fourier, *Selections*, 64.

18 Ibid. 66.

19 Ibid. 166.

Chapter 8: E.1027, Cap Martin

1 Ivan Žaknić, *The Final Testament of Père Corbu: A Translation and Interpretation of Mise au point* (New Haven, CT, 1997), 67.

2 Charles Baudelaire, *The Flowers of Evil*, trans. William Aggeler (Fresno, CA, 1954), 185.

3 Peter Adam, *Eileen Gray* (London, 1987), 217.

4 Ibid. 309–10.

5 Ibid. 309.

6 Sang Lee and Ruth Baumeister (eds), *The Domestic and the Foreign in Architecture* (Rotterdam, 2007), 122.

7 Adam, 220.

8 Ibid. 334.

9 Ibid. 335–6.

10 Beatriz Colomina, 'War on Architecture: E.1027', in *Assemblage* no. 20, April 1993, 28–9.

11 Loos, 167.

12 Beatriz Colomina, *Privacy and Publicity* (Cambridge, MA, 1994) 234.

13 Walter Benjamin, 'Surrealism' in Jennings and Eiland (eds), *Selected Writings*, Vol 2, part 1, 1927–30 (Harvard, 2005), 209.

14 Ovid, *Metamorphoses*, trans. Brookes More (Boston, 1922). http://www.perseus.tufts.edu/hopper/text?doc=Perseus%3Atext%3A1999.02.0028%3Abook%3D4%3Acard%3D55

15 Sigmund Freud, *An Infantile Neurosis and other works*, The Standard Edition Vol. XVII (London, 1955), 237.

16 The economic aspect of sex and architecture is a subject that deserves a chapter in itself. Until very recently the poor could only dream of having a room of their own. Unlike the aristocratic Pyramus and Thisbe, the 'mechanicals' who played them probably occupied one- or two-room dwellings where sex was inevitably a more public act. Without separate suites of rooms or dynastic lineages to preserve, sexuality was less architecturally controlled for Greek slaves, medieval peasants and working-class families of the mid-twentieth century. Indeed, personal private space remains a dream for much of the world's population, with the result that – in China, for example – public intimacy of a degree rarely seen in the West is necessitated by cramped domestic conditions.

17 Virginia Woolf, *A Room of One's Own* (London, 2004), 101–2.

18 Adam, 257.

19 Walter Benjamin, 'The Destructive Character', trans. Edmund Jephcott, in *Selected Writings Vol. 2, part 2: 1931–34*, ed. Michael Jennings, Howard Eiland and Gary Smith (Cambridge, MA, 2005), 542.

20 Bertholt Brecht, 'Ten Poems from a Reader for Those Who Live in Cities', in *Poems 1913–1956* (London, 1987), 131.

Chapter 9: Finsbury Health Centre, London

1   Marcel Proust, *Pleasures and Days*, trans. Andrew Brown (London, 2004), 6.

2   *Sunday Telegraph*, 3 July 1994.

3   Elizabeth Darling, *Re-Forming Britain: Narratives of Modernity Before Reconstruction* (London, 2007), 54.

4   Innes Pearse and Lucy Crocker, *The Peckham Experiment: A Study in the Living Structure of Society* (London, 1943), 241.

5   Thomas Mann, *The Magic Mountain*, trans. John E. Woods (New York, 2005), 8.

6   Paul Overy, *Light, Air and Openness: Modern Architecture Between the Wars* (London, 2007), 80.

7   John Allan, *Berthold Lubetkin: Architecture and the Tradition of Progress* (London, 1992), 29.

8   John Thompson and Grace Goldin, *The Hospital: A Social and Architectural History* (New Haven and London, 1975), 37.

9   Christine Stevenson, *Medicine and Magnificence: British Hospital and Asylum Architecture, 1660–1815* (New Haven and London, 2000), 187.

10 Thompson and Goldin, 159.

11 Owen Hatherley, 'Trip to an Exurban Hospital', on *Sit Down Man, You're a Bloody Tragedy*, 25 January 2009. http://nastybrutalistandshort.blogspot.co.uk/2009/01/trip-to-exurban-hospital.html

12 Allan, 366.

13 WHO, 2012. http://www.who.int/tb/publications/factsheet_global.pdf

Chapter 10: Footbridge, Rio de Janeiro

1   Peter Godfrey, 'Swerve with Verve: Oscar Niemeyer, the Architect who Eradicated the Straight Line', *Independent*, 18 April 2010.

2   Oscar Niemeyer, *The Curves of Time* (London, 2000), 3.

3   Obituary of Oscar Niemeyer, *Daily Star of Lebanon*, 7 December 2012.

4   Mike Davis, *Planet of Slums* (London, 2006), 9.

5   Ibid. 19.

6   Catherine Osborn, 'A History of Favela Upgrades', www.rioonwatch.org, 27 September 2012. http://rioonwatch.org/?p=5295

7   Marx used the phrase in his review of Daumer's *The Religion of the New Age* in the

Neuen Rheinischen Zeitung no. 2, February 1850. http://www.mlwerke.de/me/me07/me07_198.htm

8   Rod Burgess, 'Self-Help Housing Advocacy: A Curious Form of Radicalism', in *Self-Help Housing: A Critique*, ed. Peter Ward (1982) 55–97, 92.

9   David Harvey, *Rebel Cities* (London, 2012), 54.

Select Bibliography

Adam, Peter, *Eileen Gray* (London, 1987)

Adorno, Theodor, *In Search of Wagner*, trans. Rodney Livingstone (London, 1991 edition)

Alberti, Leon Battista, *On the Art of Building*, trans. J. Rykwert, N. Leach and R. Tavernor (Cambridge, MA, 1988)

Allan, John, *Berthold Lubetkin: Architecture and the Tradition of Progress* (London, 2013)

Arnade, Peter, *Beggars, Iconoclasts, and Civic Patriots: The Political Culture of the Dutch Revolt* (Ithaca, NY, 2008)

Attiret, Jean-Denis, *A Letter from F. Attiret*, trans. Harry Beaumont (London, 1752) http://inside.bard.edu/~louis/gardens/attiretaccount.html

Banham, Reyner, *A Concrete Atlantis: US Industrial Building and European Modern Architecture, 1900-1925* (Cambridge, MA, 1986)

Barmé, Geremie, 'The Garden of Perfect Brightness: A Life in Ruins', in *East Asian History* no. 11, June 1996

Beckett, Samuel, *First Love* (London, 1973)

Bell, Gertrude, *Amurath to Amurath* (London, 1924), http://www.presscom.co.uk/amrath/amurath.html

—, *Diaries*, http://www.gerty.ncl.ac.uk/diary_details.php?diary_id=1176

Benjamin, Walter, *One-Way Street and Other Writings* (London, 1979)

—, *Selected Writings* ed. Michael Jennings, Howard Eiland and Gary Smith (Cambridge, MA, 2004–6)

Berman, Marshall, *All That is Solid Melts Into Air* (New York, 1987)

Bernhardsson, Magnus, *Reclaiming a Plundered Past: Archaeology and Nation Building in Modern Iraq* (Austin, TX, 2005)

Bevan, Robert, *The Destruction of Memory: Architecture at War* (London, 2006)

Brook, Daniel, 'The Architect of 9/11', *Slate*, September 10 2009, http://www.slate.com/articles/news_and_politics/dispatches/features/2009/the_architect_of_911/what_can_we_learn_about_mohamed_atta_from_his_work_as_a_student_of_urban_planning.html

Bucci, Federico, *Albert Kahn: Architect of Ford* (Princeton, 1993)

Burgess, Rod, 'Self-Help Housing Advocacy: A Curious Form of Radicalism', in *Self-Help Housing: A Critique*, ed. Peter Ward (London, 1982)

Carlson, Marvin, *Places of Performance: The Semiotics of Theatre Architecture* (Ithaca, NY, 1989)

Carlyle, Thomas, *The French Revolution* (London, 1966 edition)

Céline, Louis-Ferdinand, *Voyage au bout de la nuit* (Paris, 1962 edition)

Champlin, Edward, *Nero* (Cambridge, MA, 2003)

Chi, Xiao, *The Chinese Garden as Lyric Enclave* (Ann Arbor, MI, 2001)

Clunas, Craig, *Fruitful Sites: Garden Culture in Ming Dynasty China* (London, 1996)

Colomina, Beatriz, *Privacy and Publicity* (Cambridge, MA, 1994)

Conrad, Joseph, *Heart of Darkness* (London, 1994 edition)

Dacos, Nicole, *The Loggia of Raphael: A Vatican Art Treasure* (New York, 2008)

Darling, Elizabeth, *Re-Forming Britain: Narratives of Modernity Before Reconstruction* (London, 2007)

Davis, Mike, *Planet of Slums* (London, 2006)

de La Grange, Henry-Louis, *Gustav Mahler* (Oxford, 1995–2008)

Forty, Adrian, *Words and Buildings* (London, 2000)

Foucault, Michel, *Language, Counter-Memory, Practice*, trans. Donald Bouchard and Sherry Simon (Ithaca, NY, 1980)

Fourier, Charles, *Selections from the Works of Charles Fourier*, trans. Julia Franklin (London, 1901), http://www.archive.org/stream/selectionsfromwoofourgoog#page/n2/mode/2up

—, *The Theory of the Four Movements*, eds. Ian Patterson and Gareth Stedman Jones (Cambridge, 1996)

—, *The Utopian Vision of Charles Fourier*, trans. Jonathan Beecher and Richard Bienvenu (London, 1972)

Glendinning, Miles and Stefan Muthesius, *Tower Block: Modern Public Housing in England, Scotland, Wales and Northern Ireland* (New Haven, CT, 1993)

- Harpham, Geoffrey, *On the Grotesque: Strategies of Contradiction in Art and Literature* (Princeton, NJ, 1982)

Harvey, David, *Rebel Cities* (London, 2012)

Hatherley, Owen, *A Guide to the New Ruins of Great Britain* (London, 2010)

—, *A New Kind of Bleak: Journeys Through Urban Britain* (London, 2012)

Hays, K. Michael, *Modernism and the Posthumanist Subject: The Architecture of Hannes Meyer and Ludwig Hilberseimer* (Cambridge, MA, 1992)

Hunwick, John, *Timbuktu and the Songhay Empire* (London, 2003)

Kayser, Wolfgang, *The Grotesque in Art and Literature* (Bloomington, IN, 1963)

Koolhaas, Rem, *Delirious New York* (New York, 1994)

Koss, Juliet, *Modernism After Wagner* (Minneapolis, MN, 2010)

Kracauer, Siegfried, 'Cult of Distraction: On Berlin's Picture Palaces', trans. Thomas Levin, *New German Critique* no. 40, winter 1987

—, *The Mass Ornament: Weimar Essays*, trans. Thomas Levin (Cambridge, MA, 1995)

—, *The Salaried Masses*, trans. Quintin Hoare (London, 1998)

Loos, Adolf, *Ornament and Crime: Selected Essays*, trans. Michael Mitchell (Riverside, CA, 1998)

Lusebrink, Hans Jürgen and Rolf Reichardt, *The Bastille: A History of a Symbol of Despotism and Freedom*, trans. Norbert Schürer (London, 1997)

Mandeville, Bernard, *The Fable of the Bees* (London, 1989)

Mann, Thomas, *The Magic Mountain*, trans. John E. Woods (New York, 2005)

Marx, Karl, *The Eighteenth Brumaire of Louis Bonaparte*, trans. Saul K. Padover, http://www.marxists.org/archive/marx/works/1852/18th-brumaire/

Meades, Jonathan, *Museum Without Walls* (London, 2012)

Minton, Anna, *Ground Control: Fear and Happiness in the Twenty First Century City* (London, 2012)

Mumford, Lewis, *The Culture of Cities* (London, 1938)

Newman, Ernest, *The Life of Richard Wagner* (New York, 1941)

Newsinger, John, 'Elgin in China', in *New Left Review* 15, May–June 2002, http://www.math.jussieu.fr/~harris/elgin.pdf

Niemeyer, Oscar, *The Curves of Time* (London, 2000)

Nietzsche, Friedrich, *The Case of Wagner*, trans. Anthony Ludovici (Edinburgh and London, 1911)

—, *Untimely Meditations*, trans. R.J. Hollingdale (Cambridge, 1983)

O'Dell, Emily, 'Slaying Saints and Torching Texts', on jadaliyya.com, 1 February 2013, http://www.jadaliyya.com/pages/index/9915/slaying-saints-and-torching-texts

Osborn, Catherine, 'A History of Favela Upgrades', www.rioonwatch.org, 27 September 2012, http://rioonwatch.org/?p=5295

Ovid, *Metamorphoses*, trans. Brookes More (Boston, 1922), http://www.perseus.tufts.edu/hopper/text?doc=Perseus%3Atext%3A1999.02.0028%3Abook%3D4%3Acard%3D55

Pevsner, Nikolaus, *Outline of European Architecture* (London, 1962)

Ruskin, John, *The Seven Lamps of Architecture* (New York, 1981 edition)

Rykwert, Joseph, *On Adam's House in Paradise: The Idea of the Primitive Hut in Architectural History* (Cambridge, MA, 1981)

Schwartz, Frederic, *The Werkbund: Design Theory and Culture Before the First World War* (New Haven, CT, 1996)

—, *Blind Spots: Critical Theory and the History of Art in Twentieth-Century Germany* (New Haven, CT, 2005)

Semper, Gottfried, *Style in the Technical and Tectonic Arts*, trans. Mallgrave and Robinson (Los Angeles, CA, 2004)

Sinclair, Upton, *The Flivver King* (Chicago, IL, 2010 edition)

Spence, Jonathan, *The Search for Modern China* (New York, 1990)

Spufford, Francis, *Red Plenty* (London, 2010)

Stevenson, Christine, *Medicine and Magnificence: British Hospital and Asylum Architecture, 1660–1815* (New Haven and London, 2000)

Suetonius, *The Lives of the Caesars*, trans. J.C. Rolfe (Cambridge, MA, 1914), http://penelope.uchicago.edu/Thayer/E/Roman/Texts/Suetonius/12Caesars/Nero*.html

Tacitus, *The Annals*, trans. Alfred John Church and William Jackson Brodribb (New York, 1942), http://classics.mit.edu/Tacitus/annals.mb.txt

Tafuri, Manfredo, 'The Disenchanted Mountain: The Skyscraper and the City', in *The American City: From the Civil War to the New Deal* (Cambridge, MA, 1979)

—, *Theories and History of Architecture*, trans. Giorgio Verrecchia (London, 1980)

Tavernor, Robert, *On Alberti and the Art of Building* (New Haven, 1998)

Thompson, John and Grace Goldin, *The Hospital: A Social and Architectural History* (New Haven and London, 1975)

Thoreau, Henry, *Walden* (Oxford, 2008 edition)

Vidler, Anthony, *Claude-Nicolas Ledoux: Architecture and Social Reform at the End of the Ancien Régime* (Cambridge, MA, 1990)

Vitruvius, *On Architecture*, trans. Richard Schofield (London, 2009)

Watts, Steven, *The People's Tycoon: Henry Ford and the American Century* (New York, 2005)

Whyte, William H., *The Social Life of Small Urban Spaces* (Washington, 1980)

Wolseley, G.J., *Narrative of the War With China in 1860* (London, 1862), http://www.archive.org/stream/narrativeofwarwi00wols/narrativeofwarwi00wols_djvu.txt

Woolf, Virginia, *A Room of One's Own* (London, 2004 edition)

Xueqin, Cao, *A Dream of Red Mansions* trans. Yang Xianyi and Gladys Yang (Beijing, 1994)

Young, James, 'The Counter-Monument: Memory against Itself in Germany Today', *Critical Inquiry*, 18, 2, winter 1992

Acknowledgements

The idea of writing this book would never have occurred to me without the prompting of Isabel Wilkinson, and it wouldn't have got much further than an idea without the encouragement (and irresistible charm) of Rachel Mills, Annabel Merullo and Tim Binding at Peters Fraser and Dunlop. At Bloomsbury, I thank Richard Atkinson for commissioning the book, and Bill Swainson, whose enthusiasm and expertise helped me over the finishing line. I must also express my gratitude to Professor Fred Schwartz at University College London, for his patience and support while I dodged my academic responsibilities, and for the rigorous example set by his own work; I can only hope that I have not sunk too far below his standard here. Buyun Chen kindly put me up in New York and offered her expert advice on the Garden of Perfect Brightness (any errors remaining in that chapter are of course my own), and Steve and Helen Baker assisted with translating Céline. My colleagues at the *Architectural Review* have also helped me in innumerable ways; and I must thank the Fiells for pointing me in their direction. Finally, I would like to thank Abi Wilkinson and Nathalie Zdrojewski for helping me through an occasionally trying couple of years, Owen Kyffin for his invaluable advice, and the man from Hostel Detroit who drove me to the Rouge.

Index

A NOTE ON THE AUTHOR

Tom Wilkinson is History Editor of the *Architectural Review*. He is writing a doctoral thesis on art history at University College London, where he has taught an undergraduate course on architectural history. He has lived in Shanghai and Berlin, and currently lives in East London.

A NOTE ON THE TYPE

Granjon is an old-style, fine text serif typeface designed in 1928 for Linotype by George William Jones (1860–1942), and based on the Garamond typeface. It is named after the sixteenth-century French printer, publisher and lettercutter Robert Granjon, who is noted in particular for his beautiful italic types.